True Innocence

Joseph M. Perkins
Author

eBook Cover Designs
Cover Illustrator

Jack L Stickney
Editor

EBook 12/11/15

Revised 03/26/2016

Disclaimer: All opinions, interpretations, and theories are the sole responsibility of the author. No religious organization has reviewed or endorsed these materials.

I dedicate this book and my life to helping the 'ninety and nine' who have allowed the enemies of God to lead them down forbidden paths. My hope is that they might return to the out-stretched arms of their Savior Jesus Christ.

Author's Note

All the stories in this book are true. All of the names have been changed except for my special son Joseph and me the author to protect the innocent.

Contents

Introduction

I don't profess to be perfect or a professional counselor. But in my experience as a son, brother, father, friend (and having served in various church callings) I have received counsel and given counsel to others. I have a deep love for my immediate and extended family; whether in this life or the post mortal life to come. I have a deep love for my faith and for the Holy words of God's Prophets; both past and present. I have a deep love for God and his son Jesus Christ, our brother. I also have love for all people.

I believe that the people of the world are in desperate need of answers to their questions; questions regarding the life altering things that happen to us all. How could this happen? Why is it happening, and when will we get real help for the perplexing problems of our day? We live in a world where the evil actions of others are often attributed to 'mental illnesses'.

Perhaps we need a wake-up call; a call to repentance. A call to action! Is it time to look in a new direction? Is it reasonable to accept that the guilty in many cases (involving rape, incest, and child abuse, and substance abuse, violence of any sort, murder, and even suicide) are simply funneled into a diagnosis of mental illness? Can a son or daughter of God who commits a violent act instantaneously become insane or mentally ill simply because the authorities or courts so declare? Do doctors, psychologists, and other educated professional counselors have all the answers? Can so-called anti-depressants or other prescription drugs be the panacea for depression, violence, murder, or suicide?

These questions (along with many others) involving every range of society could be answered with this simple question: Have these evil, violent acts decreased or increased in the world today?

We are an electronic world in an information age. Young children grow up with electronics at their fingertips. We can find anything on the internet if we search long enough. Life is fast-paced. Many are self-absorbed in social media and entertainment in its many forms. Countless dollars are spent for thrills. Wives and children for many have become trophies. If we could learn from history, we could solve many of today's problems. Have we forgotten God? The bible is the greatest history book ever written. Many profess to be religious, yet have never bothered to read or study the holy texts of the past.

For example, among members of the US military, there was an average of one suicide per day in 2011. In 2014, just 3 short years later – there were 22 per day, and that number is still growing at alarming rates. The United States has the greatest military power ever created by mankind. Yet the top Generals have stated, "Everything has been tried, and we simply don't have the weapon to defeat this <u>unseen</u> enemy." Suicide is closing in at the top of the charts for cause of death. There are now over one million suicides per year in the world today. This is true destruction of epic proportions.

A very pointed clue to the real guilty party comes from the statement made by the military generals. I underlined the word, "<u>unseen</u>" because it is that clue. This book will remove multiple masks, exposing the true identity of the two enemies of God and mankind. The first is very visible and completely mortal. The second is unseen but has a military-like presence of an estimated 30 billion soldiers at his command: a third of the hosts of heaven.

Let's take one enemy at a time, the <u>visible</u> one first. You see and deal with it every moment of every day. Its identity is: the 'natural man' or 'natural woman'. Our individual physical body of flesh and its appetites IS that enemy. Yet, our mortal body houses a perfect immortal spirit. Our spirit can never die, but can and will be controlled by the natural man if we choose to allow it through exercise of our moral agency. That priceless gift of agency is bestowed upon every child born to this earth by God, the Creator of our spirits.

Then, God our Eternal Father gave us an even greater gift to combat the two enemies which is, 'enmity' placed in the seed of the woman (mothers). This enmity is the, 'Light of Christ'. Just imagine every child born to this world has the spirit of Jesus Christ within them. This spirit gives each of us the knowledge and ability to choose right from wrong. During this formative time, when the Light of Christ is working within them, is when we need to teach our children light and truth. Our homes may not be perfect, but we should never give up on our children no matter how hard life may become.

You and I will, from time to time, fail in our quest for perfection; and allow the natural man to control our actions by committing sin and transgressing. And yes, we still have to deal with other humans and their weaknesses every day of our lives too. Thankfully, Judgment will come from God, based on our individual works.

Next, let's examine the <u>unseen</u> enemy. In Ephesians 6:12, the Apostle Paul states that the greater enemy is the unseen one (the ". . . rulers of darkness of this world . . ."). He (Satan and his followers) is unseen because he is a spirit, made up of spirit matter: he cannot be viewed with the 'natural' eye. He also has many disguises to mask his true identity. With a third of the hosts of heaven (who are spirits as well) at his command, we may feel outnumbered and hopeless. The scriptures say there will be 'more for us than against us' (see Kings 6:16). Satan is their leader and master. His ultimate goal is to take possession of our physical bodies and destroy the souls of men. Remember these two statements: You and I have the power to "bruise [his] head" and He only has the power to "bruise [our] heel." (Moses 4:21)

(Returning to Ephesians 6:10-11 & 13-24) Paul explains the armor that can shield us; along with the weapons to conquer and defeat the enemy of all righteousness. We must gain a perfect understanding of Satan, his weapons, and his evil tactics. Knowing His methods will make him totally visible. I testify he is real, he knows us by name, he was there, in the preexistence with us until he and his followers were cast down to earth. He knows us, and he knows those who will be the leaders of men. I testify that the most righteous individuals born to this earth will deal **personally** with the fiery darts of Satan himself. We must take a **STAND** for righteousness, all the days of our life.

If Satan takes over our body then we are subject to him. He cannot directly kill anyone, but CAN indirectly convince a person to murder or commit suicide. Satan and his followers had no veil of forgetfulness placed over their eyes. This was illustrated when the Savior approached someone possessed with evil or unclean spirits; they would exclaim, "Son of God leave us alone." They knew Him and knew that they were not worthy to be in His presence. During Christ's earthly ministry, in every village, town, and city into which He travelled; He cast out demons from many, as the scriptures testify.

This book relates many of these scriptural accounts of people like one called Legion, Mary Magdalene, and the only child of a pleading father; all of whom were possessed with demons. These special sons and daughters of God were chained, placed in tombs and judged as being insane or crazy. If this were true, then how (after the evil spirits were cast out), did they instantly become normal; and then, desire to follow Jesus as one of his disciples?

I start this book with the personal story of my son Joseph who, at the age of 23, committed suicide. I've also included many other touching accounts of suicide victims, and sacred personal revelations and visions. Most notably, I talk of preventive measures and clear solutions which have never fully been brought before the general public. A word about so-called 'action groups'. Caution is advised; they are seeking for good, but they don't acknowledge many important truths and important facts from the Holy Scriptures.

We humans (natural man) and Satan are both enemies of God. Natural Man and Satan permeate all religions, every political persuasion, every country, every race and gender.

This book called, "True Innocence" should become a companion to the Holy Scriptures in every home. Reading and re-reading this book will help you know the enemy, and teach your family how to combat its influence.

The understanding of how Satan influences homosexuality, secret combinations (secret societies) and the general tumult in the world today is essential to all mankind. Further, the issues of depression, substance abuse, drugs, suicide, mass murders, violence, rape, incest, abortion, child abuse and etc., all point directly to the influence of the two enemies of God. They are all related; each leading to the others. By contrast, the Savior Jesus Christ gives the doctrine of salvation and eternal life. Through the atonement, all mankind can escape the chains and bondage that Satan demands.

I'll present scriptures that will enlighten your mind to the truth. You may say as many have said, 'I've read the scriptures many times, but simply overlooked these truths as I sought the Good Word of the Gospel.'

Something to think about as you read this book: How many people 'out there' are possessed and dangerous to you and your family? Could it be someone in my neighborhood, a family member, a close friend, co-worker, or a stranger? I encourage you to look inward, and begin to clean the inner vessel first. Go to the mirror and ask yourself, "Are there any evil spirits within me at this very moment? If your natural man and your spirit are present and aligned in the goal of Eternal Life, then you're on the right path. Then you are able to look outward to help others. I know there are multitudes who have allowed Satan to take up residency in their bodies. Because of this, anything evil is possible in this world. I testify that the counsel in this book is true; and the counsel it contains is needed in the entire world today.

CHAPTER 1

Joseph My 'Sonny Boy' - Birth / Early years

I'm the third child of seven children. I grew up with love and learned the lesson of honesty at my mother's knee. She taught me about a loving Heavenly Father and of two plans; Jesus Christ's Plan of Happiness; and of Satan's Plan of Misery and Woe. She taught me that a record of my life was being kept of the good and bad I did. I thought (as many do) that my Heavenly Father expected me to go through life with perfection. Needless to say, I made my share of mistakes, and eventually learned for myself that God's plan only included one perfect being: Jesus Christ. Along the way, I've learned that He loves me; and is able to rescue each of us, if we will acknowledge our mistakes and repent. I've come to know he won't force me to do right – that proper choices have to be of my own free will. It is my greatest desire to be home again with my family; my Heavenly Parents and my friend, and Brother Jesus Christ who paid the ultimate price for each and every sinner.

I'm a fortunate man. I was able to marry the girl of my youth – my High School sweetheart. We were married in 1977. After a year and a half, we were blessed with a daughter. Our Emily was a beautiful little girl with her mom's looks and my big eyes. I was so happy to have a little girl.

Thirteen months later, another little girl blessed our home. Lilly looked like my aunt Kathleen and my Mom. She was a total opposite from the dark eyed, dark haired Emily. Our little blue eyed, toe headed Lilly was just as much Daddy's girl as was her older sister. When Lilly was born, the Doctor said, "This baby is a boy he looks just like his dad." Then he said, "Oops! This baby is a girl, her bottom half is like her mom." I went into momentary shock! I had thought all throughout the pregnancy that this baby was going to be a boy. We laughed at the time and have since joked about my reaction as the story has been retold over the years.

What a blessing these two girls have been to our family! I'm so proud of them. They are talented, smart, spiritual and wonderful mothers.

Two and a half years later, we were finally blessed with our first boy. Just as with the girls, Cassie experienced complications. This baby was three pounds bigger than our girls. When his head was delivered his shoulders got stuck. With some maneuvering his body was finally delivered. This was definitely a boy! I was jumping up and down yelling, "I got my boy!" After a short cry, he was having trouble breathing and began being unresponsive. He was rushed to the nursery and I went with them. Our family had been waiting and had only seen Cassie taken to the recovery room. They began to get nervous wondering where the baby and Dad were. When our boy was stabilized, I was finally able to get our parents and girls; and give them the great news. I had my 'Sonny Boy'! We named him Joseph after me. Over the years, I would usually call him Sonny, Sonny Boy or Little Joe. Cassie called him Joseph, Joe, or Joseph Shawn Perkins to get his attention (usually when he was in trouble). His siblings simply called him Joe.

He was medium colored, with big blue eyes and dark hair. He was 21 inches long and weighed 8'10". He was handsome even as a baby. He slept all night from birth. It was apparent from the start he wasn't petite like his sisters. He grew so fast, we used to call him our 'butterball'. He liked to play with his sisters, but he liked boy things: trucks, balls, planes, dogs, and etc. The girls wanted him to play the part of Prince Charming but he hated that and would always try to change the part to a Lawman, Super Hero or Athlete.

We had a playhouse in the yard, inherited from my wife's childhood. One day the girls wanted him to dress up in one of the dresses the girls would put on. That was the last straw! From then on Little Joe and the neighborhood boys would be the tormenters of the girls. He may have looked like Prince Charming, and would protect them from evil villains, but he would NOT dress up!

From the start, we knew Joseph was shy. A trait he inherited from both Cassie and I. Early on, our parents thought he couldn't talk; because he didn't talk unless he was around one of us. We both had younger brothers (his uncles) with which he enjoyed playing. At about the age of three, he was finally confident enough to start talking around others, but even then he didn't say much.

At the time of Joe's birth, I was serving as a Counselor in our Ward Bishopric. When he was 5 months old, I at the age of 25, was called to be Bishop of our new Ward. It was challenging but I made sure I spent quality time with my kids. They accompanied me to meetings at times and they were, for the most part, good for their mother. When Sonny was finally able to go the Ward Nursery, he refused because he didn't see any men. Troy and Sherron Porter were soon called to be the leaders and he instantly took a liking to Troy. Although he was still shy, he was able to go to class with his new found 'friend'.

As he grew he had many childhood friends including: Justin, Doug, the Henry twins, and Kurt. And, he was quickly learning that his actions had consequences. One day, he and the Henry twins were throwing dirt clods at a neighboring barn, when a window was broken. Out ran the owner to see who had damaged his property. He called the police and came over to discuss the damages and restitution. The fright of this farmer (who had lost his arm in an accident years before) with the 'hook arm', and the police questioning, nearly scared the boys to death. No charges were filed, but the boys learned to respect the property of others.

We have always had a big yard and garden. One summer some shovels went missing. After questioning the kids, Little Joe admitted that he had taken them to the 'field' and that he and Kurt were digging a big hole. When asked why, he promptly replied he was trying to dig down to hell and ask Satan, "Why he made people do bad things?" Even at a young age, he wanted to know, "Why?" As parents, we try to teach our kids right from wrong. We tried to explain that he, 'Wouldn't be able to dig down to find Satan', but the best thing he could do was, 'To choose to do right'. Then, Satan would have no power over him.

Joseph finally got a brother at age 3 ½. He was so excited when Grant was born. He was a good brother – kind and loving. When he was 5, Rick was born. He loved having two brothers to be able to take a stand against the older sisters when needed. He was quite often a tease, yet he was very compassionate. If the younger boys would get into trouble, he would feel their pain, and not want them to face the consequences of their actions. Over the years they had lots of adventures and a strong bond – a band of brothers. He was also a great ally for the girls when they needed his support.

One day after kindergarten, we heard him yell, "Look Mom and Dad; see what the big boys taught me." As we turned to look, we were horrified as we saw him standing on his bike seat going down our steep driveway. Just then, he hit a bump and flew head first over the handlebars landing on this head, neck, and back. He was unconscious and had blood all over his face. We grabbed him and rushed to the hospital. It was determined he had a concussion, and the inside of his mouth required many stitches to repair the damage to his mouth and lip. We were told that when he was in his twenties he could possibly lose his teeth. Looking back now, I wish I could have taught him the lesson that you don't have to do what the older or 'cool' boys do; just do what is right. Try to be a leader not a follower.

He also had a quiet sense of humor. Once, while I was fulfilling a speaking assignment in another ward, Cassie was ill, so I took the kids with me. The girls sat on the front row, but Sonny Boy wanted to be with me on the stand. As I was speaking, I noticed the congregation was laughing and I couldn't figure out why. After all, I was giving a talk on a serious subject. I looked down to my girls for support and they were pointing to the side of the pulpit at Joe. I looked over to see him pulling faces at the audience. I quickly put a stop to the behavior but not without some embarrassment. I thought to myself, 'This kid isn't as shy as I thought'! Years later, when we moved to a new area, our family was asked to speak in Church and introduce ourselves (as is the tradition in the LDS faith). All was well until it was Joe's turn to speak. Even though he had practiced and we felt he was prepared, he didn't come to the pulpit when it was his turn. Cassie went to his side to give him encouragement but his reply was an adamant, NO! He said, "I'm a kid and don't have to talk if I don't want to". Over the years we noticed he didn't have any speaking assignments in Church. We eventually found out that whenever it was his turn to talk he simply told his leaders, "No!"

Cassie's family loves to fish. I learned patience for fishing from her family while we were dating. Each year we'd take our kids to the trout farm where they could easily catch fish and have a good experience. Also, when they were small, we took fishing trips with our families to Idaho. I quickly learned that if you had kids fishing you didn't [fish]. As the adult, you were kept busy preparing the lines, baiting the hooks, helping cast the line, netting the fish they caught, handling the fish and removing the hook, putting on new hooks, sinkers and bait; and then starting the whole process over again. Little Joe taught me on that trip that he had more patience than I. He would sit quietly and as still as a statue until, sure enough, he would catch a fish. I have a picture of that trip that is a constant reminder of how fast he could learn even at a young age. He really took to the sport and fished from then on. His specialty became fishing for catfish on the Snake River.

Many times, he and his friends, would go raccoon hunting and then (using lanterns), fish the river.

Once Cassie was worried that Joseph and his friend Tim were so busy fishing that they hadn't had time to eat; and was determined to take them some food. She fixed a dinner and then we were off to find them. We found them not too far from their favorite fishing spot. Joe was so surprised and appreciative of the time and effort we took to make sure he had some nourishment. He thanked us over and over again.

At nine years old he surprised us one Sunday during the Sacrament Prayer. He told Cassie the prayer was, 'Wrong'. She asked how he knew and he emphatically showed her by opening up to the Sacrament Prayers in his scriptures. Later, when he became a Priest and was able to bless the symbols of the Sacrament, he only participated when it was absolutely needed. When he did bless the Sacrament he gave the prayers with thought and meaning. In our Ward, the young Priest and his father together would bless the Sacrament the first Sunday after the boy was ordained [a Priest]. I cherish that experience we had together.

Once he was asked to the dishes. He replied that it was a, "Woman's job". I overheard him and told him that as a consequence, his job for the next week was to do the dishes. He didn't like it, but by the end of the week, he had learned that he could still be 'cool' and help his mother. He always did his household chores early and efficiently so he could go on to the things he enjoyed. This work ethic served him well the rest of his life.

One night, he was told it was his turn to pray. He said a ten-second prayer and again (as a learning experience) he was told he would have to give the Family Prayer for the next week. By the end of a weeks' time, he had truly begun to talk to his Father in Heaven. He had grown from the experience, and so had our family.

Sonny Boy loved to play sports. At the age of 8, he played baseball with the twelve year old age group. He was young, but earned his place on the field and in the batting order. He was naturally skilled and when a ball was hit to him, he caught it. He liked to swing early when batting which had a tendency to result in a goodly number of foul balls. Once his team was playing their 'rival' team and as he walked up to the plate, the crowd for the opposing team began mocking this 'little guy' and yelling, "Easy out!" He got up to bat and swung twice before hitting the ball foul. He proceeded to hit it foul 8 more times, before hitting a double over the heads of the outfield. He seldom struck out and was an outstanding hitter with the ability to read a pitcher and adjust to hit the ball. He could play anywhere and could really field a ball. He had long legs and could cover a great distance fast. He was fortunate to always play on a championship team.

As he entered High School he tried out for the Freshman Baseball Team, but both he and his friend Larry were cut from the team during 'tryouts'. No one could accept it, given his experience and prowess in the youth leagues. The boys were told they could stay if they wanted to be 'practice players', but they would not see any 'playing time'. The other guys on the team told the coach, of his value on the field and why he should be on the team. These kids even went as far as trying to get their parents involved in the effort (since they had all seen him play over the years). But, no, the coach had made up his mind. Over the next year, Joe decided he would try out again. At parent teacher conference, Cassie talked to the Varsity Coach (who was also his Math teacher) and was told he would not be considered; because he had been labeled as having a 'negative attitude' by the Freshman Coach. That was all it took and he vowed to never try out again. He supported his friends in their sports but that was where it ended. It was at this time (when he had been disappointed by sports politics) that he started to seriously get into working a regular part-time job. He worked at a dairy and loved it. Soon the money started to come in and his thoughts turned to getting his own car.

For the rest of my life I will miss Sonny on our family bow hunting trips. He liked to take Cassie and Sherry (our granddaughter) in the truck to road hunt because (as he would always say) Sherry was his, "Good luck charm". He wasn't a 'trophy' hunter. He would hunt until he bagged a two-point buck and he would be done hunting. The first time he put a deer in the truck and Sherry saw its tongue hanging out and its glazed eyes – she cried. He asked her, "Do you like deer steaks". She said, "Yes". Then he explained that Heavenly Father had 'blessed us with the meat' and she was reconciled to the hunting process. The first time I shot a trophy deer, it wasn't killed outright and we had to wait for it to die. We tracked it for a long time and over many miles, but it seemed just as determined not to die as I was determined not to lose my trophy. It took all evening, all night and the next morning until it died. Little Joe stayed with me the whole time; and I'll never forget how happy and excited he was for me.

Joe always had brotherly love, even if he was hurt by his brother. During a particular bow hunt, he and Grant had gone down to our hunting spot early with my parents and Uncle Kent. Due to work constraints, we couldn't get there until the next day. On the way there, we stopped and bought a BB gun for Rick who had earned his own (as had done the other boys). As we drove, I taught the rules of our family 'hunter safety program'. He had passed the regular State-required Hunter Safety course, but needed to know our family guidelines. As we arrived at camp, Rick started bragging about how his gun was 'better than the other boy's guns'. This went on all night and into the next day. Joe had about enough and began to tease him relentlessly about what a 'bad aim' he had, and tell him he could 'never hit what he aimed for'. Grant and I had gone with my parents and brother to hunt. Joe had gotten his deer the first day so this left him, Rick and Cassie in camp. While Cassie was doing the breakfast dishes, Joe went off into the brush to 'answer the call of nature'. He headed down the hill with paper in hand, and Rick went uphill to shoot his BB gun. As she worked, she noticed him pump the gun as hard as he could. She guessed that he was going to show his brother he COULD hit whatever he intended to shoot.

Suddenly Cassie heard Joseph screaming for her (and concerned) ran to see what was wrong. With his pants still down and squatting he yelled, "Rick just shot me in the butt!" Cassie helped him to camp and checked his injury. The BB hadn't lodged in the skin so she applied some ointment on the large welt. Cassie was boiling as she yelled to Rick to 'bring her the gun' so she could 'put it away for a year'. He wasn't about to lose his new prized possession and didn't respond. She told him he'd better bring the gun to her or she would 'destroy it'. Thinking I would save him from the consequences, he started running up the mountain to find me. She ran after him angrier than she had ever been with one of our children. Joseph knew his mom was serious and started yelling for Rick to 'bring the gun to Mom'. Hoping to get him to come back, Joseph yelled that she, "Wouldn't destroy it if he would just bring it" to her. Rick kept yelling that he had just been aiming at a leaf, and then a branch, and then a bird but that the BB had 'dropped' (from its intended target). Because his story kept changing, Cassie knew he was lying. Seeing his mom run off, he got concerned that she would have a heart attack or something and die. He yelled, "I'll catch him" and even though his run was a hobble, but he finally caught Rick. He brought the gun back to Cassie who then severely reprimanded Rick telling him that he could have 'killed his brother'. He was bawling, she was yelling and Joe was limping. Cassie was very wound up by then and told Rick he had to learn a lesson for not following the rules, and he would lose the gun. She took the BB gun and broke it into pieces against a tree, then threw the pieces into the fire. Then both boys were bawling because Rick had lost his BB gun. When we came back to camp, all three were bawling. Cassie was crying because Joseph could have been seriously hurt or killed; and the boys for the loss of the gun. Grant was then upset feeling his brother's pain. I was angry because the gun had been expensive and could have been saved by just locking it up for a year. We still laugh today about that hard-learned lesson; but what we remember most is Little Joe's willingness to forgive.

My first son could fix anything, and was our 'electronics man'; he could dismantle, repair and reassemble anything. I'm not the best when it comes to repairing electronics and marveled at his ability. Whenever I would work on anything that needed assembly he would observe for a while, get tired of watching me be challenged, and then offer to complete the project (which he always did in what seemed record time). He was always helping me or someone else.

Although he was shy he went to the school dances and enjoyed everything but the photos of him and his date. We have many pictures of him in a tux running from the camera. He took a dance class in high school to try to get more comfortable. He and his friends thought it was cool until they had to dance with the 'all' the girls, including the ones that were 'less than petite'. On the night of one of their performances, his partner broke her skirt zipper while being lifted over his back. She blamed him for an 'improper lift'; and he blamed her because (as he put it), He hadn't forced her to 'eat so much'. Cassie was very upset with him and told him (as she has with all our kids) to, 'look on the heart' and the 'inner beauty'. Over the years, most of the girls he dated told us he was their favorite date because he was very 'fun to be with'. Although shy, he had a great sense of humor.

He was a toilet paper king. He and his friends never were caught 'in the act', but on occasion they had to 'lay low' in a ditch or field until the coast was clear. Once, the whole night passed before they could get home. That morning, when he showed us his 'handiwork', I could see why they had to stay out of sight: the house was a masterpiece!

He and his friends loved to play electronic games. Word of his skill got around and people from far and wide would call him to get the inside 'tips and tricks' so they could advance to the scores and levels he had. As parents, we generally felt that the games were a waste of time. On the other hand video games (compared to other trouble that kids can get into) might not be a bad alternative as long as the games aren't the violent type. Sonny Boy never let the games stand in the way of family interaction. Often he would be playing a game, but would stop if his nieces (our granddaughters) came over to visit. He would pop them some popcorn, put in a movie and watch it with them over and over again. Their relationship was such that many times they woke him up to tell him of their latest adventure. He would never be angry or impatient with them; instead he would just listen to them talk or watch a movie with them. Sometimes we would try to run interference for him so he could get his sleep; he would simply tell us, "It's okay, I love those kids!"

One day, Cassie was near our family room window doing the ironing. Our three granddaughters were there and were pestering grandma insisting that there was a monster in the window-well. She told them that the window-well had a cover placed on it that prevented any 'monster' from getting in. Eventually they were so persistent; Cassie turned around and saw a large, big toothed rat looking back at her. She screamed and so did the girls. Joe came running in, without his glasses (he was legally blind without them) asking, "What's wrong!" All he could understand through the screams was, "Monster in the window!" He felt his way back to his room and grabbed his glasses. When he got back and looked in the window he jumped and they started screaming again. Knowing just what had to be done, he grabbed his pellet gun, shot the rat and removed it; once again saving the day, just as he had many times before with their mothers (his sisters)!

When his dairy job ended during his senior year of High School, he wanted to find a better paying job with a possible future. He got a job working an hour away at a 'DC' (Distribution Center) unloading trucks. At the time, he had his fill with school and was convinced it was time to enter the work force full time. There were many who tried to talk to him about staying in school. His computer teacher had even told him that that he had special talent that could take him far in the industry, if he just stayed in school. But he had become bored and just wanted to have the wages to afford his fast car. As you read Joseph's story, you're witnessing how the 'natural man' began taking over, and the Spirit of God began to fade from his life. Satan's chains were starting to over-shadow his life, and his agency was slowly being destroyed one step at a time.

CHAPTER 2

Joseph's Last Year on Earth

At the outset I want to testify of the Plan of Salvation and my love of Heavenly Father, my love of the Savior Jesus Christ, my love for my eternal companion, and my love for my five children, their companions and my grandchildren. We are sincerely trying to become an 'eternal family'. Becoming an eternal family requires a lot of work and attention, but is well worth the time required to teach, learn, and grow.

I know this Plan of Happiness was presented to each of us in our pre-mortal existence and we accepted that there would be trials and tribulations in this life. We knew that there would be pain and sorrow from making bad decisions and that Satan is a reality. We knew there would be opposition to our efforts to become like God. We understood that Satan's attacks would be personal for each of us. So, how are we to understand the scripture that reads, "Men are that they might have joy?"

We knew and accepted that each challenge we encountered would give us growth and experience. Ultimately we could learn to emulate Jesus Christ which could enable us to become like our Heavenly Father. We had faith in God's Plan to send His Son to atone for our sins, to the end that the demands of justice might be satisfied. We had the promise that the Lord Jesus Christ would support us, carry us, lighten our burdens, dull our pain, appease our sorrows, remove our guilt, soften our disappointments, and save us from physical death and spiritual death through his grace and our repentance. This would enable us to return back to the Father and live with Him for all eternity.

I don't know that the pre-mortal Joseph chose suicide as his way back to the post-mortal existence. I DO believe that the Lord orchestrates circumstances and situations that will give us growth in areas that will be beneficial to us. Perhaps our decisions and actions become examples and opportunities that others will use to help them in their life. I believe that Joseph chose me and Cassie as his earthly parents because he knew that we would be able to make it through the test of his suicide; and the loss of a son through the evil plan of Satan.

It was a challenging trial then, and continues to be even today. Similarly, I trust that he knew that the rest of his family along with extended relatives would be able to handle this tragedy through the great love we have for one another. Still, I know that I'll never feel total joy until I can embrace my son again and know that we will be a forever family for all eternity. Then, and only then, will I experience that TOTAL JOY spoken of in the scriptures when my family is complete and together in the Celestial Kingdom with the Father and the Son.

As I mentioned, Joe had 'Senioritis' and was bored to death at school. He liked fast cars and he was ready to move on. He eventually qualified for graduation, but only attended his Ceremony after an argument with Cassie. As soon as it was over, school became a distant memory.

One night after work, his older friends at the 'DC' talked him into drinking with them at a local bar frequented by the workers. Up to this point in his life, he had been the designated driver for friends at school and had never taken a drink. After the bar, he waited awhile before starting home. He was concerned knowing Cassie would be worrying about where he was and why he has late getting home. As luck would have it, he was pulled over by the police because one of his headlights was burned out. His precious car was impounded and he was arrested and taken to the County Jail where he stayed until morning when we were contacted.

Joseph was humiliated. He knew better and had witnessed others sick from drugs and alcohol. The price he had to pay for his ticket and the impound fee were steep and he was required to wear an ankle bracelet for tracking his location. He hated being on the wrong side of the law. We told him that, in our eyes, he had paid his 'debt to society'; and that he should just 'learn from the experience', leave it in the past and 'move on'.

At this time in his life his High School buddies were starting to go on [LDS] missions, off to trade school or college; and the girls he had dated were starting to get married. This left a gaping void in his life. He convinced himself that because he had made some mistakes, no self-respecting girl he knew would want anything to do with him. This is an example of how Satan works; since nothing could have been farther from reality. All of the girls who had dated Joe in his teenage years told us that they always had 'a lot of fun' on their dates; and many told us that they would have loved to go on a date with him. He felt lost. We began to see evidence that he was starting to question our religious-based standards and his own faith. By his behavior, it was apparent that 'living by the rules' was more and more 'restrictive' and made him feel like a 'captive'. He wanted to move out and his 'drinking friends' were supportive of him; and those who 'break the rules' always want companionship. It's not as 'fun' alone when there are others who offer 'support' in their 'bad behavior'. But, Sonny was somewhat of a loner and he was fine on his own; he could drink, smoke, experiment with drugs and be a one-man-party.

About this time, Cassie was putting laundry away and noticed a light in his closet; she found a marijuana plant growing inside. She promptly disposed of it and confronted Joseph. He explained that marijuana growing was a lucrative business and that, 'lots of people were doing it'. Of course this reasoning fell upon deaf ears as she explained that in our family we obey the laws of the land. Certainly she wasn't going to allow the drug in our home or in the possession of her son. It's easy to see that the influence of Satan desensitizes the mind and soul to the natural consequences of illegal activities. Unhappiness and misery loves company, and he eventually moved in with his friends.

Little Joe continued to work at the distribution center and found that he had real talent for the work. He was meticulous and organized, able to devise ways to get the job done faster, and still maintain high quality. This resulted in him winning several awards and setting several records that still stand today. Cassie liked the fact that they did drug testing which gave her some peace of mind.

He soon discovered that that living away from home was expensive; particularly when he was spending his hard-earned cash on bad habits. He asked if he could move back home and we gladly accepted him back with open arms. Upon moving back, he began to be the 'old' Joseph. While he had been on his own, someone had tried to get him to leave the religion of his youth. He showed Cassie some anti-LDS materials that he had been given and said, "Mom, you need to know your enemy. These people will try to test every testimony of Christ and you need to know how they believe." His spirit still knew the truth he had been taught; he realized these things were incorrect, and false doctrine. Still, he wasn't ready to come back to regular church attendance. In fact, he only set foot in a church four times after graduation: his sisters' wedding receptions, his uncle's mission farewell and when his niece Sherry was baptized. Occasionally, he would still drink and party with his new 'friends'.

During this time, his relationship with Cassie remained as strong as ever. They talked daily; he told her things that most boys would never dare talk about with their mother. She listened and was his friend, but also tried to steer him to a better path. She knew it was best for him to decide when the time would be right for the changes his life needed. Often he would look down on his short mom from his six-foot, three-inch frame and mess up her hair saying, "Madre, I love the way your hair is fixed."

When Cassie asked why he didn't 'have his friends over', he would say, 'They aren't like our family'. Once one of his friends named Charlie did come by to pick Joe up. He wasn't ready so Cassie invited him to stay and have dinner with us. Charlie agreed, and we had a good time getting to know him. The next day, he thanked his mom and said he was, "Surprised that [she] asked Charlie to eat." Cassie replied, "You and your friends are always welcome in our home", and added with a stern look, "But there'll be no drinking or smoking!" After that, his friends came more often.

Cassie listens to the Spirit of the Holy Ghost and has been warned many times of impending trouble. She has also been directed in how to help our family. One day while folding the laundry, she was impressed to put Joseph's pants away in his closet not on his bed (for him to put away) as she usually did. She shrugged off the feeling twice, but on the third time she obeyed. She started to put the fresh clothing on top of the pants stack, but was impressed to put the clean ones underneath. When she lifted them up, there lay a pornographic calendar. When he came home, Cassie confronted him and discovered that he had purchased it on a trip to Wendover, when he turned 21; and didn't think anything was 'wrong' with it. He tried to argue that 'everyone had some' but obviously that argument wasn't going to work. Cassie was unwavering that such filth wouldn't be allowed in our home. She explained that our home was sacred and that kind of material was NEVER to be brought into our home again. She explained that women are treasures of God, and asked how he would feel if it were '[her], [his] sisters or nieces 'who were exploited in such a way. He thought for a moment, and although he was upset that she had destroyed the calendar, he said she was, 'right'. He promised that he wouldn't do it again.

While partying one night at a friend's home, he was introduced to Tracy, a 'spunky' girl with whom he had a lot in common; he fell head over heels for her. His siblings were upset because she was so different from the girls he had dated before. Cassie asked him why he 'was interested in her', he replied, "I know what she has been through, and she knows what I've been through. I want to help her and I can change her." She had come to this country as a young girl and had to learn to speak English. She had found it tough to find good friends and ended up in a rough crowd. Joe could speak her language.

Not long after they met, they were engaged to be married. On weekends, they would party with their friends. One night, he was pulled over by the police and cited for Driving under the Influence (DUI). He was taken to jail and his precious blue Mazda was impounded again. When he appeared in court, he was ordered to spend two days in jail, fined, and required to undergo counseling through the County Health Department. When Cassie picked him up at the jail on Monday morning, he was shaking badly and had tears streaming down his face. On the way home, she stopped to get gas. Joseph jumped out of the car and ran into the store. He brought out a package of cigarettes, sat on a bench outside the store, and smoked every last one. All Cassie could do was sit in the car and cry. Although she knew he smoked, she had never actually smoked in front of her before then. When he got into the car he apologized, but still shaking and crying he said, "I hope the Sheriff's Department all go to hell! They're supposed to protect people and they don't!" Cassie tried to explain that they were just doing their job; drunk drivers are dangerous on the road and that they have to do their job to protect the public. This of course didn't console him, and he never did say why he hated them so badly. We would only later find out his reason.

That night, his friends threw him a party to celebrate his getting out of jail. Joe's girlfriend Tracy got into a fight with some of the other women; he was so upset that he left the party alone and began to drive home. He stopped for gas along the way; and as he pulled away from the station, he was stopped by the police. They told him one of his taillights wasn't working. The officer suspected he was impaired and the field sobriety test confirmed his suspicions. He was taken to jail, booked for DUI, and his car impounded again.

We were very upset when we got the word of his arrest. Not only because of the DUI, but also because there were some indications that the police stop was under false pretenses, rather than for reasonable suspicion. We discovered there were witnesses at the gas station who stated that his light was working. Later it was discovered that one of the women Tracy had fought with at the party was the tipster who had called the police with the false report of the taillight. This woman thought Tracy was with him, and she was trying to get back at her. Because we believe in personal responsibility for actions (you got yourself into trouble; now face the consequences), we didn't hire a lawyer for his defense; he would have to take the services of the court-assigned attorney. In hindsight, perhaps we should have hired one (even if we couldn't afford it). As we'd find out later, in our County if you aren't represented by an attorney, the Judge has a tendency to be harsher in his rulings and penalties. It began to dawn on us that when a person is 'in the system' it's very difficult to get out. When he appeared in court, he was given a 30-day jail sentence. During the week before he was to start serving his time, Cassie felt strongly that we should have a special Family Home Evening for him before he reported to jail.

She had received some inspiration on the Family Night topic one day while in the garden picking apples. On the tree were 'good' apples and 'bad' apples. This started the wheels turning and she remembered a conversation with a young man at work who had told her he was the black sheep of his family (essentially the 'rotten' apple). Cassie called our parents and children and asked each of them if they would write a short letter telling Joseph just how much they loved him. She felt that such a thing would be timely because she recently had a very disturbing dream. The dream was that Joseph shot himself in the head with his pistol. He was an avid shooter who loved to target shoot with his family and friends. He preferred pistol shooting not caring much for rifles except for hunting. The dream was very distinct about it being a pistol that was used (in the dream) to kill himself. The dream scared her so badly she retrieved his two pistols, hid them, and never mentioned the dream to any of us.

The night arrived for our special Family Home Evening for Joseph. The next day he was to report to the jail to serve his sentence. The whole family was there, but he declined to attend, and instead said he would, "Listen from his bedroom". We began the evening with Cassie telling the story of her friend Carl from work. She held up a good apple, one with a worm hole, one with a lot of worm holes, a mushy soft one and a moldy hard shriveled one. As she talked, she looked up and saw him sitting on the edge of a chair, listening intently from his room. She explained that it didn't matter if a person was a 'choice grade-A' 'apple' or a shriveled seemingly unusable one; all had a use and a purpose. If an 'apple' has a blemish or defect, that defect can be removed, and the apple used. She talked of how even an apparently 'rotten' apple could be used to fertilize the soil; or the seeds that remain could be nurtured and grow into a healthy tree that produces good fruit. She looked at Joseph and said, "In our family, there are no rotten apples;

none of us are perfect either, but we stand by, help and love each other. Each of us has great worth in the sight of God.

That began what is now a family tradition; when we have Family Night, we pick one person, and each in turn, tell them why we love them. Joseph sat quietly as one by one we expressed our love and appreciation for him. Cassie then gave him a special little box that contained all the letters that we had written to him. We found out later, that night had been the first time he had planned to kill himself; because he never wanted to go to jail again. After family prayer and when everyone was in bed, he looked for, but couldn't find his pistols, so he sat on his bed and wrote a letter. With his anxious mind calmed, he read each letter that had been written to him; then turned to his scriptures. His scriptures hadn't been opened in a long time. He read until he fell asleep. In the morning, he began to serve the next 4 weeks in jail.

When we returned home from the jail, Cassie went to his room and found his open scriptures, and the open box full of tear-stained letters. She also found the letter he had written:

"I'm sorry I'm not the person you wanted me to be, but I still love you all. No matter what I have ever said, I have been blessed with the best family anyone could ever wish for. You were all the best. I just didn't belong. I have too many things I've wanted to do with my life and it won't happen now with the way I have ended up, but that don't matter now – All that matters is I love you all. I just wasn't meant to come to a family as good as the one I have. I know you guys hate my girlfriend (we didn't) and will never treat her with respect, when I'm gone. P.S. Tell the Sheriff's Dept. to go to hell from me. I'm never going back to jail ever! I'll miss you. Joseph."

God bless an inspired mother whose efforts that night averted a tragedy. We had genuinely been blessed and he was still ours. During his incarceration, he could only receive visitors once a week. With our visits and letters, we were able to keep him encouraged and focused on the future. He paid his price to society and came out ready to start over.

The terms of Little Joe's release required that he attend counseling sessions and have regular drug tests. On one occasion after a counseling session he said, "I hate counselors, they think they can blame everything on your family. They don't want you to admit you chose to make the wrong choices yourself." Still, he continued his counseling and drug tests and had nearly completed the requirements of his probation at the time of his death. He worked hard to complete what was required but he felt defeated. We continued to love him unconditionally in hopes that he could get on the right track.

Life can be such a complex thing. The question of how a person's life experiences mold them into who they become is a challenging one. Why does one person with similar upbringing and genes turn out so differently than another? How's it that one person seems to just 'deal with' the challenges they've had; and another has a tragic outcome? Take abuse as an example. This is an issue that only recently has been talked about openly. Perhaps, in years past, if it had been dealt with differently, things would be better today. When Emily, Lilly and Sonny Boy were young they were abused by a twelve-year old neighbor boy. Our kids were threatened not to tell; but eventually (when the boy moved), they came forward. Each of our children had to deal with it in order to move on. Could it be that his experience of being attacked while in jail that first time, opened old unhealed wounds?

Cassie and I both have had family members that were alcoholics. This was a great concern for us considering there may be a genetic predisposition that we want to avoid. So, we never drink alcoholic beverages, nor had the desire to try them. From experience, we knew that Joseph was a sad and depressed drunk; and felt the sorrow of the world. Only once did he bring alcohol into our home. Cassie found him once passed out on the couch with his arm dangling to the floor and a bottle still in his hand. She was so incensed, she woke him up and told him alcohol was not allowed in our home. He cried that he was just 'no good'. She didn't accept that. She told him he was just as good as everyone in the family, and he needed to stop letting himself down. He never drank at home again, but would give into peer pressure and drink with his friends. He stopped smoking several times claiming that it was, "All in the mind" and you could, "Stop if you really wanted". He was learning that battling addiction was more difficult than he originally convinced himself.

Joseph was invited to our oldest granddaughter Sherry's baptism; but told us he wouldn't be there. Sherry had a special bond with 'Uncle Joseph' because she was shy like him. We knew she would feel bad if he weren't there. We even suggested that he didn't have to dress up, but he still refused. As the baptism services began, we could all feel his absence. During the opening hymn, Cassie glanced over her should and elbowed me; Joseph was there! He wasn't dressed up, he was wearing his earrings, he smelled like smoke but he had tears pouring down his face. We were never so happy to see our son. When the services were over, he told Sherry that he wouldn't have missed it for the world, and that he was so glad he came. Later in a pensive moment he told Cassie, "Mom, one day I'll come back to church and go to the temple." His heart was always in the right place.

When Joe was nineteen he got a tattoo. Emily was the first to see it as she was taking some clean laundry to his room. He was stretched out on his bed sleeping; and there it was the 'grim reaper' as big as life on his shoulder. Emily started screaming and ran downstairs to tell us what she had seen. She knew how we felt about tattoos, and expected us to 'do something' about it. Cassie's response didn't surprise me knowing he worked with young people and knew how they think, she said, "Let's wait for him to show it to us." Of course like a good husband (wanting to be on the same page and support Cassie's statement in front of the kids), I had to bite my tongue. He certainly heard the commotion downstairs, and when he did come down he said, "You probably hate me, but I wanted to get a tattoo."

Cassie asked to look at the tattoo and said, "Whoever gave it to you is a good artist!" I bit my tongue again. Being a good mother then said, "I always hoped you would present the body you were given at birth back to Father in Heaven, clean, unblemished and pure as you were given it. He passed that off and admitted it was a painful experience but that, "Next time, the reaper will have color!" and then, "I'll be getting more after that." He never went back to get more tattoos. In fact, he would later say, "Getting that 'tat' was a stupid mistake and a big waste of money." We had always taught him correct principles, and it was very apparent to us that Satan wanted this boy badly; and we needed to fight harder than the evil one to keep him on a better path.

By December of 2005 (only four months before Joseph's death), I was so busy with my business and full time job I basically lost track of the boys lives. They were working odd shifts, and with my day job, I was only able to see them in passing for only a few minutes each day. It was at this time I had an eye opening experience that really caught my attention. It was as if a sledge hammer had just hit me upside the head. It made me realize that I must not have been listening to the Spirit as I should. I began to realize that they were really in a spiritually dangerous situation that could literally be life threatening

Besides my full-time job I had started a small business spin-balancing commercial aircraft air conditioning parts. At this time, part of what was consuming my time was the pressure of $5000.00 worth of parts to process in the shop; and I was behind schedule. I had a strict deadline to finish the work, and even had to take a couple of days off from my regular job to complete the work on time for my customers. Things had been going really well all morning. Then about midday, everything seemed to fall apart. As I look back upon it now, I'm not sure if the Holy Ghost was trying to get my attention; or pure evil had entered the garage.

As I was standing at one of my work benches, out of nowhere a very large venomous black widow spider fell on the bench in front of my reaching hand (just before I picked up a tool). The spider landed on its back giving me full view of the ominous red hourglass shape on the abdomen. That instant of recognition gave me just enough time to pull back my hand, grab a tool, and kill her before I was bitten. I incredulously looked up at the ceiling only to find it white and very clean; no sign of spider webs. If I hadn't been alert before, I definitely was awake now! I took a breath and walked over to another bench to the computerized balancing machine to continue the process balancing parts. To my amazement, the machine went haywire. It began speaking to me in German, and then in French. I hadn't touched any of the controls, and no matter what I tried I couldn't get it to go back to English.

I called the manufacturer, but because it was late in the day on the East Coast, there wasn't an answer. I was at a loss; first a black widow out of nowhere, and then 45 minutes of total chaos and panic. Not knowing what to do with work critical to the business at a complete stand still; I instantly went to my knees in prayer. I heard the still small voice of the Holy Ghost saying, "Wake up! Your sons Joseph and Grant are being taken over by the evil one." At that moment, I heard them arrive home from work. I immediately went to my bedroom and knelt again in fervent prayer. As I arose from my knees, I immediately began a fast for my sons. I needed answers from Heavenly Father about how to best help my boys resist the power of the destroyer. I returned to the shop and found everything back to normal with the machine. As I dove back into the work, my mind was racing about what had transpired. I continued with a prayer in my heart that I would be guided to the answers I needed.

It was a long night and during that 24-hour period, the spirit of revelation began to flow into my mind. I waited patiently for the two boys to arrive home from work. As they arrived, I asked them if they would sit with me so we could talk, and they agreed. I told them of the experience I had the previous day and I could tell that both were paying attention out of their love for me and our mutual respect. I voiced some concerns about the direction their lives had taken, and under the direction of the spirit, I told the story of George Ritchie. In his book, *Return from Tomorrow,* Mr. Ritchie recounts the story of his nine-minute death. During those disembodied nine minutes, his spirit was escorted to where he could see people who appeared to be in a bar. When they took too many drinks and lost control of their senses, a demon would dive into the person through the crown of his head. These evil spirits were waiting for the opportunity to enter the body of these humans.

I told Joseph and Grant how much I loved them and how much God loves them. I told them they are in the same condition as the people George Richie witnessed while carried away in the spirit. I told them that the Spirit tells me that you each need priesthood blessings to cast out the evil ones. The priesthood of God is real and a great blessing to the sons and daughters of man. I will forever remember their opposite responses. Grant said, "Will you do it right now for me." Then Joe jokingly interjected, "NO! I casted out the evil from Grant and I felt the evil spirit leave." He abruptly went to his room. I followed him and said, "Joseph, please let me give you a priesthood blessing; if for no other reason than out of respect for your Dad." He still adamantly refused. I begged him, but "NO" was still the answer as he left the house.

He had never refused a priesthood blessing in his previous 23 years of life. I knew at that moment he was being controlled by Satan. His agency had been enchained by evil spirits. It wasn't 'him' that told me 'No'; it was the evil ones inside of him who were doing the talking. Many tears flowed that day for my son, and many prayers followed in the days ahead.

After Joe and Tracy were engaged, she decided the ring wasn't big enough. He wanted to become more responsible and buy a bigger ring. That meant that he needed to pay off his fines. He worked very hard and, in many ways, things got back to normal. He loved being with his fiancé and loved her mother's cooking. Tracy's parents are good people with a belief in God and it seemed that the prayers of two sets of parents were being answered. Our last Christmas together, he was surprised we included Tracy as one of the family and gave her a gift. He had thought that we wouldn't accept her for the things she had done; but he was wrong. (As had been the case with the spouses of all our children), she was part of our family now. He also couldn't believe we had also given him a gift. He said, "I didn't think I was worth anything, and I can't believe what you gave me. Thanks Mom and Dad!" We told him many times we loved him as our son, and also in a Christ-like way; because we all make mistakes.

As Valentine's Day approached, Cassie felt impressed that we should take our whole family to dinner. We had a private room and enjoyed a great time with our parents, our children, their spouses (or in the case of Joseph his fiancé) and our grandchildren. We told all of our kids and their families that we loved them, and that we were a forever family. As each family member left, they thanked us. Joe and his fiancé hugged us, my parents and Cassie's mom and told us they loved us very much; it was such a great day!

On Valentine's Day he called Cassie and wanted to know what 'she was doing'? She said she was, "Smelling the red roses [I] had sent [her]. Joseph said, "Mom isn't it cool I gave my sweetheart red roses too!" He went on to say how important it was for him to love and take care of her. He wanted to get married that summer and he was starting to feel his God-given right to be a husband and caregiver to his future wife.

Little Joe felt bad about his entanglements with the law and particularly that he had lost his driving privileges. But he was paying his fines and working hard to make things right. Grant now worked with him at the DC and was his transportation. Because of several head injuries, Grant had to go about learning his new job in his own way. Joe worked closely with him giving him tips that would help him get the hang of the job. During one conversation with Cassie, he told her, "Grant takes his time learning things, but when he does get it I'm so proud; and you should be proud too!" They had a very close bond since the day Grant was born, and Little Joe held him in his arms. Grant started to drink and do things that he knew were not good for him and seemed to be going down the same path from which we were trying to rescue him. Unlike Joe however, Grant listened to our advice and wanted to change. Grant was making his own choices. Once, in a heated moment, I blamed him for the course Grant was taking. I wish I could take those words back.

Joseph was a depressed drunk, and when was feeling low (or got into trouble) he would call Lilly. She counseled him to keep going to counseling, and change his life by returning to the truths he was taught in [our] home. She told him that the best way to do that was to 'change friends' and 'start over'. After one conversation Lilly called me very concerned thinking Joe could be 'suicidal'. I didn't accept it as true. How could my 'Sonny Boy' be considering such a terrible thing? Obviously, I was in denial.

Joe and Tracy had many bumps and hurdles to overcome because of the choices they had made, and continued to make. He talked about wanting to stop drinking; she didn't want him to change. Rebellion was still 'cool' to her. They often argued about the things couples discuss as they plan for their marriage. He wanted children and she didn't. She told him several times that if she ever got pregnant, she would 'abort the baby'. Mean and hurtful things were likely said on both sides. By the end, things were going terribly wrong in their relationship.

CHAPTER 3

The Last Week, Suicide, and Days Following

Even after ten years, this is honestly the most difficult section to write. These very personal feelings and thoughts are almost beyond expression. I pray the Lord's blessing to be with me as I portray these moments of tragedy, love, hope, and faith; and how they work into the Great Plan of Happiness our Father in Heaven has laid out for each of us.

There have been many tears through this experience; and there certainly will be many more before my mortal experience ends. I must remember that Joseph is in a better place, and Satan has no part in his life now. He truly is in the arms of his Savior Jesus Christ. My hope is you will be able to sense the sorrow and grief as if you were me, Joseph's father. I pray that the Lord's spirit might touch you the reader in such a way that you will know you are never alone in this journey of life no matter the pain, the trial, or the sin.

Heavenly Father loves each of us beyond our comprehension; and this love is completely unconditional. He will never allow any trial, pain or circumstance to come our way that we won't be able to overcome thanks to His Son's Atoning Sacrifice. And may I add, no parent should ever have to bury a child except for natural causes. This has been the greatest trial of my life.

On February 28, 2006, Cassie's Uncle Dean took his own life just five days before we lost our son Joseph to suicide. This special man was one of the very best people Cassie and I have ever known. He had served in many leadership roles in the LDS church and in his employment. I had served side-by-side with him on the Stake High Council, and his goodness was evident in everything he did. A year before the end of his life, he and his wife Caroline had been called on an LDS mission to serve in the Thailand Bangkok Mission. While there, he developed severe pain in his head and was hospitalized. They soon discovered that he had acquired a blood clot on the frontal lobe of his brain; that was affecting his emotion and learning centers. This forced them to return home early from their mission. Dean became very depressed, and he wasn't himself. The brain injury was affecting his thinking ability, rationale, and other cogitative functions of his mind. The two forms of medication he was prescribed had side-effects such as depression and suicidal thoughts. Caroline had to watch him closely all the time for signs that his behavior was changing to a state detrimental to his well-being. Because of his condition and the medication, this wasn't the Dean that we had known for so many years; he just wasn't himself anymore.

On the day of his death, Caroline had left him for a few minutes when she heard the gunshot. She ran to his side only to find her dear companion of 45 years lying dead. He had placed the muzzle of his .305 caliber hunting rifle under his chin and pulled the trigger.

We knew he wasn't in his right mind, and wasn't 'himself' as he pulled the trigger. In other words, this was not the Christ-like Dean that had ended his life; but this was a manifestation of the mental illness, brought on by the use of medications (for his condition) that had severe side effects.

Cassie and I honestly felt it was okay for Dean to go at any time the Lord had appointed. Looking back on it now, we think this time-frame was chosen so Joseph would have someone special to greet him from the spirit world. Dean really knew Joseph, knew of his shyness, and loved him unconditionally. Caroline also has faith that he accepted the call to teach those (who have given into the natural man and Satan's influence) on the other side of the veil – helping in their healing and progression.

Later that afternoon, when I was telling Sonny of the death of his uncle and how it happened; he became very inquisitive of how he could have used a rifle (and not a pistol) to kill himself. This really concerned me. Had I been listening to the Spirit more closely, perhaps I would have realized he was thinking of suicide himself. As you recall, Cassie had a dream of Joseph taking his life; and in that dream, he used one of his two pistols. Cassie never told me of the dream until after Joseph's suicide. At the time she had the dream, she knew that I felt talking about such things were a 'bad omen' or 'tempting fate', and that I wouldn't have been able to handle that kind of dream. As you recall, after Cassie's dream she hid his two pistols where he wouldn't find them. I think that at the time of our conversation about Dean, two things must have entered his mind: first, how Dean was a good person; who had been true and faithful in all things; and was as close to perfection as anyone could be, had just committed suicide. And second, suicide could be done with a rifle (something to which he had access). I won't know until I'm on the other side and can ask him what was on his mind.

I never thought that one of my children would carry out such a thing as suicide; let alone feel worthless enough to consider taking their own life. As a parent, you consider that your love will carry your children through the tough times. I knew without a doubt that in Dean's case, everything would be fine. Obviously, he wasn't in his right mind; otherwise he never would have left this life, or completed his earthly mission in that way. I trust he did complete his mission, and that he was true, faithful and endured to the end. I also think he was needed to help those who allow themselves to fall into Satan's traps, start their progression on the other side of the veil. He is fulfilling a mission for Jesus Christ who will be the sole Judge of Dean's worthiness to be able to obtain a Celestial Degree of Glory at the Judgment.

Joseph was depressed and felt there was no hope. As with many who are depressed, he was in literal physical pain (and someone or something), had convinced him his body wasn't worth the pain and sorrow; that he just needed to get rid of this body. To stay here just meant more pain, sorrow, hurt feelings, hatred, and darkness. I believe in my heart, it was an evil demon or spirits that had taken control of Joseph. I know with all my heart, that if he had been willing, had a desire, and been able to receive the Priesthood Blessing I had offered him; the evil that had invaded his life could have been cast aside and given him new hope in life; and just one more chance to escape the chains that bound him.

Many things were going on in our lives, and just like any other family, it had been an extremely busy week. Work, church, kids, grandkids and daily life kept us busier than normal. That week was the longest stretch of not cleaning our home we had ever experienced. I had just gone through a lot of heartache and disappointment at work over trying to get a team leader job. There had been some dishonesty from the management team and I was trying to decide whether to move to another job on the other side of the plant, 5 miles away. Then it was the phone call about the tragic death of Uncle Dean who (to me) could have been my blood brother; he actually loved me that way. Also, Grant had a court date for his DUI, and we were preparing for a family fast for that Sunday, March 5.

We knew alcohol was one of the great tools used by Satan in taking Joseph down, and we didn't want another son to fall also. As you can see, the stress and strain on my family at that particular time was a great burden. Not only did we have a viewing Sunday night and a funeral on Monday; we also had court on Monday with Grant. We didn't know what would happen in the early morning hours of the coming Sunday. On Friday I had requested funeral leave for Monday; and asked if I could make a decision about the job when I returned to work. On Saturday our individual family members began fasting for Grant.

I want to make a confession and tell you to be careful for what you pray for. Heavenly Father knows what the best answer is to each and every prayer. The answer may not be what you would like; but in His wisdom He knows the best way to bring growth to you and to those for whom you are praying. I know that if we go to Him with a contrite spirit, a broken heart, and a righteous desire, we will get the answer we seek.

In my prayers I was pleading my Grant's case to the Father in the name of Jesus Christ. I asked that he would be able to break away from the bad influences in his life. I prayed that he would have the strength to make his own way, stop being a follower; and make right and good decisions. This would mean that Grant would have to push away his best friend, coworker; and brother, Joe. Grant was the work driver because Little Joe had lost his driving privilege in the course of his DUI's. Grant would now have to lead, instead of follow brother and his friends. Grant loved his brother with all his heart, but now he was facing the same consequences of jail time and loss of his driver's license; and because of loss of transportation and criminal prosecution, the possibility of them both losing their jobs.

This was the most difficult prayer I can ever remember expressing to my Heavenly Father. I prayed that Grant wouldn't have to go to jail; I prayed that the judge would soften his heart towards my son and feel mercy for him; I prayed that I could cast out the evil one and give Grant a priesthood blessing at the end of our fast; and I prayed that he would feel remorse, want to repent, and come unto Christ. I know now that Heavenly Father knew of the challenges we would soon be facing. I also know that He knew we would be able to get through the pain of that trial. At that time, I questioned; but now after the trial, I know with the Lords help, we can overcome any test of our faith.

On Saturday evening, he and Grant took off with Tracy to go to a friend's party (drinking) in Ogden. I had told Grant that the family was fasting for him, and asked that he come home early enough to be able to attend church meetings with the family; and try to have the Spirit with him for Sunday. Emily had brought Sherry and Violet over to spend the weekend with us. Cassie had taken Lilly, her daughter Susan, Violet and Sherry shopping for Easter dresses. When I asked Cassie "Why", she replied, "I don't know why. I just feel like it is a very important day." When they returned, Lilly and Susan went home. We had dinner and played games with the girls until Rick came home from his date. It got late, and we were getting tired of waiting up for them to get home. So, we ended the evening with Family Prayer, and put out sleeping bags and blankets on our bedroom floor for the girls. I turned on the front porch light and wearily went to bed.

Our family never stayed up very late especially the night before the Sabbath. This Saturday night was very 'out of the norm' for us. We always tried to get to bed early especially on Fast Sunday and church began early at 9 o'clock. This night, it was 1 a.m. before Cassie and I got in bed. The two granddaughters were sleeping comfortably on the floor, with their sleeping bags and favorite blankets.

At approximately 5:30 a.m., Grant, Joseph and Tracy came home. All three were loud, and the noise woke up everyone except our two granddaughters. Rick remembers awakening for a few seconds then falling back to sleep. I did the same, but drowsily drifted in and out of sleep. Cassie has always been a very light sleeper, and just stayed in bed and listened. The Lord works in such mysterious ways. We now realize that our late evening caused us to be so tired, that it wasn't meant for us to hear or try to stop what was going to happen in the hours ahead.

Grant went right to his room to get ready to shower and retire to bed. Joseph knocked on our door, opened it slightly and said, "Sorry mom and dad we're so late. Tracy is here waiting for her brother to come and get her." Cassie asked, "Are you going to the viewing for Dean tonight with the rest of us? " He said, "No, I want to remember him the way he was when I saw him last." He then uttered the last words I'll ever hear him say in this life. "Mom and Dad I love you, Good night!" We were so tired we said we 'loved him too' as he closed the door. I drifted back to sleep.

Grant was in the shower, and Cassie heard his bedroom door open and asked, "Who's in there?" Joseph answered and said he needed to 'put some stuff away for Grant'. Cassie thought nothing of it since occasionally their clothes got mixed up. We know now that is when he took Rick's .270 caliber rifle from the gun cabinet. She heard him close the door and go back down stairs. Cassie just assumed Tracy was gone. Grant finished his shower and went to bed. All was quiet and Cassie drifted off to sleep.

About half an hour later, Cassie was awakened by arguing coming from our family room. Joseph and Tracy were shouting at each other, and yelling profanities (using the "F" word over and over again) until it woke me up. Cassie just listened but after a few minutes, she had enough of that behavior and got out of bed. She went down the hall to the stairs in her night gown and called out, "What's going on down there? Do I need to call the police?" Joseph and Tracy came to the stairs; "Just go to bed Mom we're okay, we're just having a 'conversation'." But Cassie was very persistent and said, "It doesn't sound like you're just having a 'conversation' Joseph. If you both really love each other, you will stop speaking to each other in this manner!" She asked, "Does Tracy need a ride home?" He said, "No, she's waiting for her brother to come." Cassie also said she wouldn't 'allow that language in our home'. To which Joseph replied, "Sorry Mom, don't worry; everything is okay" and they went to Joseph's room.

Cassie has always been an early morning riser, but was tired and went back to bed. Soon, they were arguing again, and not wanting to have to listen to it anymore, she got up and started vacuuming the living room. I heard the conversation between Little Joe and Cassie until the vacuuming began, but nothing after that. When the arguing continued, Cassie turned off the vacuum and yelled at him again, that she was going to 'call the police if they didn't stop the arguing and yelling'.

He came back upstairs, and said that their, "Argument was over" and that her "Brother was on his way." Suddenly in a complete change of mood and tone he said, "Go ahead and call the cops mom! I want to report you for stealing my pistols. You'll be the one going to jail for stealing my pistols and hiding them from me." This really scared Cassie because of her dream. She asked why he 'needed his pistols' and he said so he and his friends could 'go to the shooting range' (as they had done many times before). She recognized he was in a 'bad' way, and that something serious had happened between him and Tracy that morning. Tracy told Cassie she was 'going outside to wait for her ride'. She looked outside to see them smoking. He had never done that at our home because he knew we didn't allow it. At this point, she came back to bed and again drifted back to sleep. She didn't hear him come back in the house.

Everyone in our family knew their relationship wasn't a good one. Rick witnessed her striking him in the face, and he wouldn't retaliate. It was a volatile relationship. Tracy wanted a bigger engagement ring; and he was trying to pay off his debt, so he could afford one. She was involved in drugs, but he wasn't; and he told her that he wouldn't have anything do with her if she kept 'using'. She had also been telling him 'you should just kill yourself'. I'm sure she was impaired during these times, and wasn't herself. We knew that when Joseph was under the influence of alcohol, he was a depressed, self-loathing, and sad drunk. Over their time together, she had thought that she might be pregnant. She would tell him she didn't want his baby, and if she became pregnant, she would have an abortion. They argued about money. She would get upset that much of his money was going to pay fines and bills. She didn't work and lacked the skills to help budget wisely. It was a bad situation and the relationship was doomed to fail; yet he loved her and kept trying to 'keep it together'.

As we would find out later, she had pushed all of Joseph's 'hot buttons' that previous night. Possibly the worst of it, she had told him she wanted to break off the engagement. Her reason: she wanted to be with a woman. Apparently, He had caught her flirting with a woman at the party; setting off their initial argument of the evening. This knowledge would be devastating to any young man who loves a young woman.

At about 7 a.m., Cassie was in a deep sleep dreaming about Joseph as a boy running down a hill with a dandelion in his hand. In the background of the dream, she could hear footsteps running up a flight of stairs, and a door slamming shut. As the dream continued, she noticed how cute and innocent he was. She reminisced of him being an explorer and lover of nature. They had always had a good relationship and she was enjoying the memories of his childhood. Just as he blew the dandelion seeds at her saying, "Look Mom!" with his beautiful smile and pretty big blue eyes – She awoke to the sound of a gunshot. She jumped from the bed yelling, "Joe, I think Joseph just shot himself!"

Before I go on, I want to set the scene of Joseph's preparations to take his own life. He did something that, at the time we noticed it, seemed very strange; we didn't know what to make of it. I now believe it was his way of showing his love to his younger brothers one last time. He had put on a shirt of Rick's, Grant's shoes, and a jacket we had given him for Christmas. These last actions of love have consoled us as we realize love extends beyond the grave. It brings so much joy and peace to my soul to know of the power of prayer and fasting and the healing power of the ministering of Angels. For a moment in time, the veil was removed and the windows of heaven were opened; and the love of God was present during this very trying time.

Moments before Cassie's fateful words, I had an 'experience'; whether it was my spirit, my physical body, or both I don't know. What I remember is sitting up in bed, and as a father and a priesthood holder, I raised my right arm to the square and commanded the evil spirits to leave our home in the name of Jesus Christ. I think the evil ones had already convinced Joseph to pull the trigger, but by my authority as a father and Elder in Israel, I had cast out the demons, that had taken over his body, before his spirit left this world. I'm sure Satan thought he had 'won'; but as you read the following verses of scripture, you'll know as I know that Satan 'lost' when it comes to my Sonny Boy, Joseph:

> "Ye cannot say, when ye are brought to that awful crisis that I will repent, that I will return to my God. Nay, ye cannot say this; for that same spirit which doth possess your bodies at the time
>
> that ye go out of this life, that same spirit will have power to possess your body in that eternal world.
>
> For behold, if ye have procrastinated the day of your repentance even until death, behold, ye have become subjected to the spirit of the devil, and he doth seal you his; therefore, the Spirit of the Lord hath withdrawn from you, and hath no place in you, and the devil hath all power over you; and this is the final state of the wicked." (*The Book of Mormon,* Alma 34:34-35)

I believe that the Spirit of the Lord had taken over my spirit; in order for me to save Joseph from spirit prison and the possession of Satan before departing this life into the Spirit World. I've thanked my Heavenly Father many times for those few moments of exercising my priesthood power and authority. I testify that by Joseph having a .2165 blood-alcohol level in his system, he was not himself; and did not have full control of his reasoning power at the time of his suicide. I testify that he is in Paradise because the Grace of God allowed me to exercise my Patriarchal authority in my home and in behalf of my son. My son Joseph wasn't a wicked man; he was very meek, loving and kind to everyone.

As I fell back into a deep sleep, that's when I heard Cassie jump from the bed saying, "Joe, I think Joseph just shot himself." I was trying to wake up and make sense of what she had said, when I heard Cassie screaming my name in the most mournful and horrible way possible. It took me a moment to comprehend whether this was real or a dream. I jumped from the bed and threw on my clothes!

Cassie had run downstairs and paused at his closed door. Wondering if she had jumped to a wrong conclusion, she stopped, and softly (in case he was asleep) asked, "Joseph, are you okay?" There was not a response. She opened the door and came face to face with the worst thing any person, let alone a parent, should have to witness. The child who she had carried, borne, loved, nurtured, and taught - lay dead. In that moment of shock (I believe her spirit tried to protect her mind from the gory scene), her eyes moved to the top of the wall and she wondered, 'What is that gray thing sticking out of the wall'? It was part of his skull. His beautiful handsome face was ripped apart. Half of it was gone the other lay on his shoulder. She witnessed the spinal fluid and blood spraying over the walls, bed and floor. She was momentarily paralyzed from the scene that lay before her; then she screamed my name. She needed to hold her first born son, the child she had carried, her precious baby; but she had the restraint not to cradle his body, knowing she could never be pulled from him if she did.

Time Stood Still. She wondered if anyone could hear her screams, and turned and ran up the stairs to find me, our granddaughters and our two sons coming out of our rooms. Rick asked what was wrong and she screamed that, 'Joseph was dead - he killed himself with a rifle'. I nearly went down – I think I even forgot my granddaughters were there. Rick shoved Cassie out of the way and yelled to call 911. As he ran down the stairs he yelled, "Mom and Dad I'll save him!" All Cassie could say was, "No – he's dead." Rick started to scream in anguish, "He's dead, he's dead!" In anger now, he ran up the stairs yelling, "Where's Tracy?"

As I entered Joe's room, I experienced the tunnel vision, and the deafening silence of the moment. I couldn't hear anyone or anything. It was as if, it was just Joseph and me; and yet he wasn't there, just his lifeless body. Hollywood could not create a more horrible scene. I remember the shock of seeing what was left after placing the barrel of the gun in his mouth and pulling the trigger. It was as if a bomb had gone off in that small bedroom. I was overcome with grief; I couldn't recognize my own son! I looked around the room for Tracy. I was afraid she was dead too, but thankfully she wasn't there. Realizing this was real; I dragged myself up the stairs and went to the entrance of our living room. Grant passed me as he ran downstairs to see if he could help. It was then that I smelled the alcohol on him. In all the chaos, our granddaughters had started to go down the stairs to see what was going on. Thankfully the boys stopped them before they could view the horrible scene. The last thing he would want is for these young girls to be traumatized by the sight of his body in that condition. It was a blessing that they were stopped amid all the confusion and commotion.

Grant started to scream that he was, 'Going to kill Tracy for this!' He came upstairs and threw up. Cassie was on her cell phone trying to call for help. Being in shock, her fingers kept punching the wrong number. I asked again what we should do. Cassie was trying to comfort our boys and granddaughters so I said, "Someone, grab the house phone, dial 911, and I'll talk to them." As I sat at our table, numb and mechanically answering questions; I felt I was in the middle of a bad dream. Eventually, I could hear the siren of the ambulance. I asked, "Why are they using sirens? Don't they understand my boy is dead? His head is gone!" Just then the First Responders (our neighbors across the street) and the Highway Patrol arrived. Soon, more officers, detectives and the Sheriff's Department were on the scene. Our home became an open book with our family the main characters on display for the world to see. We tried to answer the questions to the best of our ability; as we tried to piece together the circumstances of Joseph's death; and determine who might have witnessed anything or been involved in any way.

As the investigation progressed, we discovered where Tracy had been during and after the shooting. When he told her of his intention to kill himself, she immediately left his room and the house. She was waiting on the front porch step for her brother to pick her up, when she heard the gunshot. She became hysterical and started running down the street. She tried to call Joe, hoping he hadn't done what he had threatened. We were told that the police located her half a mile down the road, crouched in a ditch.

To this day, Tracy hasn't been forthcoming with us about what was said or done to push Joseph to do such a horrible thing as suicide. We know there were probably many contributing factors. The questions that have arisen many times in our minds are: Could she have stopped him? Did she see the rifle? If so, why didn't she call out for help? Or, did she tell him like so many times before, "Go ahead; you should kill yourself." We may never know the full story until we meet Joseph again. One thing we CAN say with certainty is: we have forgiven Tracy. Since his death, we have treated her as our own daughter. We know this is the Christ-like thing to do; and what Joseph would have wanted us to do.

The First Responders (who had been through suicide in their extended family) were very kind and caring. They helped Cassie calm down enough to call our family who we needed for comfort during this time of shock and grief.

Cassie called Lilly first. Lilly had trouble getting pregnant in the past and Cassie was afraid the shock of the news might cause her to have a miscarriage (she was carrying her son Tom at the time). When Lilly answered, she screamed, "I need to talk to Joseph!" Lilly said, "Joe isn't here" (and thought that perhaps something had happened to me). Cassie said, "I mean I need to talk to Lee (Lilly's husband)." Lilly explained he had 'left earlier on the truck'. Cassie said, "Okay", and hung up. She dialed Lee's parents and asked them to, 'Call Lee and go gently tell Lilly the bad news'. In the meantime, Lilly had called Lee and told him she thought 'Joe was dead!' Lilly heard the farm radio phone ring in the background. As she stayed on the line, she could hear enough of Lee's conversation, that her fears were confirmed. Lee's parents picked her up and rushed to our house to help with Emily's girls. Lee was able to arrange for another driver to take his load, and he headed immediately to our home to do whatever he could.

Cassie next called her younger sister Amy's home. She told George (her brother-in-law) the sad news, and asked him to get word to her 'mother, and the rest of the family'. Then, she requested that he go to Emily's home and bring her to get her daughters. Every family member that got the news, started to scream in anguish at Joseph's loss. They were all still reeling from the death of Uncle Dean.

Next, Cassie called another sister Sally. She cried and lamented over the tragedy; then gaining control of her emotions she said, "We'll get right in the car and come to help however we can" (They lived in

Idaho Falls which was a two-hour drive). Her husband called their mom and asked if George and Amy were there yet. She said, "No" and asked, "What's going on? Are the grandchildren OK? Has there been an accident?" He said, "They'll fill you in when they get there."

Thinking George and Amy would be there, Cassie dialed her mom. She again indicated that they 'hadn't arrived', and again asked about 'the grandchildren'. Cassie just said 'No' to her questions, and asked her to have them call when they arrive. Her mom became very adamant that Cassie tell her 'what was wrong'. Cassie finally said, "Joseph killed himself." She started screaming and threw the phone down, just as Amy and George knocked on the door. They could hear 'Mom' crying and screaming, and after some knocking and yelling for her to unlock the door, they were able to get in to help her. They got her dressed and drove off to tell Emily the terrible news.

I called my parents, and of course they responded as had the others. In their grief, shock, and confusion, they thought they were talking to Cassie. They called my siblings. In the meantime, Amy, George, and Cassie's Mom arrived at Emily's apartment. But at the same moment, Rick called and told Emily 'Joe's dead'. She asked, "How" and Rick blurted out, "He shot his head off." At this gory image, Emily screamed and ran out of her apartment; just as they were getting out of the car. Emily fell into their arms as they cried together over the awful loss of Joseph's life.

At the 9 a.m. start of our local ward church services, they announced what had happened. One of Joseph's best friends was blessing his baby that morning. He jumped up from his seat sobbing and left to call Grant; hoping this was just some sick joke. Many and varied are the ways people far and wide heard and received the news. The top headline news on television that day was the occurrence of a 'domestic violence situation' in a small Utah town. They showed a photo of our home and of Tracy as they spoke of Joseph's death. The news story was difficult to watch, but also served to contact our extended family and friends in two states. The 911 call ran for two days as the investigation continued. For good or ill, news of tragedy travels fast. One thing is certain: Joseph was well-liked, and his death has had a lasting effect on many people; family friends and strangers.

As things at home slowed to a numbing lull, Lee's dad (Thomas) gave us each a priesthood blessing. The First Responders (EMT's) lived just across the street, and opened their home to us and our visitors; so the authorities could finish their investigation and the cleanup begin. The Ward, under the direction of the Relief Society sisters, provided food for our family and friends. Lee and my brother Tyler were asked to be volunteers to help clean up the room.

Family and friends poured in like sunshine through the clouds on that cold spring day. The crocus, tulips, and daffodils were just starting emerge from the ground; reminding us, in an even more personal way now, of the Atonement and Resurrection and their promise of 'new beginnings'. My parents graciously invited us to spend a few days with them. We decided it would be good to stay at my parents' home at least that night. During the day, both our families came in large numbers to offer their support. Members from our current ward and every area, in which we had ever lived, called or came to embrace us and offer their aid and sympathy. Even friends from our youth and our places of work took the time and the effort to come. A tragic death can be very traumatic but can be made a treasure by dear people that in some way help ease your pain and suffering.

Needless to say, we didn't make it to Uncle Dean's viewing (visitation) or funeral; we planned our son's. The next day our immediate family members met at the funeral home and florist to make arrangements. The funeral services were planned with the necessary people called to speak, provide the music, and sing. Together we selected a forest-green casket decorated with pine trees. We chose his burial spot at a small local cemetery, his burial clothing and the photos that would help tell his life story. Our children showed their love and faith as they helped with every aspect of what would be our final tribute to a son and brother who was loved beyond words to express.

Still, I was in denial saying, "That wasn't my son! My son wouldn't do that!" I didn't want to leave his side. I truthfully didn't want life to go on. I felt as lifeless as his body lying there on his bedroom floor. All I wanted was to go with him to the 'other side' of the veil; our post-earth life existence. As I mentioned, many Ward members left church services to come render Christ-like service to us by preparing meals and expressing their love for us. It was really this Christ like love that sustained us, supported us, and made it bearable to survive this huge trial.

By staying with my parents, we were able to reflect, calm down and prepare for the funeral. I wanted the funeral to proceed as soon as possible. Then again, in Cassie's great wisdom, she could see we needed to have time to grieve, gather our thoughts and wait a week. Accordingly, we held the viewing the following Sunday evening; and the funeral on Monday morning.

I'm so grateful she was listening to the Spirit. This time was needed in order to overcome our emotions; and give her the courage she needed to be able to speak at our son's funeral service. She felt speaking (although it would be very difficult) was necessary for her closure, and to express her love for a very close and special son. To me Joseph was my 'Sonny Boy'. The love for our son and our other four children is stronger than death itself; it is eternal.

As I remember it, time seemed to stand still at this point; minutes seemed to be hours, and hours seemed to be days. The tragic scene kept running through our minds over and over again. There was no recrimination, finger-pointing, or feelings of regret. Cassie and I had been grateful to take Joseph back into our home; to give him his own bedroom and privacy at a time when had didn't have money or anywhere else to turn. There were times, after each arrest, that some would say, "Give him a dose of reality, some tough love; kick him out!" We felt inspired that sometimes, 'tough love' is to do what the Savior would do; and that's forgiving 'seven times seventy'.

Cassie and me would counsel with him and discuss the rules while in our home (such as no alcohol, drugs, or tobacco). We loved him unconditionally, and gave him a roof over his head. This gave us the opportunity to see him and talk to him every day. I know that Heavenly Father knows the end from the beginning; and gave us these special moments that we could cherish when he was gone. These kinds of priceless, loving moments help to build our hope and faith in a brighter future when we may see Joseph again.

Ask yourself: if you as a parent were in a similar circumstance; could you forgive yourself (when tragedy strikes) had you not taken your child back when they were in a dire situation? Would your child have shortened his life much more? Would he have been totally alone in his death? Ultimately, the value and support of a caring family can't be expressed in words.

How would we feel if we didn't have our Heavenly Father and his son Jesus Christ there to catch us when we've fallen into sin? The spirit may withdraw, but they stand ready (perhaps at a distance) with their eyes longingly affixed upon us; waiting for us to forsake the sin and repent. They never leave us alone, nor will they ever stop loving us unconditionally.

Cassie and I will always miss Joseph but we have no regrets for the time we had together before he left this life. I pray every day that no other parent, brother, sister or child will ever have to suffer through a trial such as this. Suicide is final; there is no 'coming back'. Often, there isn't closure because there are no answers to the questions: 'Why'. Especially when there aren't notes or letters left behind; or that final chance to tell a loved one how much you love them. We were fortunate to hear these words from Joseph one last time, "Dad and Mom I love you; good night."

The evening of the first day, was the beginning of many opportunities for the veil to be removed. Cassie and I were at Dad and Mom's when Emily arrived with her two daughters Sherry and Violet. I was having one of those emotional breakdowns, where the tears flowed freely. Little five-year old Violet looked up at me and said, "Grandpa, why are you crying? Joseph is all right. Can't you see him standing there next to you?" The honest innocence of these little ones is a gift of God. If we as adults could only see with our spiritual eyes, what wonders might come to our view! These little children are so clean and pure of heart that they have an unmatched 'closeness' to Father in Heaven. The angels on the other side of the veil were working their miracles that day as well.

One of my close friends in a city 20 miles away, called our home within the first hours after Joseph's death. As Cassie answered the phone he said, "Cassie what's wrong? The Spirit (just like I'm talking to you right now) said to me twice: "Call Joe's house, there's something wrong.""

My good friend Steve was serving as a High Councilman in a neighboring Stake. He was on his way to meet with the Bishopric of the ward where he had been assigned to speak that day. He explains the experience this way: "I realized I hadn't made time for personal prayer before arriving at the meeting house. Before I knocked on the Bishop's door, I started praying silently when a spirit appeared in front of me and introduced himself as 'Joseph'. I had never seen him before but he had beautiful dark hair and big blue eyes. He said, "You're talk will be fine; and everything else will be fine too." Then he disappeared.

As Steve entered the prayer meeting, he described what had just happened. The Bishopric had already heard about my son's suicide earlier that morning; and explained it to Steve. Later, when Steve got up to speak in the meeting, the Spirit bore witness to him that he needed to say, "We are not to judge the parents or the young man who died; only the Savior can judge these situations."

Monday finally arrived; there had been no sleep the past night, only tears. In the next couple of days the veil covering our eyes was very thin and it became a very special time of communication between those here and spirits from the other side.

On the third day after Joseph's death, Grant had a visit from his older brother. Grant was finally getting some sleep on a friend's couch. He had just fallen asleep, when he felt three taps on his shoulder. Looking up, he saw Joseph standing at the side of the couch above the floor. Grant could 'hear' Joseph speaking but his lips weren't moving. Joseph asked, "Are you ready?" Grant's replied, "Ready for what?" "Are you ready to go on a mission for me?" "No", was Grant's reply. Joseph: "Not that kind of mission." (Grant was very shy and doubted his own ability to teach and be a missionary). "I want you to prepare yourself for the blessings of the Temple; and then take my name through the Temple so we can be with Dad and Mom together forever." Grant committed to his brother that he would get himself ready, and go to the temple; and then, do (by proxy) Joseph's temple work. This ended the visit. This visit is a demonstration of the continued love God has for us even after death and into the journey of the afterlife. Here Joseph was given the opportunity to help Grant understand the eternal nature of the family; and encourage him to pursue a better course with his life. How fortunate Grant was to have had such an experience soon after his brother's death!

In the *Book of Mormon* a Prophet describes what happens to the spirits of those who die. Here are the words of Alma to his son Corianton:

> "Now, concerning the state of the soul between death and the resurrection—Behold, it has been made known unto me by an angel, that the spirits of all men, as soon as they are departed from this mortal body, yea, the spirits of all men, whether they be good or evil, are taken home to that God who gave them life.

And then shall it come to pass, that the spirits of those who are righteous are received into a state of happiness, which is called paradise, a state of rest, a state of peace, where they shall rest from all their troubles and from all care, and sorrow.

And then shall it come to pass, that the spirits of the wicked, yea, who are evil—for behold, they have no part nor portion of the Spirit of the Lord; for behold, they chose evil works rather than good; therefore the spirit of the devil did enter into them, and take possession of their house—and these shall be cast out into outer darkness; there shall be weeping, and wailing, and gnashing of teeth, and this because of their own iniquity, being led captive by the will of the devil." (*The Book of Mormon,* Alma 40:11-13)

Based on the words of Alma, a prophet of God (as well as other scriptures) and my personal witness, I testify that my son Joseph returned to Jesus Christ, the God of this earth, and was given an assignment (in paradise) to return. He visited his brother Grant to preach repentance to him so that he might be encouraged to become worthy to receive the Holy Priesthood and go to the Temple; first for himself, and then for his brother. This work in the temple would lay the foundation for us to be an eternal family - forever. Had Joseph been deemed 'evil' or 'wicked', upon his arrival in the afterlife, he would have been sent to the 'spirit prison', and not have the opportunity to return and counsel his brother.

So, did this experience really motivate Grant to change? The answer is a resounding, 'Yes'! Since Joseph's death, many wonderful changes have taken place in his life. On February 8, 2007 he went to the Temple for his own Endowment, and had his marriage 'solemnized' as he and his beautiful eternal companion Farrah were Sealed for 'Time and all Eternity'.

On March 10, 2007 Grant performed Joseph's temple ordinances finally fulfilling his commitment to his older brother. We all felt his presence (and many others from beyond the veil) in the Temple that day. The Spirit bore witness to Grant that his brother was there by his side during the whole temple experience.

I also had a very special experience Tuesday night (March 7th) two days after Joseph's death. As I was showering at my parent's home, my mind was racing in many directions.   The tears were flowing uncontrollably as the water from the shower washed them away. Many questions flooded my mind: Why now? Why my son? Why, when I had been asking in frequent and sincere prayer to receive inspiration for: 'How can I help Joseph back to the Gospel of Jesus Christ? Will he have an eternal companion? What about children? These are questions that any loving parent has for their living children; but Joseph had left this his probationary state without these opportunities.

As the last question flashed through my mind, a vision opened before my eyes. I saw the face of a beautiful young woman in her 20s with a beautiful smile. She had pretty, long, brownish hair. Her appearance exuded the compassion and love of someone who could work with troubled youth. The impression I was given was that somehow, this woman would be a part of his afterlife. A short time later I was sharing my experience with Emily. She had experienced the same impression (and as we compared timeframes) about the same time when she was home in her apartment.

This experience gave me an overwhelming feeling of peace and love; not only for my son, but also my Heavenly Father and his Plan of Happiness. Knowing Joseph was progressing and working out his salvation was a comfort to me. I accept as true that when we leave this life (if we have the right attitude and a great desire to repent of the sins with which we die), then we can change over time, and through the tender mercies of our Savior. The earthly 'distractions' are gone, and we will no longer be bombarded, harassed, and tempted by Satan and his followers. The level of our eternal progress (when we die) depends significantly on how we live during this, our time on earth. Are we keeping the commandments, coming unto Christ, showing unconditional love to everyone, and most especially striving to become like our Savior Jesus Christ? Are we making the atonement a part of our everyday life; and praying to our Heavenly Father expressing thanks and asking for his help every day? That progress can and does continue beyond this mortal sphere.

As the rest of the week proceeded, we received calls from all over the United States expressing their sorrow and condolences for our loss. There was such a great outpouring of love, which carried us through this ordeal; we couldn't have done it on our own. Even the funeral home felt the out-pouring of love from our dear friends as they assisted with taking care of the funeral arrangements. There were even coworkers who approached management to donate some of their vacation time (so I could remain home with my family as long as needed). The week following Joseph's death was the longest week of my life. The first three days, I had no desire to continue with life; I only wanted to be with my Sonny Boy. As time went on, I came to know and understand that Heavenly Father's plan was that on March 5th, 2006 was Joseph's appointed day to leave this earthly life.

As I mentioned before, there were many spiritual experiences during this time. Following are some of those experiences; and some personal feelings of family members. These were expressed following the situation with which we suddenly were faced: this thing called 'suicide'. There are statistics readily available that indicate when a family loses a child to suicide, some families are torn apart by divorce; or another family member or close friends also commits suicide. It is my belief that Satan and his followers try to influence those who are racked with grief, by placing recriminating thought into their minds. As an example, pointing fingers of blame at other family members. As I relate a few of these experiences of my family, I think you'll see this thankfully wasn't the case with us. This potentially devastating situation turned into a blessing of greater knowledge of the 'Plan' of our Heavenly Father, significant spiritual growth, and increased love for one another.

I'll start first with my mother, Joseph's grandmother, and her feelings after she witnessed what this did to me. The way my grief expressed itself was deep feelings of defeat and depression. Of all the family members affected by his suicide, I believe my mother was the only one that expressed 'anger'. She was angry that Joseph had hurt her son in such a way as this. She saw how I was completely devastated to the point that I didn't even have the strength to lift my head from my lap. She couldn't believe Joseph could have done this to his family. She knew that Cassie and I loved our children and grandchildren more than life itself. We would give our own lives if necessary to save our children and grandchildren. It may be hard to believe, but she was the only one that really had anger as her first emotion of the circumstances of Joseph's death.

Please understand that not all of the emotional responses were immediate. Some were expressed and explained days and even years after the suicide. Some of the emotion came flooding out in moments when it wouldn't be expected; masking my mother's true feelings at the time. Knowing that anger is of Satan, and not of our Heavenly Father; her feelings have been reconciled over time and today are of love and understanding.

When we read in the Bible, 'Heavenly Father was *angry* with his children', the original translated meaning is *disappointment*. We were all disappointed in Joseph, and the hurt his actions caused. Many expressed that disappointment as anger when we were blamed for his suicide. It's difficult to express the hurt those penetrating words caused as they pierced our hearts. In reality, our love for each of our children transcends anything we can express. Heavenly Father is my witness of this love for it is literally 'Godly love'.

Our daughter Emily expressed her feelings several times during the months following Joseph's suicide. She felt jealous toward him for the attention he had received. Let me explain; Emily felt that she had gone through much more pain and sorrow than Joseph. She reasoned, how could this be fair? She'd been through many more trials including, debilitating physical pain, mental anguish, and abuse. Here she was, a single mother trying to raise two little girls in the aftermath of two bad divorces. It was a high stress situation trying to be both father (provider) and mother (nurturer) to the girls (which by all observations she was doing very well). Yet she felt that Joseph had taken the easy way out. On one occasion, I took the opportunity to explain that Joseph wasn't going to have it easy. In fact, of all the wrong things that he had done in his life, taking his own life would be his most difficult to overcome. The repentance process [for him] had become significantly more difficult because he no longer had his mortal body. As a loving father, I also counseled her to never mention suicide as one of her own feelings; by doing so, Satan and his followers know, and establish an influence in her life to carry out that suicidal thought.

Lilly was the strong one through this whole ordeal. You may recall that our family had begun a fast for Grant. As her small family knelt in family prayer they felt impressed to also pray for Joe. Lilly was very close to him and empathized with his struggles; she also knew that he was suicidal. They prayed that night that Grant would be able to 'break the bands of sin he had gotten entangled in' and also prayed that Joe would be able to 'have a witness like that of Alma the Younger'; that he would undergo a 'life changing experience to change his route in life'. The early morning of the suicide, Lee and Lilly couldn't asleep; they both felt something was wrong. Not being able to sleep, Lee decided to leave early for his trucking run. It was then that Lilly received the call from Cassie moments after the suicide was discovered (as was described above). As I related there, that first hour was chaotic.

Lee's parents went to Lilly's home to get her and bring her to our home. Lilly remained so calm and was the single voice of reason there at the time. Upon arriving, Lilly (seeing Cassie crying hysterically), calmly went to her, gave her a hug and said, "It'll be okay mom." Rick started to tell what 'Joe and the room looked like'. She could hear someone crying down the hall and found Grant in a panic because he didn't know how to console me. Lilly walked into my room, I was catatonic. Lilly recounted her trying to console me by telling me, "It'll be okay dad." In complete denial I said, [to Grant and Lilly] "Go down there and turn the body over to get the wallet, so you can call the kid's parents." Lilly said, "Dad its Joe!" I replied, "My son couldn't have done that to himself." Lilly continued to calm me in a loving way and said, "Heavenly Father answered our prayers? We prayed for Joe to have an experience so he couldn't get worse!" That made me upset and I said, "Do you think Heavenly Father would answer a prayer this way?" "Dad, you need a blessing", she said. Minutes later when we had been helped to the neighbor's home, Lee's father offered me a blessing. Once the blessing was pronounced, I looked up with tears in my eyes at Lilly and said, "I do believe Heavenly Father answered our prayers." My eyes had been opened to accept this was how Joseph would be able to have progression.

The scriptures tell us very clearly that it's more difficult to repent in the spirit world (without a body) than here in mortality. Yet it has become my belief that, for Joseph to continue his progression, that separation needed to occur. Ultimately Jesus Christ will judge each of us in His mercy and loving-kindness based on our heart. I choose to believe that Joseph's heart was pure as he departed this life.

Rick is my youngest son. The love he has for his oldest brother transcends the impossible. His greatest desire that morning was, 'I'm going to go save my brother'. Of course logically he knew he couldn't put him back together; but his love was greater than the impossible. This is the familial love or unconditional love we should have every day for our fellow man; but most especially, for the members of our own family; the greatest organization on the earth. Ask yourself, "To whom do I show the most love: my friends, my coworkers, my family (brothers, sisters, mother and father)? Life can be short or long and the days of our life are numbered. May we show unconditional love toward each other, so when that moment comes that our loved ones are gone, we won't have any regrets.

Cassie had such a great relationship with Joseph. Even though she wasn't happy with his lifestyle choices, or some of the people he associated with, her love for him was unconditional. What a burden she carried of the dream (that she feared would become reality) of his suicide! For several months she kept the dream to herself so as not to burden others; all the while, knowing within her heart that day would come. Joseph knew his mother loved him and would accept his fiancée with loving arms when other family members were not as willing.

The morning of the suicide, Cassie and Rick were the only ones to hear the gun shot. She was the first to see his body, and knew he was gone. She would be the one to miss the daily phone calls from him just asking how she was doing. She would be the one to miss just wanting to hear his voice again telling her how much he loved her. Cassie was an inspiration to us all during that first week. She was the strong one trying to keep the rest of us together. I believe no other person could have handled the circumstances of this terrible situation better than she did.

Grant was not only Joseph's brother, but also his best friend. You recall that the family was fasting and praying for Grant who had a court date on Monday, March 7. Grant would be facing the same judge on a DUI charge, and knew he would be going to jail; the question remaining was, 'For how long? Joe had convinced Grant that he should do everything possible to avoid jail; because of the evil people that were there. He told Grant not to go to the showers because there would be 10 or 15 men trying to rape him, and he would lose. Only later did we find out that this had happened to Joseph when he had been in the County Jail for only two days.

Grant was very scared that the same thing would happen to him. He had told Joe that he would rather die than go to jail to be raped by the other inmates. In fact, Grant had written a suicide note addressed to our family explaining his love for us; and the reason he was going to end his life. We didn't find the note until about six months later when we were packing to move. The letter was found in the top of his closet by Farrah, his fiancé. I'm convinced that Joseph thought if Grant committed suicide, he would get the blame for Grant's actions, by his family and friends. I believe Joseph also considered taking his own life as a way to save his brother's life. When that letter was found, I knew I could have lost two sons to suicide. Feelings of being a worthless parent overcame me; and I begged forgiveness of my Heavenly Father in prayer many times.

The judge postponed the court date for two months in deference to our family situation with Joseph's suicide. As you can imagine, Grant blamed himself for the loss of his older brother; and felt depressed and defeated. It was only by the power of prayer, priesthood blessings, and the support of a loving family (including his girlfriend and future wife Farrah) that he was helped him through this difficult time. Even though, at the time, he wasn't living a Gospel-centered lifestyle, he was blessed. He and others were blessed to have Joseph's spirit come and keep hope alive in each of us. Our greatest goal is to have an Eternal Family.

Lastly, I'll share my feelings. I was definitely in complete denial and could not accept that one of my children had done this. I felt the love in our home should have prevented any total loss of hope in any of our family members. Many things were running through my mind such as past prayerful conversations with my Heavenly Father concerning Joseph. As I talked to Father, I told Him that I felt I had the faith of Alma and King Mosiah; great fathers and prophets of the book of Mormon. In the book of Mosiah we read the words of Alma involving his son Alma. This is the story of Alma the younger and the sons of Mosiah:

> "Now the sons of Mosiah were numbered among the unbelievers; and also one of the sons of Alma was numbered among them, he being called Alma, after his father; nevertheless, he became a very wicked and an idolatrous man. And he was a man of many words, and did speak much flattery to the people; therefore he led many of the people to do after the manner of his iniquities.
>
> And he became a great hinderment to the prosperity of the church of God; stealing away the hearts of the people; causing much dissension among the people; giving a chance for the enemy of God to exercise his power over them.
>
> And now it came to pass that while he was going about to destroy the church of God, for he did go about secretly with the sons of Mosiah seeking to destroy the church, and to lead astray the people of the Lord, contrary to the commandments of God, or even the king—
>
> And as I said unto you, as they were going about rebelling against God, behold, the angel of the Lord appeared unto them; and he descended as it were in a cloud; and he spake as it were with a voice of thunder, which caused the earth to shake upon

which they stood;

And so great was their astonishment, that they fell to the earth, and understood not the words which he spake unto them.

Nevertheless he cried again, saying: Alma, arise and stand forth, for why persecutest thou the church of God? For the Lord hath said: This is my church, and I will establish it; and nothing shall overthrow it, save it is the transgression of my people.

And again, the angel said: Behold, the Lord hath heard the prayers of his people, and also the prayers of his servant, Alma, who is thy father; for he has prayed with much faith concerning thee that thou mightest be brought to the knowledge of the truth; therefore, for this purpose have I come to convince thee of the power and authority of God, that the prayers of his servants might be answered according to their faith." (*The Book of Mormon,* Mosiah 27:8-14)

The words of the Angel to Alma, relating the prayers of a pleading father reverberated in my mind in this moment as I thought of my son's situation. Why did I not have the faith of Alma? Why couldn't I bring my son back to the fold of God? Why didn't he get another chance to repent and enjoy the blessings of the Atonement of Jesus Christ? I literally asked many times in fasting and prayer for the same miracle that Alma received for his son; and now knowing that prayer would never be answered in the same way for my son Joseph, was devastating. Was I so unworthy that I couldn't have my prayers answered the same way as Alma's prayers? Let's review how Alma's prayers were finally answered:

"And now the astonishment of Alma was so great that he became dumb, that he could not open his mouth; yea, and he became weak, even that he could not move his hands; therefore he was taken by those that were with him, and carried helpless, even until he was laid before his father.

And they rehearsed unto his father all that had happened unto them; and his father rejoiced, for he knew that it was the power of God.

And he caused that a multitude should be gathered together that they might witness what the Lord had done for his son, and also for those that were with him.

And he caused that the priests should assemble themselves together; and they began to fast, and to pray to the Lord their God that he would open the mouth of Alma, that he might speak, and also that his limbs might receive their strength—that the eyes of the people might be opened to see and know of the goodness and glory of God.

And it came to pass after they had fasted and prayed for the space of two days and two nights, the limbs of Alma received their strength, and he stood up and began to speak unto them, bidding them to be of good comfort:

For, said he, I have repented of my sins, and have been redeemed of the Lord; behold I am born of the Spirit.

And the Lord said unto me: Marvel not that all mankind, yea, men and women, all nations, kindreds, tongues and people, must be born again; yea, born of God, changed from their carnal and fallen state, to a state of righteousness, being redeemed of God, becoming his sons and daughters;

And thus they become new creatures; and unless they do this, they can in nowise inherit the kingdom of God." (*The Book of Mormon,* Mosiah 27:19-26)

It took an Angel sent from God to awaken Alma the younger and the sons of Mosiah. It was done because of the love and the faith of their fathers, mothers, and the people of the church. They (those sons) were literally driving the people away from the Church of God in open rebellion and yet, they were given another chance. Alma the younger himself testifies of the reason his father's prayers were answered in the way they were as we read in verse 35 (Mosiah 27).

"And they traveled throughout all the land of Zarahemla, and among all the people who were under the reign of king Mosiah, zealously striving to repair all the injuries which they had done to the church, confessing all their sins, and publishing all the things which they had seen, and explaining the prophecies and the scriptures to all who desired to hear them."

You see, Alma the younger and the sons of Mosiah had to UNDO the damage they had done by going to every person and asking forgiveness for damaging their testimonies of the gospel of Jesus Christ. If they were to pass away from this life, this could never happen from the spirit world. At the time of Joseph's death I was disappointed in my Heavenly Father for not answering my prayers in his behalf. For two or three days after Joseph's death, all I wanted was to be with him in death. Thoughts of suicide never crossed my mind; I simply wanted to be with my son. It's taken many years to recognize and understand that my prayers were answered; but in the Lord's way; the best way for Joseph. No, he didn't drive people away from the church; he did commit sin like we all do; but his continued progression (which was a direct answer to my prayers) was to be better done in the spirit world.

I testify that our prayers as fathers and mothers are answered for our children in the Lord's wisdom. I testify that God our Eternal Father knows each of us individually by name; and we are each loved beyond our ability to comprehend. He knows our hearts, our thoughts, and intentions. I have received a personal witness, that in the time Joseph has been gone, his progression toward perfection has continued. He has realized the blessings of the Temple ordinances, which will have enabled him to grow and progress in a miraculous way; better than he would, had he stayed on earth. That knowledge doesn't lessen the pain we still endure as we miss him every day. Often, the tears flow uncontrollably when we hear one of Joseph's funeral hymns at church or on the radio. Life isn't easy when you can't reach out and embrace someone you love. Cassie and I anticipate that these tender moments from beyond the veil will continue in the future; and we recognize that without each other's companionship, and our family around us, life would hold less meaning for us all.

When we pray with faith and love in the name of our Savior Jesus Christ, we may have confidence that the Father will answer every prayer, in his way, and in his time. We must trust that this is the appointed way, and have faith that the answers will come. We should be patient, always striving to understanding that the Lord is in charge. As we keep His commandments, and endure our trials and tribulations well; we will be blessed. And let us have 'ears to hear' the Still Small Voice of the Holy Ghost that testifies of the truth.

As you can imagine, Joseph's room was a disaster. First his belongings had to be removed; and an attempt made to locate the bullet. It was never found. It took the commercial cleaning and restoration service two days to remove the carpet, closet door, the room door and the drywall. When all was complete, we ended up with his golf clubs and the little box that contained the letters from each of us. We also had the very special letter that Joseph had written to us on that family night we held for him. That family night will never be forgotten. Cassie had the dream that Joseph would soon be gone, and hoped this night of expressing our appreciation for him, could help him in some way. Joseph felt the spirit of those words, then without being asked, wrote a letter back to us. It was brief, but to the point. The spirit of what he said could really be felt as he expressed the love and gratitude he had for each member of his family. Cassie's idea really bore fruit as it was apparent he was actually touched by the words each had written. We each expressed our individual love for him which was our expression of 'Godly' love. I know that Joseph knew, at that moment, his family would always be there for him; no matter what the situation. I also believe he knew that love extended beyond death. I know he continues to feel our love as he tries to work out his eternal progression in the Spirit World.

CHAPTER 4

Viewing, Funeral and Burial

The date is Sunday March 12, one week after our son's death. We waited a week before having the viewing and the funeral. Cassie felt very strongly we needed that time to pull things together for the arrangements, rest our souls, and prepare. Rick also had a ball tournament in St. George that we wanted to support him in; to lend at least some normalcy to our shattered situation. The news media was still parked in our yard doing updates and story follow-up. Even though we could have gone home (the cleanup of Joseph's room had been completed), we spent a few more days at my parents' home just to rest our nerves, hearts and spirits. Quite frankly, we needed the courage to go on. We needed to make sure that all of our friends and family were notified of Joseph's death; and plan the funeral (including asking those we desired to speak and take part in the service). Had it not been for the overwhelming love, support and concern of our Ward members, family and friends; I know I could not have made it through this a horrible tragedy. A parent never dreams that they will be in the position of burying a child; it's supposed to be the other way around. I kept saying to myself and others, "I'm not so certain I would have agreed to this trial before coming to earth." In all reality, a part of me died that morning my son died.

His viewing was the evening of March 12th. As a family, each one of us felt the need to attend our regular church services that afternoon. God has always been a big part of our lives and we needed his strength. We arrived for Sacrament Meeting early. Emily, Lilly and their families attended our Ward to give Cassie and I all the support they could. Nearly every ward member came to us and embraced our family. Our Bishop announced the details of the viewing that evening and the funeral the next day. Many members of our ward couldn't believe that we had attended our meetings at this time of our bereavement. We explained that we had wanted to partake of the Holy Sacrament and receive blessings from our Heavenly Father to sustain and carry us through this trial. We also felt we needed to show faith in the Atoning Sacrifice of our Savior.

Earlier in the week (as we were attending to the details at the funeral home), the mortician told us that sometimes they are able to restore a shooting victims appearance so that they might be viewed by the family. He offered to do this so we could see his face at the family viewing. The alternative would be to have the bandages cover his head. We decided we wanted to remember how handsome he was before that tragic day, and asked to have his bandages remain. Prior to the public viewing, we invited our immediate family to view his body in the casket; and then it would be closed for the public visitation. The evening of the viewing arrived, and our family congregated at the funeral home to see the body of our Joseph for the last time perhaps before his resurrection day.

Before the casket was opened, I told our children that this would only be his mortal body, and that although we felt his spirit there, it wasn't in his body that lay in the casket. As the casket was opened, I cannot express in words the empty feeling that we each felt knowing we wouldn't see him again for the length of our mortal lives. The pain we all felt was unbearable, but our knowledge of the Plan of Salvation, and the rescuing power of the Atonement, along with the love of so many others, supported and lifted us through this moment of grief.

He was dressed in a blue shirt, tie, pants and socks as his burial clothing. Cassie was upset because she hadn't thought about shoes. At any rate, his left foot was rigid and in a position that would have prevented a shoe to be worn. Those of us, who had seen his shattered face, felt it a good decision to have his face remain bandaged. Emily was quite upset and vocal because she wanted to see her brother's face one last time. Each of us paid our last respects, and said a personal 'goodbye'. Cassie clung to his hand for a while and then gently laid it in his lap, knowing that if she were patient, until his body and spirit were reunited in the resurrection, he could hold her hand again. The casket was closed, and we took our places near the side of our special son Joseph. The doors were opened and the viewing began.

Even after all this time, the tears still flow freely when talking about the details of those two sad weeks. I'll never forget any of the details, and the pain of every moment surrounding the loss of a child. Yes, we believe he's in a better place; but I miss him so much and can't wait to embrace him and express my love for him again. I know that when that moment comes, he will never leave me again.

The people started to pour into the funeral home by the hundreds. To the outside observer it might appear that perhaps a great local leader or church official had just passed away. The community was very supportive, and we were able to see at least one person (often many more) from every LDS ward in which we had ever lived during our 30 years of marriage. There were friends from our youth to the present, coworkers, family and neighbors. Joseph's friends came like a flood. These good friends were genuinely living up to their baptismal covenants and 'mourning with those that mourn, and comforting those who stand in need of comfort'. We never before knew that Joseph had so many girls that had wanted to be his date, or his girlfriend or even his spouse! The line of well-wishers wanting to pay their respects eventually stretched outside the building and into the parking area.

As the visitation progressed, we received word that Tracy and her family had arrived to show their last respects. We had only met Tracy briefly once or twice; and never met her family. It had been natural for us as a family (due to the volatility of their relationship and the circumstances of Joseph's death) to question how we might feel, act and respond to her when we next met. Each member of our family had to decide whether to take the high path and be Christ-like; or to be resentful and bitter. We saw her approach (along with her brother, sisters, mother and stepfather); we could see their pained hearts and long faces. I'm sure they were wondering how we'd accept them when once face-to-face at Joseph's casket.

We discovered later, that Tracy's family had insisted she be there to show love and support to Joseph's family. As she approached, she first faced the boys Grant and Rick; then the girls Emily and Lilly. I was very proud of them as they embraced her and her family just as Christ would do in the same situation: as part of our family. I also embraced Tracy and told her and her family members that I loved them and have no ill feelings toward them. I also told them, "We need one another to get through this time of sorrow".

We wanted to be there for Tracy. We knew she had been taken in by the Sheriff and questioned about the circumstances surrounding Joseph's death. We also knew that she would soon be back in court concerning outstanding warrants; and likely face jail time. What we didn't know at the time: she was carrying Joseph's child.

As the evening ended, it was really hard to leave Joseph at the funeral home knowing that tomorrow Monday, March 13, 2006 would bring the funeral and burial of our loving son and brother.

That morning as we arrived at the chapel, we could see that our Ward Relief Society sisters and the funeral director had arrived early to prepare for the one-hour viewing prior to the funeral service. These friends were like extended family; they had been so kind and supportive from the first moment of this tragedy, and willing to help in any way possible. The inspection department where I worked closed so my coworkers, manager and an HR representative could come to support us in our time of need. As it had been for the viewing, the number in attendance at the funeral was unbelievable. The funeral director told me it was one of the largest turnouts for a funeral he had seen in many years.

After the viewing prior to the funeral was complete, my father offered the family prayer. The casket was moved toward the chapel as our family solemnly followed behind. The congregation was standing as we entered the chapel and we were seated at the front, near the casket. Bishop Hunter was conducting the meeting and asked the attendees to be seated; and introduced the program.

My brother Peter gave the invocation followed by a Special Musical Number (four ward members singing a medley of hymns). Lilly read the obituary and spoke briefly sharing some of the special thoughts and feelings each of Joseph's brothers and sisters had expressed privately about their brother.

What follows are transcripts of the three main speakers at the funeral. The reason for including the complete talks is to show that we are just an ordinary family. Joseph was an ordinary son, growing up in a typical town; we are no different than any other family than you might encounter anywhere in the world; and we believe that each of us is a brother and sister in the extremity of our circumstances. We are each sons and daughters of a Heavenly Father who loves us unconditionally; and He is there for us no matter our situations. Please pay special attention to the words of a loving mother; and the doctrine of Apostles and Prophets that is quoted by my brother and brother-in-law in their talks. These words give us hope that even those who commit the act of suicide, forgiveness is possible. That is through the knowledge and the reassurance that Jesus the Christ is the ultimate Judge; and only He knows the content of our hearts. Jesus Christ is the mediator between us and The Father. He will plead our case because he has suffered every pain that we will ever experience in this life. His mercies are extended to all of God's children. That means every child born to this earth; or any other of God's planetary creations.

Cassie was the first speaker. What a beacon of strength she had been during this first week following Joseph's death; I personally could not have done it alone. I now quote Cassie's talk:

"To the Sheriff's Department, all the law enforcement officers, Highway Patrol officers and EMTs we want to thank you along with friends and family members. We give you special thanks and want you to know we love you and want you to know that Joseph loved you as well. In Mosiah 4:9 we read:

"Believe in God; believe that he is, and that he created all things, both in heaven and in earth; believe that he has all wisdom, and all power, both in heaven and in earth; believe that man doth not comprehend all the things which the Lord can comprehend."

During this last week we've had a special witness from the Spirit for we know that Joseph is in a better place for his progression. We know that Joseph couldn't progress any further here, he's now in the hands of our Savior and now he can progress. I now want to share some special experiences that we had with this special son. He was due on my birthday but decided to come three days later. He was 3 pounds larger than Lilly and 2 pounds larger than Emily. It was such a hard labor, and when he was born he was 'knocked out'; and after they revived him, the doctor said, "[Joe] you've finally got your son". I told the doctor, "That's not my son! His mouth is too big". That's probably the only time that I thought his mouth was too big; he was always shy but he also was a 'tease' and very fun to be around. I think it took 2 1/2 or 3 years before any of the grandparents on either side heard him even speak; he just kept to himself or his brothers and sisters.

When he was 2 1/2 years old he became very ill, and I was up with him all night. He had a very high fever, and finally in the middle of the night I awakened Joe to tell him that I had done all I could do: he needed to have a priesthood blessing. Joe got up and gave him a blessing. As the blessing was completed, the fever broke. We had a picture of the Savior at the head of our bed; and with Little Joseph looking up at the picture said, "Daddy I'm in the hands of my Savior (pointing up at him) and I'm going to be okay." We know he's in the hands of the Savior now.

With two older sisters Joseph had to play with all the time, it was a good thing he had a couple of uncles that were about the same age or a little older. Emily and Lilly dressed Joseph up as their Prince charming and he had to play that role for them. When he was five years old Joe and I were working out in the front yard, Joseph hollered at us at the head of our hundred foot driveway. He was standing on the seat of his bike with hands down on the handlebars saying, "Look what the big boys have taught me!" He proceeded down the driveway, tumbling over the handlebars, and hitting his face on the cement driveway. He passed out, banging up his face and teeth; we actually thought we had lost him then. We took him to the emergency room to have his mouth stitched up.

Joseph loved to play with trucks, and he had a toy backhoe that he used to play with in the sand pile out back of our house. He would say he was doing, "Just like Grandpa Richards." Then one day the Henry twins came over, and Joseph and them when out to the big field (to a big dirt hill) and began throwing dirt clods and rocks. Joseph having a great arm could throw farther than the others. Well, one rock hit a window on the farmer's barn and broke it. The farmer came out and chased the boys to our house. The farmer had lost one of his arms years ago, so he had a hook on one arm. He called the police and they came to our home. Joseph and his friends hid behind us for they honestly thought this 'Captain Hook' (as the farmer was called) was going to get them and take them away. He learned an important lesson there that day to make the wrong right.

He started kindergarten three days before his birthday. He stood up at 'show and tell' and told his class that he had the 'Oldest mother in the school' because it was 'Her birthday today and she turned 30'. He was just that way. That summer he started playing baseball and he loved the game. Joe recalls when he was eight years old (which is really too young to play in Minor Little League) he was on the team with his Uncle Kent. The next year Joseph was nine and Kent was 12. They came to play a team that hadn't lost a game in three years. They were beating us, and it was Joseph's turn at bat; the last batter or ninth batter. Joe was coaching on third and little Joseph (the youngest in the game) hit two foul balls right by his dad's head; and then smashed the ball over the third baseman's head for a standup double. It motivated the older boys to come alive at the bat, and they won the game. He was shy, but he was a fighter, and a winner; that's just the way he was. When he was in Senior Little League, he was the home run king; he could play anywhere on the field, and never complained. It really hurt him when he could no longer play baseball, because he was such a good player. Each of our kids were good athletes, but Joseph out did them all. It was unfairly taken away from him; but we've reconciled with that, and it's okay.

Back when his was younger, the girls came running to me and told me that Joseph had just shot the TV. I ran into the other room and found a hole in the TV. Joseph had taken his bow and arrow and shot the TV. He said, "I was trying to get the bad guys mom!" So, we had a hole in our TV for a little while; that was Joseph. He and Kurt (our next door neighbor boy), were best of friends for many years. One day they were out between the two houses digging a big hole. I had been out yelling at him to come home and eat (several times), and finally I got mad and went over there and asked him, "What are you doing? "I'm digging this hole trying to find Satan and ask him why he makes us do bad things."

When he was nine or ten years old, we were sitting in Sacrament Meeting and the Priest had just offered the prayer. Joseph said to me, "He did it wrong" I said, "No, he said it right." Joseph pulled out his scriptures and read the correct words; and yes, it was said wrong. The Bishop knew it was wrong as well, and he had the Priest redo it. I asked him how he knew [it had been wrong] he said, "I know the scriptures mom", and Joseph did. When he was younger, he read a lot of the scriptures and he knew they were true.

He and I had a very unique relationship, and we enjoyed many talks together. Not every mom can say that their son would tell them every bad thing he did; he kind of used me as his 'bishop'. I know his sins and I knew his joys of life. I knew his pranks with his friends that he pulled on others. When was a little bit older, he hated to do chores. I asked him to do the dishes one time (he didn't know that Joe at come home early from work) and he made the comment that, "The dishes are women's work." That was the wrong thing to say. His dad overheard, and for the next week, Joseph did the dishes. But Joseph was a good worker, he knew how to work.

Another time, Joseph gave little short prayers whenever he would pray. When we had our family prayer every night, each of us would take a night when it was our turn to pray. It was Joseph's turn and the prayer was so short, that Joe looked at Joseph and said to him, "You need to learn to know the Savior, so you will say the prayer every night for the next week; until you can feel the love of your Heavenly Father and your Savior Jesus Christ." Joseph said, "Dad I can't; dad I can't." Joe said, "Yes you can!" About the third night, Joseph offered such a beautiful prayer; it was as if he was literally talking to his Heavenly

Father. We were all overcome by the spirit, and tears were flowing from our eyes. Joseph now had a relationship with his Savior.

When he was milking cows at the William's dairy, he really loved the job because he enjoyed fresh milk. One Winter Sunday morning at about 4 a.m., Joseph called home. I answered the phone and Joseph said, "I need Dad's help right now!" Joe's a sound sleeper, so it took a few minutes to wake him up. Joe put on his pajama bottoms and slippers, and I put on my high heels and my dress coat; and off we were to the dairy to see what was up. When we got there Joseph said, "What are you wearing those things for? I have a dead cow and I need some help pulling it out of the stall." So we did what we could, but afterward had to throw away the clothes we were wearing.

Joseph had a lot of fun in Boy Scouts. He enjoyed his scout leaders, the Young Men leaders in our ward, and in other wards; he talked about them all the time. He loved to snowboard. I came home from work one day Joseph was downstairs watching TV. He was watching a movie about snowboarding in some resorts in Utah. Joseph mentioned that he had been there and done what they were doing (jumping off cliffs and enjoying themselves). I begged him not to do it anymore because it scared me so badly. All he would just say was, "It's okay mom; it's cool."

Joseph enjoyed being a prankster on the phone. He knew some Spanish and could talk with a Japanese or Arabic accent with people on the phone. He even did it to me one time. He was such a joy to raise. We talked every day and that will undoubtedly be missed. That closeness we had expressed love better than anything else. He would always say that he loved me and his dad; he wasn't afraid to say, "I love you." He enjoyed flipping my hair after I just got it done. "Hi 'Madre'; you shouldn't have fixed your hair, it looked okay before."

In the last year, Joseph had been in a lot of pain. He's gone through a lot of things that others could not do. We knew how hard it was for him both physically and mentally to carry on. He got a DUI and had to spend two days in jail and it was just devastating to him. When he got out, the tears just flowed and he said, "I'm never going to go back there; I can't and I won't." The day he got out of jail he wanted to go celebrate with his friends; they drank, and he was pulled over again. He was ready to give up then; life to him wasn't worth it anymore. It was a real struggle for him because he knew that jail would happen again; and this time it was possible that the jail time could be six months.

Thankfully, the sentence was for 30-days. The day before Joseph would spend a month in jail, we had a special Family Home Evening. Each member of the family expressed their love for him in a written letter. Grandparents, brothers and sisters, and nieces all wrote letters and they were placed in a small metal box as if it was a mailbox. Little did we know, that night he had planned to commit suicide so he wouldn't have to go back to jail. The letters with their expressions of love changed his mind. Joseph knew his family was going to be there for him no matter what. Instead, Joseph read those letters and wrote a letter back telling us as a family that he knew we loved him.

I must tell you this: my son taught me more about Christ-like love, than any teacher or verse of scripture. As we visited him in jail, the scripture came to my mind, 'when you have visited me in prison you have visited the Savior'. When he came home, we made a big poster for him, and he was so happy to be back home. He started coming to every family night, listening and enjoying his family instead of leaving and going someplace else.

In January of every year, my job required me to work every day of the month. This particular January, I was working the swing shift. About mid-month I called home and told Joe that through the spirit, I knew what we needed to do for family night around Valentine's Day in February. I told him that we needed to have a dinner with grandparents, our children, and grandchildren. So, on the Saturday before Valentines we got together at our favorite restaurant. Joe and I wrote a special note to each of our family members expressing our love for them. We had a beautiful time. We knew their weaknesses, but we loved them all unconditionally; and told them we'd 'be there for them no matter what'. We knew that Joseph loved his brothers, sisters, and grandparents; but had a hard time expressing that love because of his shyness. That night, he embraced each of us there and told us he loved us.

Joseph you were our 'sunshine' and you were your Dad's 'Sonny Boy'; it was a pleasure to raise you. Before I heard the fatal gunshot, I was dreaming of Joseph as a little boy running through a field with the breeze blowing through his hair, the sunshine reflecting on his forehead, and a big smile across his face. I know the Lord was preparing me for what was to happen. I've had a years' worth of experiences that have prepared me for this day. I know that Joseph is okay and that we will see him again. I know that his uncle Dean was there when this happened. I know my father was there and turned me around after I entered his room so I wouldn't see any more. I was the first to see my son after the gunshot and it seemed like a long time before the others came down the stairs.

Thanks to our special neighbors who allowed me to scream and cry and vent my emotions of mourning. To our family and friends that came so quickly that morning, it meant so much to us; it lifted our burden in a time of need. The phone has rung off the hook with expressions of love and questions of, 'What can we do for you'? We'll be okay. We are comforted by your prayers and can feel the love of the Savior. We love Joseph so much. It was such a privilege to have him in our lives for these 23 1/2 years. We were blessed with a great son and he will always be missed. I say these things in the name of Jesus Christ, Amen."

Musical Number: *The Test* - Sung by Cindy and Troy Longworth

The next speaker was Sam Perkins; my elder brother and Joseph's uncle. This is his talk:

"Those two songs were so beautiful; music truly brings the Spirit into any meeting. I'm so honored to speak today for Joe and Cassie and their family; I love them so much. I pray the Lord will bless me and be with me as I speak, that I might say the things that I've prepared (and in my heart). That I'll be able to control my emotions, and that the Spirit will be with me. Joe and Cassie are so strong; I know that this test and trial that you're going through will bless and strengthen you. I have witnessed in my own life many times (and the lives of many others) that faith is strengthened in the Savior Jesus Christ after going through trials. The family will grow from this and become stronger when the next trial comes.

A week ago (Saturday morning), Joe and his son Grant and my Dad came to my home. They had been out hunting for deer antler sheds. Many of you know that Joe balances snowmobile clutches, so they stopped at my home to pick up my snowmobile clutch. We were talking about balancing clutches, and then we just started talking about trials. I mentioned the biography of Joseph Smith and the trials that he went through with the early saints. Joe mentioned this month's First Presidency Message on the Stillman and Pond family, and how the father lost nine children and his wife coming across the plains to Utah. At the time, I wondered why we were talking about that; and then the next morning, I knew exactly why with Joseph taking his life. The family asked me to talk about the atonement and the resurrection.

I would like to share a talk from President Faust with you for a couple of minutes. Through the Spirit, I think that we all need to hear this; he's talking about 'how dear are the sheep that have wandered'. It's a conference talk of April 06, 2003. I think everyone in here has children or grandchildren that have made mistakes and his words give us hope in these cases. Quoting from his address:

> "I must first begin by testifying that the will of the Lord to parents throughout the church is contained in *Doctrine and Covenants Section 68 verse 25*:

> "And again, inasmuch as parents have children in Zion, or in any of her stakes which are organized, that teach them not to understand the doctrine of repentance, faith in Christ the Son of the living God, and of baptism and the gift of the Holy Ghost by the laying on of the hands, when eight years old, the sin be upon the heads of the parents."

Parents are instructed to teach their children to pray and walk up rightly before the Lord. Fathers, grandfathers and even great-grandfathers should learn their responsibility to teach these things to their children. As a servant of the living Lord Jesus Christ I urge parents to heed this counsel and live it." Then he talks about those who are good parents:

> "Those are they who have earnestly and lovingly tried to teach correct principles and doctrines of Christ. They had been examples of praying and walking up rightly before the Lord. This is true even when some of the children become disobedient or worldly. Children come into this world with their own individual spirits and personalities. Some children would question or challenge any situation in any circumstance. And there are others that are such a joy to raise and follow the counsel of their parents. Successful parents are ones that struggle and try to do the best they can with what they have in their own family circumstances."

I personally testify that Joe and Cassie have done all of this. I know they would do anything for their children they love them so much. And they have taught them well; this is the part that I would like to talk about or emphasize the most. Continuing with President Faust's words:

"The Prophet Joseph Smith never taught, or declared, a more comforting doctrine. The Eternal Sealing of good and faithful parents and divine promises to faithful parents in the cause of truth; would not only save themselves, but likewise their posterity. Although some of the children might wander, they will eventually feel the divine tentacles reaching out after them, and bring them back to the fold. In this life or the life to come, they will return. Yes, they will have to pay that debt to justice. They will suffer for their sins that they've not repented of, and they will tread a thorny path; but it will lead them back just like the prodigal son to a loving father. The painful experience will not be in vain. Pray for your careless and disobedient children never give up on them.

Hold onto them with your faith and love them until you see the salvation of God. What's often overlooked is that the price of sin must be fully paid before redemption can come. I recognize now that this is the time to prepare to meet God. If we don't witness (in this life) a wayward child come back; the great power of the sealing temple ordinance will reach out and bring them back before the end. In the doctrine covenants we read that the repentance of the dead can be realized and they can be brought back to the presence of the Father."

These are great blessings from our Heavenly Father which really inspire me to want and keep my sacred Temple covenants: the covenants that I've made with my Heavenly Father and in his holy house. I hope that this doctrine can strengthen each of us that have children who are struggling with life's challenges; to give us hope for a better day. May we have that faith in Jesus Christ through his atonement, that we can all make it back to the presence of our Heavenly Father.

Elder Ballard a couple years ago in a conference talk gave some really good counsel. His grandson had lost his life shortly after his mission. Elder Ballard said that he had just sealed him three months previous in the Temple. And then three months later in an airplane crash he lost his life. And he tells about how important the atonement is in every situation in life and death; to know (because of Jesus Christ) he will be able to see his grandson again. How great it is to have a testimony of the atonement of Jesus Christ to know that He lives and He loves us unconditionally.

I'm so grateful to know I can be forgiven for any sin that I'll ever commit; for I've made many mistakes in my life. I know that my Savior loves me very much for I've really felt his love many times in my life; even when I've been doing something I should not have been doing, or things that I should have done but didn't do. And I know if I'll go to him and pray for forgiveness, he will be there to listen and forgive. And through the Holy Ghost who is the testifier of truth, I can know he has forgiven me. I'm grateful to my Heavenly Father who has provided a Plan for us that we all can return back to him. This plan is the atonement of Jesus Christ. I would like to now read a quote from Joseph Smith:

> "I wonder if we know the significance of the resurrection that is so fundamental to our faith. That Jesus Christ died on the cross; rose on the third day and all other doctrine is appendices to this doctrine. It is only through the name of Jesus Christ and his atonement and resurrection that makes it possible to return back to our Heavenly Father"

Before this world was, our Heavenly Father presented this great Plan. He knew that his Son would have to suffer all things and Atone for the sins of all men, even unto death. He knew his Son Jesus Christ would want to do this because He loved us all more than Himself; and He was willing to do the Lord's will making it possible for all of us to have Eternal Life. I'm grateful that He did this; enabling us to repent and to become perfect even as Jesus Christ. As an LDS Bishop for seven years, I had many people come with heavy burdens of sin. I'm happy I was able to help them through these trying times. There's nothing more special than witnessing someone find their Savior and feel of his forgiving love for them; to make it back to the straight and narrow path.

I want you to know that Jesus Christ is my Savior and my Redeemer. He is the Only Begotten Son of our Heavenly Father. He sent His son here to fulfill his great mission and that is to bring us all back to the presence of the Father. I pray that each and every one of us will do everything we can to have the Savior in our lives, and that we will get to know Him better. That we will trust in Him, and have faith in Him; that He will help us through the trials of life. For He suffered for all the sins, all the pain, and all the sorrow that we will ever go through; He knows what each of us need. If we will just go to him, he will strengthen us and carry us through the trials of life. I testify that these things are true; and I say these things in the name of Jesus Christ, Amen."

Musical Number: *Galilean Sands* - sung by Cindy and Troy Longworth
Next we heard from George Stuart, one of Joseph's uncles:

"Like Sam, I have a hard time controlling my emotions so I apologize in advance. I'm deeply humbled to be here today and share a few words with you. I'm grateful for those who've gone before me; who brought the Spirit with them and set the tone for this meeting. As I pondered on what I would say today, the message that came to mind (in which the Spirit seemed to concur) is: 'Reaching Out to the One'.

Who is the 'one'? If you think about it, we all are. For each of us there comes a point where we need a hand of fellowship and love; a friendly hello, a listening ear, and a shoulder to cry on. As we travel through the storms of life, sometimes we think to ourselves, 'Nobody understands'; but our Savior does. As Sam mentioned, the suffering of our Savior was for us. We read in *The Book of Mormon,* Alma 7, verses 11 & 12:

> "And he shall go forth, suffering pains and afflictions and temptations of every kind; and this that the word might be fulfilled which saith he will take upon him the pains and the sicknesses of his people.

> And he will take upon him death that he may loose the bands of death which bind his people; and he will take upon him their infirmities, that his bowels may be filled with mercy, according to the flesh, that he may know according to the flesh how to succor his people according to their infirmities."

There is nothing in this world that our Savior has not experienced. He has perfect empathy for us, for he suffered those things that He may be filled with perfect mercy and will succor us in times of need. Sometimes the 'one' doesn't have the faith necessary to seek out our Lord's touch in their lives. That is where the rest of us come in; we ARE our brother's keeper. We are the friends, neighbors, coworkers, classmates, Home Teachers, and Visiting Teachers of the 'one'. In Alma 5:59 & 60 we read:

> "For what shepherd is there among you having many sheep doth not watch over them, that the wolves enter not and devour his flock? And behold, if a wolf enter his flock doth he not drive him out? Yea, and at the last, if he can, he will destroy him.

And now I say unto you that the good shepherd doth call after you; and if you will hearken unto his voice he will bring you into his fold, and ye are his sheep; and he commandeth you that ye suffer no ravenous wolf to enter among you, that ye may not be destroyed.''

Let us think about this for a moment. When a pack of wolves come upon their prey, they look for the weak one; the sick one is easily spotted. The wolves will attack the 'one'. The adversary is the same way; he knows our weaknesses, and knows when he can prey upon us. He spots us in the 'herd' so to speak, and will try to take us down. We should succor and help one another to keep the adversary (or wolf) at bay. Joseph has moved on to his next phase of existence. He has found some new friends and gotten reacquainted with loved ones who have passed on before. He will be called upon to touch someone; and that he already has. It's my hope and prayer that we as friends and neighbors, loved ones, coworkers, classmates, Home Teachers, Visiting Teachers, and clergy will each make the effort necessary to reach out and touch the 'one'. It takes courage, and often times we don't see the immediate fruits of our labors.

Someday in the life of that 'one', they will find meaning and realize, 'Someone really loves me and cares about me; I matter to someone'. Often times we're afraid to approach someone. It takes courage; and we may shy away fearing possible rejection. When moved upon by the Spirit, <u>we need to act</u>.

When the Lord said to Samuel, 'find a new king'; He said, 'don't look at the man's stature or his countenance, for the Lord doesn't look upon someone as man does. For man looks on the outward appearance but the Lord looks upon the heart'. Brothers and sisters seek out the 'one'; make a difference in their life, endure with love because 'The worth of a soul is great in the eyes of the Lord'.

I testify that our Lord and Savior Jesus Christ lives; that we have a loving Father in Heaven. He knows us personally and he hears and answers our prayers. We are so blessed to have the Gospel of Jesus Christ that fills our souls with light. Of this I so testify, in the name of Jesus Christ; Amen.

Congregational Hymn: *God Be with You Till We Meet Again*

Benediction: Tyler Perkins (an Uncle)

Bishop Hunter then stood and asked the audience to rise as the pallbearers came forward to remove the casket from the chapel, and place in the hearse for travel to the town cemetery. There the funeral services would be concluded. I would be offering the prayer dedicating the gravesite.

I should give a brief explanation about this special and sacred ordinance of dedicating a grave. First, it's important to have some understanding of the Priesthood of God. One definition of 'priesthood' is: The power and authority of God given to man, to act for Jesus Christ or in the name of Jesus Christ, on the Earth. In other words, one holding the Melchizedek Priesthood can stand in place of Jesus Christ and administer Priesthood Blessings, and Priesthood Ordinances, as if they were the Lord himself. This Priesthood is given to worthy males by the 'laying on of hands' by one having the authority of Jesus Christ as given him through living prophets in our day. I was ordained a High Priest on March 7, 1982 by my Stake President in the Church of Jesus Christ of Latter-day Saints. In magnifying my Priesthood, and living worthy of such blessings, I have the authority to administer such ordinances as the dedication of a grave. If I continue worthy throughout my life, I hope to attain eternal life with my Heavenly Father and my Savior Jesus Christ.

So, it was my awesome responsibility and honor to dedicate the gravesite of my special son Joseph. You may ask the question: Why do we dedicate a gravesite? Some will say that his physical body is just being placed in the ground and we no longer need to worry about it. The LDS Church sanctions it, and I say that this plot or piece of earth should be blessed as a sacred and holy place. That it needs to be blessed and protected from the elements, from earthquakes and other natural disasters; even though the body is protected in a beautiful preserving casket and sturdy concrete vault. Along with the blessing of the site, a blessing is given that the deceased's body is prepared to come forth in the 'First Resurrection' when his spirit reunites with his mortal body and becomes immortal; to never be separated again by death.

The pallbearers, which were made up of Joseph's two brothers, and first cousins, carried the casket to the funeral hearse. The rest of the family and friends got into their vehicles to leave the chapel grounds. Many thoughts and memories were flooding my mind, and I questioned if I would ever get any better at coping with the loss. Cassie and I followed immediately behind the funeral hearse to the town cemetery. This was a drive of approximately 5 miles taking us through country roads and across bridges spanning the interstate twice.

I'll never forget looking in my rearview mirror and seeing an impressive line of cars stretching more than a mile (bumper to bumper); following us with their lights on to the cemetery. What a beautiful expression of love by so many. It was apparent they wanted to show their love and support to us through to the completion of the funeral services. They could've gone home or their separate ways, but they were there for us to the end. As one coworker related to me later; "We were fed spiritually. It was beyond words, both at the church and at the gravesite."

As we arrived at the cemetery, the Bishop remarked, "What a great family you have Joe and Cassie. To extend your love and support also to Tracy and her family; and support one another in your grief, is so commendable. Forgiveness is an eternal principle of the Lord's work."

The pallbearers removed the casket from the hearse and carried it to the grave. Family and friends moved in closer to surround that special place for the dedicational prayer, and to seek some shelter from the freezing winds that were blowing in a partially clouded sky. Before the Bishop announced my name to give the prayer, I noticed Emily approach Tracy, take her by the arm and lead her to sit with us at the side of the grave on chairs placed for the family. What an expression of love in our time of mutual mourning for Joseph! I feel certain that Joseph and our Savior Jesus Christ would have wanted it that way.

Then a miraculous thing happened. As I started the dedicatory prayer, the winds stopped and the clouds moved, giving the sun the opportunity to warm us; and we felt the love of God in our souls.

I remember a few of the words of the prayer, but most remarkably I recognize the blessings that have been fulfilled from that special priesthood ordinance in the days and years   since. During the prayer, a special vision was experienced by my granddaughter Susan who was so innocent and young at the age of four. She opened her eyes during the prayer and saw two personages of spirit standing next to me; one she described as being 'Uncle Joseph', and one described as being a 'gray and white-haired man' she didn't know. She said that the person that was with Joseph was telling him that 'it's okay' and that 'it's almost time to go' and Joseph was saying he 'wanted to stay'. The veil between this world and the next was literally removed for a moment for little Susan in that possibly once-in-a-lifetime experience. I believe it was Cassie's uncle Dean (who had passed two weeks earlier from his own suicide) standing next to Joseph. I testify that many of the words of this prayer have been fulfilled through the power of the Priesthood; which power transcends death or the grave. I now quote some of the words of the prayer:

> "Calling upon the powers of Heaven in the name of Jesus Christ and through the Holy Priesthood of God, I bless and dedicate this small plot of earth for the final resting place for the mortal body of Joseph Perkins. I bless this gravesite from the elements, earthquakes and other natural disasters that his body might be preserved and protected to come forth in the morning of the first resurrection."

I spoke to Joseph as a father and told him that, '[he] had broken our hearts' but that we had 'forgiven [him]'. I blessed him with a special father's blessing that he would be able to, 'come unto Christ and be forgiven for [his] sins through the power of the Atonement and be able to be forgiven by his Heavenly Father and overcome the demands of justice'. I blessed him to realize that this, 'mistake (this thing called suicide) would be [his] hardest and most trying challenge because [he] no longer had the flesh; but that he needed to, 'spend every moment working towards receiving the saving ordinances of the Temple by 'proxy'. I blessed him that he would be able in the spirit to, 'come to his brothers, sisters, and parents in times of need and when they struggle in this life, that [he] would be there for them'. I blessed him that he would be able to, 'come wherever they are at the most trying times'. That they would be blessed to, 'feel his presence and his support along with other ministering Angels'. Through this blessing, I also blessed his brothers and sisters to, 'commit to becoming better people, both temporally and spiritually; that they could become examples to their children and live up to the covenants that they've made with their Heavenly Father'. To prepare to, 'receive the covenants and blessings of the Temple for themselves.'

There were many other things mentioned in that prayer; and I know they will all be fulfilled through the Power of the Priesthood of God; and through our faithfulness. As I ended the prayer there was silence, reverence, and no one seemed to want to move. The Spirit was so strong, everyone seemed to want to bask in its warmth even more; and not leave Joseph's side. Joseph's close friends (although not very religiously inclined) did not want to leave. They stood surrounding the casket (kind of guarding it), staying there for some time. They didn't want to leave Tracy there alone with him.

I think I should emphasize some points of doctrine that were expressed during his funeral service:

- First, we are all sons and daughters of God. No matter rich or poor, religious or not; Heavenly Father loves us each unconditionally.
- Second, no matter what sin or condition our life seems to be in, we must keep hope alive and never give up, having faith in our Savior Jesus Christ.
- Third, the Temple Sealing is a saving ordinance that binds families together forever. On condition that we endure to the end, and are faithful to the Holy Ordinances and Covenants made in the House of the Lord.
- Fourth, the Resurrection is a true principle and blessing for every child born to this Earth.
- Fifth, we must forgive all people in all circumstances. This enables us to be forgiven for our sins and shortcomings by our Heavenly Father.
- Sixth, comfort those who stand in need of comfort and mourn with those that mourn.
- Seventh, seek out the 'one'. Love all God's children and look inward (to their heart), instead of the outward (on their appearance).
- Eighth, do not judge; 'for with what judgment ye judge, ye also shall be judged'.
- Ninth, never give up on anyone. Each of us is a child of God and has the capacity to become like God. We are each a spirit child of God, created in his image.
- And tenth, "Love one another as I have loved you" are the words of Jesus Christ our Savior and Redeemer to each of us.

Since the day we laid Joseph's mortal body to rest, many of our family have had experiences I think are worth mentioning. These experiences (and more) are a manifestation of God's love and care for His children. In the next pages, I'll relate a few of these experiences, and in other parts of this book, I'll share others.

One of the most special dreams that I've ever had I would like to give at this time which is fulfilling one of the Priesthood blessings of the prayer of grave dedication. As you recall, I blessed Joseph to come to his brothers, sisters, and parents at a time of need. I had a dream at a time I was struggling with the question of when I would be able to see

Joseph again; and see him whole again (without the injuries of his suicide). I suppose it was about a month or so after his death. Sleep was slow in coming that night; but finally I was able to fall asleep. I dreamed I was walking down a hallway and in that hallway were four closed doors. I came to one of the doors and opened it. It was a small room with white walls, and sitting at the other end of the room was who I thought was my son Grant. He had his bandaged head bowed down and was in a white robe. As I looked, I noticed the bandages began to unwind and float upward. As he looked up, I was startled because it wasn't Grant, but was Joseph instead. I exclaimed, "Oh Joseph!" As the bandages floated away from his head, and face, I noticed he had no blemishes or scars. He had his pretty black hair, no tattoos and his countenance just glowed. It was then that I realized I was witnessing a future event in Joseph's progression: his resurrection day. The Lord allowed me to see this to give me comfort and the knowledge that Joseph was going to be okay; and eventually (as all of us) resurrected beings. This very special experience will remain with me for all eternity. It gives me hope, comfort, peace, and joy beyond measure to know there is a Plan for all of us; that we may be together as a family for all time and eternity with our loving Heavenly Father and his Son Jesus Christ.

Three family members witnessed (in the daylight hours) a very special vision similar in some ways to the description that Joseph Smith testifies of in the Grove of trees when the Father and the Son visited him. No, we did not see the Father and the Son, but this is what we did see and it will never be forgotten. This special vision occurred on April 18, 2006, just five weeks after the funeral.

The circumstances that we consider brought on this special experience were that our youngest son Rick (who was a senior in high school) had been fasting and praying to know if his brother Joseph was 'okay'. This faithful prayer of a young man was answered in a very miraculous way. Rick was pitching in a game about an hour and a half away from our home. Here he was, an 18 year old who has recently lost his older brother to suicide; how devastating and depressing that was to him; and draining it was on the whole family. Rick was doing well with his pitching, but his teammates were making lots of errors, and they lost the game. Normally after a loss, the team rides home together in defeat; but something unusual happened after this game. Some of the seniors asked the coach if they could, 'ride home with [their] parents'; and the coach gave his permission.

I drove with Cassie sitting behind me, and Rick in the passenger seat beside me as we traveled home. It had rained earlier and the skies were still a little cloudy the weather was good for the ride home. It was about 8pm as we came up I-15 from Riverdale towards the 24th Street exit in Ogden; we were traveling northwest at about 65 miles per hour. We all began to notice a large black and gray cloud formation directly ahead of us. The formation appeared like ocean waves, and it was separated from any other clouds; and the sun was setting to the west side of the cloud. Suddenly a pillar of light, as bright as the sun, burst through this cloud (on the east side of the cloud away from the sun) in a perfect cylinder from the top of the cloud to nearly the ground. The first words uttered were from Cassie in the backseat she said, "Oh Joe, is this the Second Coming of Jesus Christ?" We all could discern that the phenomenon wasn't being caused by the rays of the sun, because it came from a different direction. Rick quickly reached for his cell phone and took several photos. After arriving home, Rick went to his girlfriend's home to show her the photos. The photos were somewhat overexposed from the brightness of the pillar of light. Ivie had an impression come to her mind; what if the photo exposure and contrast was adjusted? Rick opened his photo editor app and made the adjustments. What resulted sent chills down his spine! There standing in the air, is the image of a person, which appears to be dressed in a white robe with outstretched hands. The personage also appears to be standing on a round object similar to the Angel Moroni statue on the LDS Temples. Rick immediately called me and sent the four pictures to my cell phone. To me, this is a witness and an answer to a boy's prayer. If you were to ask Rick today, 'Who was that standing in that pillar of light?' he would say, "It was Joseph come to answer my prayer by showing me he was 'okay'."

Another experience I had with Joseph came about 7 years after his death. I had just gotten home from church on a Fast Sunday. What a beautiful spiritual Sabbath day it had been! Going upstairs to change my clothes, I had just been thinking about Joseph when the Spirit said, "Look at his picture sitting on your dresser"; (this was the same picture which was displayed on his casket). I picked it up and looked into his face and the image of Jesus Christ looked back at me. The scripture, "Do you have his image in your countenance" flashed before my mind. Then, another miracle: I could see his beautiful blue eyes as if with 10X magnification. I knew at that moment, his progress on the other side of the veil was possibly greater than my own; and I felt the warmth of his embrace just for a moment.

I can also testify that what we have seen is real. I also believe and testify that when we hear of people passing away and then coming back to life, what they have witnessed are the spirits in the Spirit World as, 'Ministering Angels' coming to us in our time of need. I testify they need us, and we need them, to make it through this life; and the life hereafter. As the scripture says, "There are more for us, than against us." This I say in the name of Jesus Christ; Amen.

CHAPTER 5

Forgiveness the Greatest Healer

As I complete Part I; I'm including a talk written by Cassie entitled: 'FORGIVENESS: The Greatest Healer of the Heart and Soul'. Also, a poem that I have written entitled: 'Mirror'.

FORGIVENESS:

The Greatest Healer of the Heart and Soul

By Cassie Perkins

"On the morning of March 5th, 2006, at 7:30 a.m. our lives were changed forever. I was dreaming about our son Joseph as a boy running down a grassy hill, with a dandelion in his hand. Just as he reached me, he looked me in the eye and blew the seeds into the air. At that exact moment I heard a gunshot blast. Instantly I screamed and jumped from the bed yelling, "Joe, I think Joseph just shot himself!" I ran down the stairs as fast as I could, pausing outside his door long enough to ask, "Joseph are you okay?" I guess I started to wonder if I was having a crazy dream. No this was real! My warning in a previous dream, and the promptings of the spirit during the last year, were now a reality. I knew I had hidden his pistols. I opened his door and found my son dead.

Numb and paralyzed with shock, I screamed his dads name over and over again. I knew Joseph was dead, and watched horror as his heart quit its function. I had given him birth, and was there at his death. The pain was unbearable as time stood absolutely still. I wanted to hold him, rock him, hug and kiss him as I always had. In that moment, between light and darkness, I was overcome with the Spirit. I knew who was with him when his spirit departed, and I was physically turned around so as not to have to deal with the terrible scene any longer. In that instance, I knew the veil was very thin. I knew family and friends were there to give me the strength to endure and move forward. I knew I would have to be the strong one to get my husband and family through the events that would now take place. I ran upstairs still screaming and met Joe, Rick and Grant running out of their rooms at the same time trying to dress and figure out what was wrong.

The mind goes in so many directions in a time like this. Trying to put the pieces together, and to make some sense out of the situation; it was just overwhelming. Joe was in denial as he looked for Joseph and wondered out loud, "whose boy is in Joseph's room?" Our youngest son Rick yelled, "I'll save him! Don't worry; I'll put Joe together again! It'll be okay; I promise mom." In shock, he repeated this over and over again. My son Grant was so angry. He was determined to track down Joseph's girlfriend and make her pay for what had happened. Two of our grand-daughters who had spent the night, were scared to death and in shock with all the commotion and screaming.

Joseph had come home that morning at 5:30. Grant had brought him and his girlfriend home. Joseph had come to our room and told us "I'm home mom and dad. I love you! Tracy is here. Her brother is on his way to come and get her."

Many things happened before, during and after that pivotal moment when all of our lives were changed forever. At first, the investigators did not know if it was suicide because of the scene and the timing of Rick and my sleepy recollections of hearing running up the stairs and the slamming of the door. Rick thought it was after the shot. I wasn't sure if it was before or after, and full memory of those moments didn't come for months. His girlfriend was arrested and taken in for questioning. They couldn't find any evidence on her, and the autopsy proved it was suicide. The detectives told us that even though he pulled the trigger, she was the cause. Her attitude and previous problems were what people talked about. She had treated him physically and verbally abusive during their relationship.

During the eight days, before we buried him, I was overcome with the feeling that we as a family must forgive. In our grief, we never stopped to think that she and her family might be grieving as well. A gentleman from her stake called me and told me their family was suffering too. They had immigrated to America. He wanted to assure me that they were good people. Her family had loved him as a son and knew how much he had helped her. At first, many people also thought she had pulled the trigger. They knew how mean she was to him and others. Many people shunned and judged.

On the night of his viewing, there was a family in the line that I was drawn to. I did not know them but I knew they were grieving.

When they came up to us in line, Tracy was ushered in and stopped in front of us. It would have been easy and satisfying to tell her she did not belong here. We followed the spirit and chose to forgive her and tell her we loved her and that she should go on and be the best she could be. It was heart wrenching to watch her hug my husband and beg for forgiveness, and then he told her we forgave her and took her up to the casket, where she sobbed. Just like us, she was unable to hug him one more time or say I love you or say she was sorry'.

At the funeral we did not see her. She had come a little late because of her fear of judgment by Joseph's family and friends. The service was crowded, and so was the graveside. It was so cold. Our bodies felt like our hearts - ice cold. Joe dedicated the grave and sat down with us as we just stared in disbelief. Just then, Tracy came to the coffin shaking with a red rose in her hand and placed it on the coffin. She turned and ran back to her mother. Our daughter Emily brought her back and had her sit with our family. For the first time in eight days our spirits were truly warm and we let the tender mercies of the Lord take over. Forgiveness on all of our parts wasn't easy, but the healing power it has is far greater than anything we have ever known.

Two weeks later, Tracy, still not forgiving herself, got very drunk. She was pulled over and taken to jail for DUI. With the previous trouble she had, she spent the next two months in jail. It was there, she tested positive for being pregnant. It turned out that she had become pregnant four days before Joseph's death. Eight and half months after Joseph's death, his son was born; he looks so much like his father. Things would have been so different if we hadn't been forgiving. We probably wouldn't get to see this sweet child who came to earth knowing his father wouldn't be here. We would not have been able to know Tracy's heart, her culture and her wonderful family.

Two families' prayers had been answered the morning of our son's death. Although they were not answered in any way we imagined. Our families are intertwined. We understand depression, dependency, abuse, anger and Satan's power to destroy God's precious spirits. We also know love, forgiveness, prayer, temple blessings and the love of the Master's Hand.

Many angels helped us through the bad times. A good Bishop, home and visiting teachers, neighbors, work associates, family and friends who performed countless acts of service for and behalf of our family to name a few. Visits, cards, calls, letters, flowers, and hugs are just a few ways we were helped. We were contacted by people in every Ward we have lived in. Others honestly lifted our burden and carried us.

I could be angry, but I refuse to give into Satan. Who would have to pay more than me: the young man who molested Joseph as a boy; the men he worked with that told him he couldn't have fun if he followed all of the rules, and that it was okay to drink; the men who raped him in jail when he served his two days for a DUI; his friends that knew he was an alcoholic and still presented him with situations to drink; his friends that went on missions and into the business world who didn't remember their friendship; Joseph for not telling his girlfriend he didn't have money for alcohol; the trials in Tracy's life which had left little trust for people outside her family; the person who came to the door to get some parts from my husband and told him they came just because they were dying to know if his son is the one who killed himself; the woman who made the comment that his [Joseph's] mother should have stayed home when he was young (I DID); the people who said if he had good parents and a good home this wouldn't have happened; the people who assume he used drugs and told us to our face; the woman who yelled at me saying I'm crazy for forgiving the girl or accepting her child; or the people who still turn away, as if I have the 'plague'?

We live in a world where we are constantly judged. We are losing so many of our precious ones in and out of the Church because we judge. So what if they have made one mistake or many; we all make mistakes. When we choose not to judge and extend a hand or open arms to them, we open the hand and arms of our Savior and Father in Heaven for ourselves.

I learned more about my Savior from Joseph than I learned from any other source. I wish everyone could ask (about anyone who touches our lives for good or bad), "What can I learn from them?" Just maybe, people with problems are put near us so the Savior can see how we will respond: will we be 'better' or 'bitter'? Forgiveness is so much worth the effort. I have no regrets. I've loved unconditionally. I know our son is in a better place; and I know I've become a better person. I know that our prayers and family nights were worth it. Our family has been so blessed by this one moment in time when we turned the other cheek.

It is our prayer as parents that we will all learn to forgive, never judge, and be willing to turn the other cheek; in an evil-filled world that would have us do otherwise. I'm so thankful that as a family we never gave up on Joseph. He was on his way back to us and his Father in Heaven. Alcohol was the gateway to depression for him. Suicide is not the answer for any problem. Never give up on yourself or a family member. May we all be there to gather up the lost sheep of the fold; and lovingly bring them home to us and to a loving Father in Heaven."

It's so hard to follow a woman's heartfelt touch. I love my wife of 37 years so much! Words cannot explain the love we have for each other. As I end this special section on the life of Joseph Perkins I testify he lives, his presence has and will be felt forever more. I have created this poem to go along with my special sweetheart's message on forgiveness.

MIRROR

Look upon the transgressor,
The weight of the sin.
Overwhelming him to his knees,
Once smooth, now cracked and bleeding.

Tears become steady,
Endless streams of grief.
Pains of the Son of God in Gethsemane,
And godly sorrow enter in.

Once deep wounds now healing,
The miracle of the atonement is within reach.
The burden of guilt and darkness turns to light;
So close to the journeys end.

Even knowing that the Father has erased and forgotten;
One step nearer to perfection.
The out stretched arms of a loving Father in Heaven,
Can be seen in the distance.

Then another so close to you, drives the dagger to your soul;
I can't forgive you – you are horrible.
With every fit of anger you point,
To that person in the mirror.

And then declaring the echoing words,
"You're guilty, you're a sinner."
Showing no mercy, "I demand justice";
"You must be punished the way I want."

He was so close,
But another will not forgive and forget.
The images remain, flashing in front of his face once again;
And he finds it so hard, so very hard to forgive oneself.

Can't you see! The image in the mirror is you and only you.
Don't place yourself in God's shoes.
You and I are not worthy,
To even touch the master's wounded hands and feet.

Joseph you are truly my, "Sonny Boy." Love Dad

CHAPTER 6

The Earthly Ministry of Jesus Christ

Would it be fair to say that the words contained in the four Gospels (that detail the Ministry of Jesus Christ) could also be considered the 'Doctrine of Christ'? If you are a Christian, then *every* verse of scripture containing His Gospel *is* the Word of Christ. The four Apostles Matthew, Mark, Luke, and John are the attributed authors of the Four Gospels. They were eyewitnesses to each situation, doctrine and teaching given during His Ministry. They were (to the best of their ability) dictating and writing in specific detail, the most important things for all mankind to read and understand. If we accept this be the case, and then what I describe in this chapter (using these verses of scripture), should also prove to be the Doctrine of Jesus Christ.

First, let me ask a question: In the teachings of your religious institution, have your leaders discussed the topic of evil spirits gaining control of your physical body? I would venture to say this doctrine may be read, but there is little or no detailed discussion. This critical issue is described in great detail, in the scriptures of the New Testament. I believe with all my heart, it's important for our salvation to discuss this in enough detail that we might learn and understand. The Savior himself taught these things, and they were apparently important enough to have been written, compiled, and preserved for our use as the Holy Bible. This doctrinal topic isn't pleasant to discuss, but it's essential to know who this adversary is: Satan. If we know who he is, and learn of his tactics, then we will be better able to use our God-given agency to discern and judge right from wrong; and to choose good from evil. In this chapter and others, you'll come to know and realize Satan *is* real.

In this chapter, will be a detailed description (primarily using the first three Gospels) to explain in detail what the Savior is trying to teach the people of the Earth. He gives us all the information we need to make us equal to the task of overcoming any trial we'll ever encounter in this life.

Matthew's teaching is primarily directed to the Jews. Mark is talking to the Gentiles and the Romans. Luke gives us a detailed version of Christ's life. The book of John is written to the members of Christ's church; those who are already convinced that Jesus is the Christ. I'll also use the Book of Acts whose author is the Apostle Paul. The Four Gospels cover the birth, life, earthly ministry, death, and resurrection of the Lord Jesus Christ.

My purpose in this writing is to review the three-year Ministry of Jesus Christ. It was during this time of ministry, that the parables, the miracles, the Savior's praying to his father, the one-on-one teaching of the 12 apostles, and especially where Jesus demonstrated His unconditional love for His followers as He taught them.   Truth is established in the mouth of two or three witnesses, and many of His teachings are repeated in the three Gospels. This apparent duplication allows us to see the different perspectives of the several Apostles as they address their various audiences.   Let's also keep in mind that these writings were put into their current form by inspired men, so we'd be blessed to have them in our day. It is marvelous (and one could say a miracle) that we have these compiled writings of the Old Testament and New Testaments available for our study and use.

Jesus Christ taught that we should 'come follow Him' and do the things which we have 'heard and seen' Him do. Using the proper authority, and in the name of Jesus Christ, we may call upon our Heavenly Father in all things. This authority is mentioned in Mark 7:32, Mark 16:18, Luke 13:13 and Luke 24:50 just to name a few. In these four verses of Scripture, is described the laying on of hands by a Priesthood holder who has the authority to place their hands on those who are the sick and the downtrodden; and heal them in the name of Jesus Christ.

Jesus Christ teaches his Disciples to 'become like Him' through faith, good works, and service to others; by and through the name of Jesus Christ. He teaches how to pray, how we should treat our (so-called) enemies, and how to love everyone unconditionally. He even raised the dead. He gave Power and Authority to his Apostles to do the same. They too were able to raise the dead, give sight to the blind, and teach the Doctrine of the Atonement.

Is it necessary to be an Apostle in order to have the Power and Authority of the Priesthood of God? Thanks to the 'restoration of all things' in our day, every male holder of the Holy Priesthood (if living worthily) can exercise this same 'Power to act' given by and through the laying on of hands. What about worthy women and children? They too can call upon the name of Jesus Christ and bring down the 'Powers of Heaven' through mighty faith, fasting, and prayer; to be delivered from evil, heal the sick, and bless the afflicted, *if* there is no Priesthood Holder available.

Christ also taught of the 'opposition' which is upon the Earth. Thanks to modern revelation we understand this to include one-third of the original hosts of Heaven; and their leader Lucifer (also known as Satan, the father of all lies). Let's just try to quantify what one-third of the hosts of Heaven might mean. By some estimates, there have been over 107 billion people born on Earth. If that number were to represent the two-thirds of the hosts of Heaven who followed Christ's Plan; then using simple math, one third could represent approximately 35 billion spirits that followed Satan when he was cast to the Earth. That would mean, based on an estimated current world population of 7 billion, we are outnumbered by 5 to 1! Satan and his demons seem to have a distinct advantage over the children of God here on Earth. Lest this seems like a hopeless situation, be assured that we have the advantage because God *is* on our side. I'll explain who Satan is, and who his followers are in greater detail, in another chapter.

In the first three Gospels, and the Book of Acts, there are numerous scriptural references describing the ability of Satan and his followers to gain access to physical bodies. Why would these demons try to infiltrate human bodies? A major part of their punishment for rejecting God's Plan, was they could never have a body like you and me. These 'spirit entities' can only temporarily possess the bodies of mortals; and that, only if we 'allow' it. The Savior in His teachings exposes these devils, and teaches us how to cast them out, and eliminate them from our lives. How well do you know the Savior Jesus Christ? How well do you know Satan? The closeness of our relationship with Christ will help determine how well we learn to become like Him, and cast Satan from our lives. Our knowledge of Satan and his evil ways will give us the power to reject his efforts as he tries to convince us to worship him.

As we read the following scriptures, picture in your mind the situation in which they were given; and why the Savior is teaching this doctrine. You may ask these questions in relation to our day: Are these demons and evil spirits around us now? Is there evidence of evil in the world today? Does the worlds' 'illuminated', attempt to explain this evil away as 'societal problems'; and offer simple cures that never involve religion as a solution?   I will attempt to show that *evil in all forms* originates with Satan; and that only through the Holy One of Israel, Jesus Christ can this evil be crushed.   The Savior teaches us that by keeping the Commandments, being pure of heart, and doing good to all men, we can have 'power to bind Satan' and his billions of servant demons.

Let's go to the scriptures of the *King James Version of the Holy Bible* New Testament Gospels and read some of the verses where the Master Teacher is teaching His true doctrine:

"Then saith Jesus unto him, *Get thee hence, Satan*: for it is written, Thou shalt worship the Lord thy God, and him only shalt thou serve.

Then the devil leaveth him, and, behold, angels came and ministered unto him. (Matthew 4:10-11 – *emphasis* added)

"And his fame went throughout all Syria: and they brought under him all sick people that were taken with divers diseases and torments, *and those which were possessed with devils, and those which were lunatic*, and those that had the palsy; and he healed them." (Matthew 4:24 *emphasis* added)

"When the even was come, *they brought unto him many that were possessed devils: and he cast out the spirits with his word*, and healed all that were sick:" (Matthew 8:16 – *emphasis* added)

"And when he was come to the other side into the country of the Gergesenes, there met him *two possessed with devils, coming out of the tombs, exceeding fierce*, so that no man might pass by that way.

And, behold, they cried out, saying, What have we to do with thee, Jesus, thou Son of God? art thou come hither to torment us before the time?

And there was a good way off from them an herd of many swine feeding.

So the devils besought him, saying, If thou cast us out, suffer us to go away into the herd of swine.

And he said unto them, *Go. And when they were come out, they went into the herd of swine: and, behold, the whole herd of swine ran violently down a steep place into the sea, and perished in the waters.*

And they that kept them fled, and went their ways into the city, and told every thing, and what was befallen to the *possessed of the devils*.

And, behold, the whole city came out to meet Jesus: and when they saw him, they besought him that he would depart out of their coasts. (Matthew 8:28-34 – *emphasis* added)

In the Luke (8:30) and Mark (5:9) accounts of this incident, one of the evil spirits declared itself to be an entity called 'Legion'. These evil spirits knew that Jesus was the Son of God, and they wanted to possess some kind of flesh or physical body even if it was an animal.

We see by this account that when demons take possession of a person's physical body, they (at least temporarily) remove that person's identity as a child of God.

"As they went out, behold, *they brought to him a dumb man possessed with a devil*.

And when the devil was cast out, the dumb spake: and the multitudes marveled, saying, it was never so seen in Israel.

But the Pharisees said, *he casteth out devils through the prince of the devils.*: (Matthew 9:32-34 – *emphasis* added)

"And if Satan cast out Satan, he is divided against himself; how shall then his kingdom stand?

And if I by Beelzebub cast out devils, by whom do your children cast them out? Therefore they shall be your judges.

But if I cast out devils by the Spirit of God, then the kingdom of God is come unto you.

Or else how can one enter into a strong man's house, and spoil his goods, except he first bind the strong man? And then he will spoil his house.

He that is not with me is against me; and he that gathereth not with me scattereth abroad." (Matthew 12:26-30 – *emphasis* added)

"And, behold, a woman of Canaan came out of the same coasts, and cried unto him, saying, Have mercy on me, O Lord, thou Son of David*; my daughter is grievously vexed with a devil.*

Then Jesus answered and said unto her, O woman, great is thy faith: be it unto thee even as thou wilt. *And her daughter was made whole from that very hour.*"' (Matthew 15:22 & 28 - *emphasis* added)

The Savior uses this example to teach and show that it's by this mother's faith, that her daughter was made whole; and the devil cast out.

"And when they were come to the multitude, there came to him a certain man, kneeling down to him, and saying,

Lord, have mercy on my son: for he is lunatic, and sore vexed: for ofttimes he falleth into the fire, and oft into the water.

And I brought him to thy disciples, and they could not cure him.

Then Jesus answered and said, O faithless and perverse generation, how long shall I be with you? how long shall I suffer you? bring him hither to me.

And *Jesus rebuked the devil; and he departed out of him*: and the child was cured from that very hour.

Then came the disciples to Jesus apart, and said, *Why could not we cast him out?*

And Jesus said unto them, Because of your unbelief: for verily I say unto you, If ye have faith as a grain of mustard seed, ye shall say unto this mountain, Remove hence to yonder place; and it shall remove; and nothing shall be impossible unto you.

Howbeit this kind goeth not out *but by prayer and fasting*. (Matthew 17:14-21 – *emphasis* added)

Here, a father comes to the disciples to have an evil spirit cast out of his son; but they could not do it. The Savior chastises them and explains again, what has to be done to remove an evil spirit. First, a person must have faith; and secondly, they must have the proper Priesthood Authority (going forth in fasting and prayer); *only then* he can cast out the demon. Key to this process is faith in the Lord Jesus Christ; and calling upon His name. The evil one must leave because the very name of Jesus Christ carries power over Satan and his followers.

We now move to the book of Mark. Here many of the same experiences are witnessed by another set of eyes; and testimony is borne of this doctrine, that was as essential for people in the days of Jesus

Christ, as it is in our day. This doctrine enables us to cast off the chains Satan tries to use to bind us. I testify this is true. This book openly exposes this doctrine for all to see; that the opposition, the father of lies, even Satan, *is real*. His ultimate goal is to possess the bodies that Heavenly Father created to house our spirits.

> *"And there was in their synagogue a man with an unclean spirit*; and he cried out,
>
> Saying, Let us alone; what have we to do with thee, thou Jesus of Nazareth? art thou come to destroy us? I know thee who thou art, the Holy One of God.
>
> *And Jesus rebuked him, saying, Hold thy peace, and come out of him.*
>
> And when the unclean spirit had torn him, and cried with a loud voice, he came out of him.
>
> And they were all amazed, insomuch that they questioned among themselves, saying, What thing is this? what new doctrine is this? for with authority commandeth he even the unclean spirits, and they do obey him". (Mark 1:23-27 – emphasis added)

> *'What thing is this? What new doctrine is this? For with authority commanded he even the unclean spirits, and they do obey him.'*

Here we see the evil ones know him as Jesus Christ the Son of the living God. Do we know the Savior as well as the evil one does? Could we recognize Him, if we were in His presence today?

> "And at even, when the sun did set, they brought unto him all that were diseased, and them that were *possessed with devils.*
>
> And all the city was gathered together at the door.
>
> And he healed many that were sick of divers diseases, *and cast out many devils; and suffered not the devils to speak,* because they knew him." (Mark 1:32-34 – *emphasis* added)

> And he preached in their synagogues throughout all of Galilee, *and cast out devils.* (Mark 1:39 – *emphasis* added)

> "And unclean spirits, when they saw him, fell down before him, and cried, saying, Thou art the Son of God.

And he straitly charged them that they should not make him known. (Mark 3:11-12 – *emphasis* added)

"And he ordained twelve, that they should be with him, and that he might send them forth to preach,

And to have power to heal sicknesses, and to *cast out devils*:" (Mark 3:14-15 – emphasis added)

The Savior here is giving the authority of the priesthood to the 12 Apostles; the power they now have to heal the sick and cast out devils.

"And when he was come out of the ship, immediately there met him out of the tombs a man with an unclean spirit,

Who had his dwelling among the tombs; and no man could bind him, no, not with chains:

Because that he had been often bound with fetters and chains, and the chains had been plucked asunder by him, and the fetters broken in pieces: neither could any man tame him.

And always, night and day, he was in the mountains, and in the tombs, crying, and cutting himself with stones.

But when he saw Jesus afar off, he ran and worshipped

him.

And cried with a loud voice, and said, What have I to do

With thee, Jesus, thou Son of the most high God? I adjure

thee by God, that thou torment me not.

For he said unto him, *Come out of the man, thou unclean*

spirit.

And he asked him, What is thy name? And he answered, saying, My name is Legion: for we are many.

And he besought him much that he would not send them away out of the country.

Now there was there nigh unto the mountains a great herd of swine feeding.

And all the devils besought him, saying, Send us into the swine, that we may enter into them.

And forthwith Jesus gave them leave. *And the unclean spirits went ou*t, and entered into the swine: and the herd ran violently down a steep place into the sea, (they were about two thousand;) and were choked in the sea.

And they that fed the swine fled, and told it in the city, and in the country. And they went out to see what it was that was done.

And they come to Jesus, and see him that *was possessed with the devil*, and had the legion, sitting, and clothed, and in his right mind: and they were afraid.

And they that saw it told them how it befell to him that *was possessed with the devil*, and also concerning the swine.

And they began to pray him to depart out of their coasts.

And when he was come into the ship, he that had *been possessed with the devil* prayed him that he might be with him.

Howbeit Jesus suffered him not, but saith unto him, Go home to thy friends, and tell them how great things the Lord hath done for thee, and hath had compassion on thee.

And he departed, and began to publish in Decapolis how great things Jesus had done for him: and all men did marvel." (Mark 5:2-20 – *emphasis* added)

Unlike Matthew, Mark gives the name of this individual evil spirit as 'Legion', and also mentions the 2000 other demons or devils that possessed this man's body. A special note: again the evil ones did know him as the Son of God. Also, when the man was cleansed of the demons, he wanted to continue on with Jesus. The Lord forbade him and told him to go and tell his family and friends how great the things were the Lord had done for him. Yet when the Lord had performed other miracles (such as healing the blind and raising the dead), the Savior often asked the recipient to 'tell no man'. To me, this is evidence that the doctrine of casting Satan and his followers aside (using the proper Authority of the Priesthood of God) is very important to know and understand, especially in our day.

"And he called unto him the twelve, and began to send them forth by two and two; and gave them power over unclean spirits;

And they cast out many devils, and anointed with oil many that were sick, and healed them." (Mark 6:7 & 13 – *emphasis* added)

Here the Savior called the 12 Apostles to the work, and gave them power over *unclean spirits*, which Power is the Priesthood of God. He taught them the process of the 'laying on of hands' and the use of anointing oil for the healing of the sick.

"For a certain woman, whose young daughter had an unclean spirit, heard of him, and came and fell at his feet:

The woman was a Greek, a Syrophenician by nation; and she besought him that he would *cast forth the devil out of her daughter*.

But Jesus said unto her, Let the children first be filled: for it is not meet to take the children's bread, and to cast it unto the dogs.

And she answered and said unto him, Yes, Lord: yet the dogs under the table eat of the children's crumbs.

And he said unto her, For this saying go thy way; *the devil is gone out of thy daughter*.

And when she was come to her house, *she found the devil gone out*, and her daughter laid upon the bed. (Mark 7:25-30 – *emphasis* added)

"And one of the multitude answered and said, Master, I have brought unto thee my son, which hath a dumb spirit;

And wheresoever he taketh him, he teareth him: and he foameth, and gnasheth with his teeth, and pineth away: and I spake to thy disciples that they should cast him out; and they could not.

He answereth him, and saith, O faithless generation, how long shall I be with you? how long shall I suffer you? bring him unto me.

And they brought him unto him: and when he saw him, straightway the spirit tare him; and he fell on the ground, and wallowed foaming.

And he asked his father, How long is it ago since this came unto him? And he said, Of a child.

And ofttimes it hath cast him into the fire, and into the waters, to destroy him: but if thou canst do any thing, have compassion on us, and help us.

Jesus said unto him, If thou canst believe, all things are possible to him that believeth.

And straightway the father of the child cried out, and said with tears, Lord, I believe; help thou mine unbelief.

When Jesus saw that the people came running together, *he rebuked the foul spirit*, saying unto him, Thou dumb and deaf spirit, *I charge thee, come out of him, and enter no more into him.*

And the spirit cried, and rent him sore, and came out of him: and he was as one dead; insomuch that many said, He is dead.

But Jesus took him by the hand, and lifted him up; and he

arose.

And when he was come into the house, his disciples asked him privately, Why could not we cast him out?

And he said unto them, This kind can come forth by nothing, but by prayer and fasting. (Mark 9:17-29 – *emphasis* added)

Mark tells a slightly different story than Matthew. He talks about this boy having one or several evil spirits in him for many years. This boy didn't even have the physical strength to stand after the evil ones were cast out. Then, the Savior tells his disciples that first they need to have faith, much fasting and prayer, and of course Priesthood Authority. After the evil ones left the boy, the Savior placed His hands upon his head and blessed him. His strength was restored and he was made whole.

"And John answered him, saying, Master, *we saw one casting out devils in thy name*, and he followeth not us: and we forbad him, because he followeth not us.

But Jesus said, Forbid him not: for there is no man which shall do a miracle in my name, that can lightly speak evil of me.

For he that is not against us is on our part." (Mark 9:38-40 – *emphasis* added)

Other Priesthood holders can cast out devils if they have the faith, and they've been fasting and praying. The Apostles today can't be everywhere the need may arise. What would be desirable is more worthy and righteous Priesthood holders in our midst that can help when called upon.

"Now when Jesus was risen early the first day of the week, he appeared first to *Mary Magdalene, out of whom he had cast seven devils.*" (Mark 16:9 – *emphasis* added)

This is a very interesting scripture because of who is the subject of this cleansing. We see that Satan, or one of his followers, can take over our physical body if we 'allow' it. Mary Magdalene was at the Savior's side throughout his earthly ministry, and the first to see the resurrected Lord. No matter whom we are, if we let down our guard, evil can enter in.

"And these signs shall follow them that believe; *In my name shall they cast out devils*; they shall speak with new tongues;" (Mark 16:17 – *emphasis* added)

In the name of Jesus Christ devils can be cast out. This is the only name on Earth that Satan and his evil followers MUST obey.

"And in the synagogue there was a *man, which had a spirit of an unclean devil, and cried out with a loud voice,*

Saying, Let us alone; what have we to do with thee, thou Jesus of Nazareth? art thou come to destroy us? I know thee who thou art; the Holy One of God.

And Jesus rebuked him, saying, Hold thy peace, and come out of him. And when the devil had thrown him in the midst, he came out of him, and hurt him not.

And they were all amazed, and spake among themselves, saying, What a word is this! for with authority and power *he commandeth the unclean spirits, and they come out.*" (Luke 4:33-36 – *emphasis* added)

"Now when the sun was setting, all they that had any sick with divers diseases brought them unto him; and he laid his hands on every one of them, and healed them.

And devils also came out of many, crying out, and saying, Thou art Christ the Son of God. And he rebuking them suffered them not to speak: for they knew that he was Christ." (Luke 4:40-41 – *emphasis* added)

Here again we see the laying on of hands by the Savior or another Priesthood holder. We also see that the evil ones knew he was Christ the Lord the very Son of God.

"And they that were *vexed with unclean spirits*: and they were healed." (Luke 6:18 – *emphasis* added)

"And in that same hour he cured many of their infirmities and plagues, *and of evil spirits*; and unto many that were blind he gave sight." (Luke 7:21 – emphasis added)

"And certain women, which had been *healed of evil spirits* and infirmities, Mary called Magdalene, *out of whom went seven devils.*" (Luke 8:2 – *emphasis* added)

Mary Magdalene was a Disciple of Christ. She wasn't an evil person just because evil had entered into her body. Satan preys on the more righteous, rather than those persons who don't need his help or encouragement to do evil. We also see he doesn't give those that follow him, support for long. He wants all the glory and recognition, and then once the person is taken to a self-sustaining level of evil, he moves on to his next prey. He leaves those who have fallen destitute and void of *any* spirit. No matter who you are, if evil has come into your life, there *is* hope. You can become whole again just like Mary.

"And when he went forth to land, there met him out of the city *a certain man, which had devils* long time, and ware no clothes, neither abode in any house, but in the tombs.

When he saw Jesus, he cried out, and fell down before him, and with a loud voice said, What have I to do with thee, Jesus, thou Son of God most high? I beseech thee, torment me not.

(*For he had commanded the unclean spirit to come out of the man.* For oftentimes it had caught him: and he was kept bound with chains and in fetters; and he brake the bands, and was driven of the devil into the wilderness.)

And Jesus asked him, saying, What is thy name? And he said, *Legion: because many devils were entered into him.*

And they besought him that he would not command them to go out into the deep.

And there was there an herd of many swine feeding on the mountain: and they besought him that he would suffer them to enter into them. And he suffered them.

Then went the devils out of the man, and entered into the swine: and the herd ran violently down a steep place into the lake, and were choked." (Luke 8:27-33 – *emphasis* added)

Evil spirits want to possess a physical body, even if it be that of an animal. These spirits will do anything to obtain the mortal body of one of God's sons or daughters. The antidote: we must do everything in our power to control ourselves (the natural man) and avoid even the very appearance of evil. He can't take over our body without us allowing it to happen. Remember he is at war for our souls. He has become a mastermind with the types of warfare used to gain control of us. We have ultimate power over him when we choose to follow the Savior, and choose obedience and allegiance to Him.

> *"Then he called his twelve disciples together, and gave them power and authority over all devils*, and to cure diseases." (Luke 9:1 – *emphasis* added)

We can see that dealing with evil spirits was a very important aspect and focus to the Savior Jesus Christ; the record abounds with examples during his earthly ministry. I believe this understanding is significantly more important today as these are the Last Days, foretold by the Savior and all the Prophets, ancient and modern. Satan knows the scriptures and prophecies, and that he must intensify his efforts. He knows Jesus Christ will be returning soon.

> "And, behold, a man of the company cried out, saying, Master, I beseech thee, look upon my son: for he is mine only child.
>
> And, lo, a spirit taketh him, and he suddenly crieth out; and it teareth him that he foameth again, and bruising him hardly departeth from him.

And I besought thy disciples to cast him out; and they could

not.

And Jesus answering said, O faithless and perverse generation, how long shall I be with you, and suffer you? Bring thy son hither.

And as he was yet a coming, the devil threw him down, and tare him. *And Jesus rebuked the unclean spirit*, and healed the child, and delivered him again to his father. (Luke 9:38-42 – *emphasis* added)

Illustrated here is the violence that comes to a physical body when an unclean spirit, demon or evil spirit is residing within a person. The evil can distort the person's face; change their voice, personality, and very character, as they try to destroy that person.

> *"And John answered and said, Master, we saw one casting out devils in thy name; and we forbad him, because he followeth not with us.*
>
> And Jesus said unto him, Forbid him not: for he that is not against us is for us." (Luke 9:49-50 – *emphasis* added)

> "And *the seventy* returned again with joy, saying, Lord, *even the devils are subject unto us* through thy name.
>
> And he said unto them, I beheld Satan as lightning fall from heaven.
>
> Behold, *I give unto you power to tread on serpents and scorpions, and over all the power of the enemy*: and nothing shall by any means hurt you.
>
> Notwithstanding in this rejoice not, *that the spirits are subject unto you*; but rather rejoice, because your names are written in heaven." (Luke 10:17-20 – *emphasis* added)

These verses are very important because the Savior is giving power over the demons to the Seventy or someone other than the Apostles. As I've mentioned before, all worthy persons holding the Holy Priesthood, have 'authority' over evil spirits.

"And he was casting out a devil, and it was dumb. And it came to pass, when the devil was gone out, the dumb spake; and the people wondered.

But some of them said, *He casteth out devils through Beelzebub the chief of the devils.*

And others, tempting him, sought of him a sign from heaven.

But he, knowing their thoughts, said unto them, Every kingdom divided against itself is brought to desolation; and a house divided against a house falleth.

If Satan also be divided against himself, how shall his kingdom stand? because ye say that I cast out devils through Beelzebub.

And if I by Beelzebub cast out devils, by whom do your sons cast them out? therefore shall they be your judges.

But if *I with the finger of God cast out devils,* no doubt the kingdom of God is come upon you.

When a strong man armed keepeth his palace, his goods are in peace:

But when a stronger than he shall come upon him, and overcome him, he taketh from him all his armour wherein he trusted, and divideth his spoils.

He that is not with me is against me: and he that gathereth not with me scattereth.

When the unclean spirit is gone out of a man, he walketh through dry places, seeking rest; and finding none, he saith, I will return unto my house whence I came out.

And when he cometh, he findeth it swept and garnished.

Then goeth he, and taketh to him seven other spirits more wicked than himself; and they enter in, and dwell there: and the last state of that man is worse than the first." (Luke 11:14-26 – *emphasis* added)

We see here that when an evil spirit is cast out, he doesn't give up on that person; but will bring seven (more wicked than he), to take over that person's body. We must understand that Satan never quits, he never takes breaks or vacations. He and his minions are relentless, until the goal has been reached: possession of the bodies that God has created for his sons and daughters. These are the bodies which we rightfully earned through our obedience, in our preexistent state before coming to Earth.

"And, behold, there was *a woman which had a spirit of infirmity eighteen years*, and was bowed together, and could in no wise lift up herself.

And when Jesus saw her, he called her to him, and said unto her, Woman, thou art loosed from thine infirmity.

And he laid his hands on her: and immediately she was made straight, and glorified God.

And the ruler of the synagogue answered with indignation, because that Jesus had healed on the sabbath day, and said unto the people, There are six days in which men ought to work: in them therefore come and be healed, and not on the sabbath day.

The Lord then answered him, and said, Thou hypocrite, doth not each one of you on the sabbath loose his ox or his ass from the stall, and lead him away to watering?

And ought not this woman, being a daughter of Abraham, *whom Satan hath bound, lo, these eighteen years, be loosed from this bond* on the sabbath day?" (Luke 13:11-16 – *emphasis* added)

Christ set the example and gave this woman a blessing by the laying on of hands to cast out the evil spirit.

"And he said unto them, Go ye, and tell that fox, behold, *I cast out devils*, and I do cures to end tomorrow, and the third day I shall be perfected." (Luke 13:32 – *emphasis* added)

"There came also a multitude out of the cities round about unto Jerusalem, bringing sick folks, *and them which were vexed with unclean spirits*: and they were healed every one." (Acts 5:16 – *emphasis* added)

"And this did she many days. But *Paul, being grieved, turned and said to the spirit, I command thee in the name of Jesus Christ to come out of her. And he came out the same hour.*" (Acts 16:18 – emphasis added)

The Book of Acts is another witness of the Doctrines of Christ through his Holy Apostles. Paul teaches us how and what words to use in casting out an evil spirit.

"So that from his body were brought unto the sick handkerchiefs or aprons, and the diseases departed from them, *and the evil spirits went out of them.*

Then certain of the vagabond Jews, exorcists, took upon them to call over them which had evil spirits the name of the Lord Jesus, saying, We adjure you by Jesus whom Paul preacheth.

And there were seven sons of one Sceva, a Jew, and chief of the priests, which did so.

And the evil spirit answered and said, Jesus I know, and Paul I know; but who are ye?

And the man in whom the evil spirit was leaped on them, and overcame them, and prevailed against them, so that they fled out of that house naked and wounded." (Acts 19:12-16 – emphasis added)

These verses are a good example of how a person NOT having the proper Priesthood Authority, has NO power over evil spirits. Remember, what the evil demons said, they 'know Jesus, and they knew Paul'. The sons of the Chief Priest felt they could call on Heaven to receive Power to remove evil spirits. They found they had no power, and were actually instead, each overcome by the demonic spirits. They lacked the Holy Priesthood given to them by the 'laying on of hands' given by one having 'Authority from Jesus Christ.

Can you now answer the question I proposed at the beginning of this chapter? The question was: "In the teachings of your religious institution, have your leaders discussed the topic of evil spirits gaining control of your physical body?" Hopefully, if not, they soon will be more often and openly discussed. We all need these tools to thwart the adversary in his quest to 'make us his'.

These individuals described in the above verses, are real people; just common folk like you and me. Can you empathize with, understand, and feel as they did in these circumstances? Can you 'liken' these scriptures to you? I encourage you to pick up the Holy Bible and read the full stories that surround the sited verses as they come from the eyewitness accounts of the Apostles. Place yourself in the shoes of the father whose son was possessed for years; to feel the pain and sorrow he felt for his son. This story is recorded in three of the four gospels, Matthew 17:14-21, Mark 9: 17-29, and Luke 9: 37-45.

The story of a mother dealing with a daughter who was possessed is found in Matthew 15: 22-28 and Mark 7: 25-29. And of course, the story of the man possessed by 'Legion' and perhaps as many as 2000 demons as found in Matthew 8: 28-33, Mark 5: 1-20, and Luke 8: 27-39.

And finally, the story of the woman possessed for 18 years. It's found in Luke 13: 11-16. This story is unique because the greatest criticism was directed toward Jesus Christ simply for conducting this great miracle on the Sabbath day. Please read these stories again and again, until you can picture, comprehend and even feel, the torture and pain of these real people.

How many fathers, mothers, brothers, sisters, sons, and daughters are there in the world today, suffering with the same infirmities, and don't know where to go for help? Perhaps it's you, personally witnessing and experiencing this suffering and pain. Only longing to be 'you' again, and feel joy and happiness in your life. You're never alone! Look to the scriptures and see how easy it was for the Lord Jesus Christ (in his Eternal Love) to cast out and crush the evil ones whose only desire is to take over our mortal bodies.

I've sited many scriptures from the New Testament of the Bible. Remember: the word of God is established by the 'mouth of two or three witnesses' to the truth. There are many more scriptures that support the foundation and principle I have tried to establish here. This doctrine is important enough that it's repeated over and over again; so we can understand how and what to do. Doing this, we will be able to 'endure to the end' and cast aside Satan and his followers from our lives. We must realize that this is a never-ending process; all the days of our lives. Satan will not rest until the second coming of Savior Jesus Christ; at which time he will be bound for a thousand years. Undoubtedly, there are many thousands of people in the world today who are possessed by demon spirits; and being held captive by the chains of Satan. Their perfect spirits are suppressed and crying out for help. Their loved ones grieve and pray as they watch and their lives (and that of those around them), are destroyed. These family members are begging and pleading their case to their Heavenly Father through prayer and fasting.

In the scriptural record, Jesus and his Apostles perform the casting out of evil spirits. But He is also teaching each of us that we too can have this power over Satan and his followers. Ask yourself the question: 'If Jesus Christ and the Apostles (in the small sphere of influence in which they operated) were casting out 'many' evil spirits from 'many' individuals; how many are there in the world of today harboring evil spirits within them? Their ministry of possibly only a 100 mile radius; compared to the whole world. I venture to say that the word 'many' could easily be replaced with the word 'millions'; and that is a very alarming thought. In the following scriptures the apostle John witnesses this very thing:

> "And John answered him, saying, Master, *we saw one casting out devils in thy name*, and he followeth not us: and we forbad him, because he followeth not us." (Mark 9:38 – emphasis added)

John tells Jesus that he saw someone else casting out devils in his name (Jesus Christ). And he 'forbade him' because he didn't travel with Jesus and the apostles. The Savior told John he did wrong by stopping this man. For who does these things in the name of Jesus Christ, really does walk with Christ.

> *"And John answered and said, Master, we saw one casting out devils in thy name; and we forbad him, because he followeth not with us.*
>
> And Jesus said and did him, Forbid him not: for he that is not against us is for us." (Luke 9: 49-50 – emphasis added)

This is the same story as the one in Mark 9: 38. Where Jesus tells John that those persons 'who are not against us must be for us'.

To illustrate how the power of invoking Christ's name against evil can be done, I relate the following uncorroborated true story that involved a six year old girl. She had been taught this doctrine by her parents. She was kidnapped by a stranger who took her to the local mountains with the intention of raping and killing her. He stopped the car at his destination, removed her bindings, and un-gagged her mouth. As soon as she was free, she raised her right arm to the square and called upon the powers of heaven by commanding this stranger to 'leave in the name of Jesus Christ'. As the story goes, without a single word or move in her direction, he turned, got into his car, and drove away. The little girl calmly walked down the road (approximately half a mile) to an intersection with a highway. Within a short time, a car stopped. She asked the gentleman who he was and he told her he was a local LDS Bishop. He said he was 'told by the spirit' to 'drive down this road' (instead of his regular route to work). She was taken to the authorities and reunited with her family.

As the girl's parents had done with her, I have also met with my children, their spouses, and my 12 grandchildren; and taught each of them how to handle a situation such as this. By raising their right arm to the square and commanding the evil one, in the name of Jesus Christ, to leave or to stop whatever they were doing. I can honestly say that this instruction was received and comprehended by my grandchildren as young as six-years-old. Children are innocent sons and daughters of God who loves them beyond our wildest dreams; He will be there for them at a moment's notice. When Jesus Christ's name is announced, the evil ones have to leave because they are not able to withstand even name of the Son of God.

With this in mind, does the horrible scene in Connecticut where 20 young children were shot to death come to mind? If any of the 26 people in that tragedy had this knowledge, could the end result have possibly been different? In my opinion, the answer is a resounding, 'Yes'! The 20 year old perpetrator was obviously possessed by evil, and could have been stopped without a single gunshot. He wasn't himself; he could not be himself, not crazy, not evil but possessed with evil spirits. The killing of his mother, of innocent children and teachers could only be the result of pure evil. He had to be void of self-love; or love of anyone else. It's probable that he had several demons that had taken over his body.

The question remains: 'Why?' Was it the violent video games that he played every day desensitizing him to the value of life; and the real consequences of true lethal actions? In susceptible persons, violence breeds violence and can have a definite effect on a person's mind, opening it to the influence of Satan. If you constantly watch or do certain things that in the real world are evil, then true evil has the opportunity to simply take over. The natural man is an enemy to God. Could he have been threatened with getting help? Could his medications have contributed to an altered mental state? We may never know for certain; but, I know without a doubt that someone raising their right arm to the square and commanding this young man to stop in the name of Jesus Christ would have caused him to collapse to the ground and end his killing spree. The activists for control of our guns use this and other incidents to pursue their cause. When evil is involved (gun or not), they will find a way to wreak havoc, to shed blood, or to kill.

I also believe that the mass murders in the Colorado Theater could have been stopped the same way; in the name of Jesus Christ our Master. Again, I say the teachings of Jesus Christ during his three-year ministry teach us how to handle every possible situation spawned by evil, with which we may be confronted. It's that simple.

By following His teachings, and each day becoming more Christ-like, we will be enabled to return to His presence. The scriptures tell us that there is 'opposition in all things'; but it's not the Lord's will, that anyone takes the agency of someone else. Only when the Lord himself commands one of his servants to take another's life, is it justified; and that has seldom been authorized in the world's history.

After this horrible mass murder in Sandy Hook, a very knowledgeable individual said to me that this was, 'The Lord's will'. My response was, "So, in other words, the Lord willed (or told) this young man to murder 26 people and himself?" I don't agree. Murder is taking someone else's agency or 'free will' away. We should not blame the guns (or other weapons); call the person insane, crazy, or mentally ill; or even evil. The evil ones are the followers of Satan. Satan and his followers were cast down never to have a physical body. To take over our body is their ultimate goal. After they've enticed the natural man and dimmed the light of Christ (which is given to all children born to the Earth); that is when they take over the body if allowed. In time as the Light continues to dim, additional evil spirits can take possession of the body.

Perhaps this killer in Connecticut was under the direction of Satan, and possibly many other evil demons. They used the natural man in him as a weapon of destruction. He got to that point in his life through video games, drugs, or outward influences; and evil finally took charge. When a person does evil for long periods of time, the natural man or the appetites of the flesh, submits to the demands of Satan. Perhaps his spirit and the light of Christ were so suppressed by evil spirits that the light had been turned into darkness within this young man. The evidence is strong that he had evil spirits in him, controlling his actions.

There shouldn't be blame laid on the guns or the number of bullets in a magazine. The fact of the matter is he wasn't himself. He was even commanded to take his own life in the end by the evil spirits in him. The master in this situation was not Jesus Christ or God the Father. It was simply and completely Satan, the father of all lies. One might ask the question, 'Were the evil ones killed when he committed suicide?' Or, 'What happens to the demon spirits of one who was killed?' The answer to both of these questions is simply, 'Satan and his followers are spirits and can't be killed.' Only through proper choices, and obedience to God, can we thwart this unseen enemy.

One might ask, 'What about the victims of the evil acts of men?' Those 20 children are free of sin; their spirit bodies instantly returned back to the God that created them to live with him forever. Their probation here on this Earth is over. They will become celestial beings after their resurrection. The adults (including the mass murderer), also return back to the God that created them. After an accounting of their life, the adults will be sent to paradise or spirit prison depending on their works during their life (whether they were good or evil). There they can progress if they so desire. Jesus Christ is the judge. He atoned for our sins; he knows our hearts and he knows where we stand. In the end, Satan is the loser. He no longer could possess the body of the murderer for he is dead. The demons also leave and try to possess another living person; and the cycle continues.

If the warning signs in this young man's life could have been recognized by those that were around him every day, perhaps by simply questioning behavior changes, and getting him help, this terrible event wouldn't have happened. As parents we do the best we can. If our children choose unrighteousness, we still love them and continue to do the best we can to help them. I definitely believe that more gun control or more gun laws is not the answer. We need to teach accountability for actions; not 'accept-ability' and 'excuse-ability'.

In concluding this chapter, I want to put this in the simplest terms possible; and draw a parallel between the time that Jesus walked the earth, and our time in these the last days. When Jesus cast out the evil spirits (described below), the Pharisees (or Jewish leadership class) said this:

"As they went out, behold, *they brought to him a dumb man possessed with a devil.*

And when the devil was cast out, the dumb spake: and the multitudes marveled, saying, it was never so seen in Israel.

 But the Pharisees said, *he casteth out devils through the prince of the devils.*" (Matt 9:32-34 – emphasis added)

"And he was casting out a devil, and it was dumb. And it came to pass, when the devil was gone out, the dumb spake; and the people wondered.

But some of them said, *He casteth out devils through Beelzebub the chief of the devils.*

And others, tempting him, sought of him a sign from

heaven.

But he, knowing their thoughts, said unto them, Every kingdom divided against itself is brought to desolation; and a house divided against a house falleth.

If Satan also be divided against himself, how shall his kingdom stand? because ye say that I cast out devils through Beelzebub.

And if I by Beelzebub cast out devils, by whom do your sons cast them out? therefore shall they be your judges.

But if *I with the finger of God cast out devils,* no doubt the kingdom of God is come upon you.

When a strong man armed keepeth his palace, his goods are in peace:

But when a stronger than he shall come upon him, and overcome him, he taketh from him all his armour wherein he trusted, and divideth his spoils.

He that is not with me is against me: and he that gathereth not with me scattereth.

When the unclean spirit is gone out of a man, he walketh through dry places, seeking rest; and finding none, he saith, *I will return unto my house whence I came out.*

And when he cometh, he findeth it swept and garnished.

Then goeth he, and taketh to him seven other spirits more wicked than himself; and they enter in, and dwell there: and the last state of that man is worse than the first." (Luke 11:14-26 – *emphasis* added)

The Pharisees accused this simple carpenter known as Jesus of Nazareth of being a prince of the devil. These scriptures answer several questions. One of those questions is, 'Can just anyone cast out a demon spirit?' The answer is, 'No'; if the person is possessed, then his master is the devil or Satan. In order to cast out an evil spirit the person has to be a worthy Priesthood holder. An innocent child, woman, young man, or adult man who doesn't hold any Priesthood, can command the evil ones to leave their presence, or stop an evil act. This is done by raising the right arm to the square, and in the name of Jesus Christ.

In today's world, the polls indicate that at least 20% of American's don't believe in God. This is used as justification for the so-called political correctness of removing God from our schools, our government, our Constitution, and public lives. They say it's 'offensive' to them, and they shouldn't be subjected to something they don't believe. What about the 80% that believes in God? We cannot remain silent. We must take a stand. We cannot turn away from the natural laws by which God has asked us to live. One of the 10 Commandments that have been the basis for law for thousands of years says, "Do not take the Lord God's name in vain"; yet we hear it in everyday speech. In every form of media, we hear the casual and vain use of the Lord's name. God is mocked, and we wonder why our country is in such a bad way! Recently in national news, polls indicate that 51% of Americans agree with same sex marriage. This is abomination in God's eyes. Marriage is ordained of God. God's law is marriage between one man and one woman.

Below I highlight seven scriptures from the Gospels of Matthew, Mark, and Luke to illustrate my point. You decide what the evil unclean spirits think or know of Jesus Christ:

"And, behold, they cried out, saying, What have we to do with thee, *Jesus, thou Son of God*? art thou come hither to torment us before the time?" (Matt 8:29 – *emphasis* added)

"Saying, Let us alone; what have we to do with thee, thou Jesus of Nazareth? art thou come to destroy us? I know thee who thou art, the Holy One of God." (Mark 1:24 – *emphasis* added)

"And unclean spirits, when they saw him, fell down before him, and cried, saying, thou art the Son of God." (Mark 3:11 – *emphasis* added)

"And cried with a loud voice, and said, What have I to do with thee, Jesus, thou Son of the most high God? I adjure thee by God, that thou torment me not." (Mark 5:7 – emphasis added)
"Saying, Let us alone; what have we to do with thee, thou Jesus of Nazareth? art thou come to destroy us? *I know thee who thou art; the Holy One of God.*" (Luke 4:34 – *emphasis* added)
"*And devils also came out of many, crying out, and saying, Thou art Christ the Son of God.* And he rebuking them suffered them not to speak: for they knew that he was Christ." (Luke 4:41 – *emphasis* added)

"When he saw Jesus, he cried out, and fell down before him, and with a loud voice said, What have I to do with thee, *Jesus, thou Son of God most high*? I beseech thee, torment me not." (Luke 8:28 – *emphasis* added)

Now, what do *you* think of Jesus Christ? Is Jesus Christ a part of your life? Is God the Father a part of your life? Do you have his image in your countenance? Do you get on your knees every day and pray to him, thanking him for your many blessings; and then asking with a sincere heart, with real intent to bless you to make it through another day? Thousands of people witnessed the many miracles Jesus Christ performed, yet many thought he was evil and hated him to the point that they cried, 'Crucify Him! Even His apostles questioned his Divine Nature as the Son of God on many occasions. Can you imagine Peter's pain when he realized he had denied Christ three times as was prophesied? Like Peter, we must repent and dedicate our lives to teaching and spreading the teachings of Jesus Christ abroad.

I testify of these truths; that the power of Jesus Christ is the Power of Creation. He literally *is* the Son of God; and helped create the Earth. He is our Elder Brother. You and I are sons and daughters of a living God who loves us unconditionally.

I testify that Satan lives and we should know him 'as he is'. We have the power within us to crush him, and to push him out of our lives. By living righteous lives, and calling upon the Holy Spirit to guide us through this Probationary State, we can have a 'fullness of joy' and companionship of the Spirit every day of our lives. The greatest power in the Universe is the power of Jesus Christ our Savior and Redeemer.

Jesus Christ having a mortal mother and his Father being God; He was able to see with His 'spiritual eyes'. This gave Him power to look upon the soul, and know instantly whether a person was being controlled by demons, their own spirit, or the natural man. Just imagine looking out into the world and seeing all the spirit children of God both good and evil; it's mindboggling.

I testify that He can 'make up the difference' when we fall short in our lives. He will lighten our burden in every situation, every trial, every pain, every sorrow, even unto death, through the mercies and powers of the Holy Atonement. I know I can't fully comprehend how the Savior in Gethsemane and on the hill Golgotha (where the Son of God bled and suffered for every sin that you and I would ever commit) accomplished His Infinite Atonement. But I do know I love my Savior with all my heart and soul. I testify that these things are true, in the name of Jesus Christ; Amen.

CHAPTER 7

The Natural Man, Enemy of God

Who is the 'natural man'? Of course it's the one you see in the mirror every day. He or She is the 'appetites of the flesh' or the physical body. Consequently, everyone born on Earth has to deal with the natural man or woman. The scriptures explain how the Lord feels about the natural man:

> "For the natural man is an enemy to God, and has been from the fall of Adam, and will be, forever and ever, unless he yields to the enticings of the Holy Spirit, and putteth off the natural man and becometh a saint through the atonement of Christ the Lord, and becometh as a child, submissive, meek, humble, patient, full of love, willing to submit to all things which the Lord seeth fit to inflict upon him, even as a child doth submit to his father." (*The Book of Mormon*, Mosiah 3:19)

Actually, there are really two of you in the mirror, one seen and the other unseen. The unseen, is the spirit body that God created for you. Our physical body (created by our parents) is a covering to house our perfect spirit bodies. As the scriptures put it, the body is a 'temple' that houses the spirit. We are commanded not to defile it [the body] in any way; this means both inwardly (by consuming harmful substances) and outwardly (by defacing, damaging or abusing). The spirit body, unlike the mortal body, will never die. A significant difference between our spirit and Satan's spirit is, he will never 'progress' from the time he was cast out of the pre-existent realm. Our spirits will continue to progress in knowledge and understanding until the 'perfect day' receiving all that the Father has; if we have been wise stewards by choosing good over evil.

Our spirit bodies were created in the image of God. Our spirits have been endowed with all the attributes of loving parents which include (but are not limited to): light, truth, charity, kindness, companionship, purity, virtue, patience, meekness, and charity; lowliness of heart, oneness, knowledge, wisdom, humility, and unconditional love.

These are some of the attributes of the 'natural man' in comparison: He has many weaknesses. He can hate, he is jealous, loves to make a lie, contentious, lazy, and negative; and wants to hurt others. He can be deceitful, a cheat, a thief, is selfish; and often hates himself. He is easy to anger, and often physically, emotionally and mentally abusive. He attacks the inner spirit. He is possessive, uses ungodly language, can exhibit animal characteristics; is unclean, wicked, unholy, and wants to hurt others. He glories in self, murders, enjoys the pain of others; destroys lives, and seeks revenge. He will worship Satan, be unforgiving, lustful, and envious; he can be depressed, vulgar, and immoral; and uses the Lord's name in vain. He's a blasphemer, practices witchcraft, sorcery, fornication, and adultery. The list goes on and on.

If this sounds like a classic battle between good and evil, you are right. Satan is in opposition to God. So is the battle within each of us; the appetites of the flesh vs. our perfect spirit.

The million dollar question is this, "Who is in charge in your life? The only choices in this multiple choice question are: (a.) your spirit or (b.) the natural man. Obviously the correct answer should be (a.) [Our] perfect spirit; but remember, there was only one perfect person to come to this earth. We all fall short of perfection, and instead choose the weaknesses of the flesh, many times throughout our lives. Perhaps there should be a third choice: (c.) The spirit united with the mortal body that is 'one' in all things pertaining to God; just as the Father and Son are one. I love the words of this parable entitled 'Two Wolves – A Cherokee Parable':

"An old Cherokee chief was teaching his grandson about life. "A fight is going on inside me," he said to the boy. "It is a terrible fight, and it is between two wolves." "One is evil – he is anger, envy, sorrow, regret, greed, arrogance, self-pity, guilt, resentment, inferiority, lies, false pride, superiority, self-doubt, and ego." "The other is good – he is joy, peace, love, hope, serenity, humility, kindness, benevolence, empathy, generosity, truth, compassion, and faith."

"This same fight is going on inside you - and inside every other person, too." The grandson thought about it for a minute and then asked his grandfather, "Which wolf will win?" The old chief simply replied, "The one you feed."

(Author unknown; Possibly a Cherokee parable going back at least to the 1950's; in print – but unsubstantiated)

This parable has great wisdom for all of us, and is very true in how we handle life's challenges. Do we feed the natural man, or the spirit? When we subdue and conquer the natural man, Satan cannot influence us because we are 'standing in holy places' where he is unworthy to be.

I have many personal stories where I failed; and gave into the natural man. Thanks to the principle of repentance, those 'failings' have been turned into 'learning experiences'. The personal growth gained in that process is priceless. From the depths of sorrow, feeling anger and hate; to returning full circle and receiving the blessings of God's love and total forgiveness. Because I was willing to change, overcoming the natural man has blessed me with more knowledge and personal growth. By swallowing my pride, forgiving others (or myself), and showing unconditional love, I have had the privilege of special assignments (callings) of trust; and tremendous personal character growth.

The following personal story illustrates one of those character growth opportunities. As you read, think of the 'thirty pieces of silver' that was paid in the betrayal Jesus Christ. I entitle the story: 'The 40 Dollars'.

"In the late 1970's, my older brother Sam and I were taking a hunting trip 500 miles from home. Before we departed, I told him that I was $40 short for my half of the gas money for the trip. His response was, "That'll be fine; pay it when you can." The three day coyote hunting expedition was very successful. At that time, coyote hides would bring $60 each; and we brought back 23, worth nearly $1400.

In our spare time for the next two days, we cleaned, sewed and stretched the hides for drying. In a couple of weeks they would be sold. Shortly after the work was completed, I went down to my Dad's mechanic shop to talk to him and Sam (who worked there as a mechanic). When I got there, all Sam wanted to talk about was the forty dollars I owed him. As I tried to explain that I hadn't received my pay check from work and couldn't pay him that day; without warning, he hauled off and punched me in the mouth; and then walked away as if nothing happened.

I shook off the punch, and after recovering from shock and disbelief, I made a beeline right for him. I was ready to knock his head off even though he was bigger than me. We hadn't fought since we were boys. My dad came running and jumped between us just before I reached him. I tried to remove my dad, but realized I would have hurt him in the process. Even so, he was willing to risk his own safety for his adult sons. He knew that someone would end up either in the hospital or dead if he let us get to one another. All three of us were very strong and the confrontation created a very dangerous situation.

I picked up my Dad several times, but he simply held on, effectively keeping me away from Sam. Eventually I just walked away, bleeding and dejected.

I was angry and full of rage because I felt that justice was on my side. 'Revenge to the death' I thought, if need be. No one had ever punched me without a fight to the end. Someone must be the winner, and 'I will never lose again', I thought. 'He's no longer a brother to me'. My anger and feelings of hate grew. The natural man was in complete control of my heart and soul. I was so bitter that I vowed to never pay him the money I owed. The family was divided. No more visits to the shop; and Sam and I would never speak to each other again. Forgiveness never entered my mind. I did nothing wrong, I even prayed that he would feel 'God's justice' for what he had done. My mother (who was 46 years old and eight months pregnant with my youngest brother) was totally heartbroken by the actions of her two oldest sons.

Cassie had given birth to our oldest daughter Emily the previous September. Normally, I was happy and full of the joy of life; now, the situation between me and my brother was eating me alive. But, being bull-headed, I wouldn't admit I should pay him back; and apologize for not telling him right away that I didn't have the money. My pride was causing me to justify my inaction, and I just 'didn't care'. I was running on a short fuse and my spiritual progress had seemed to come to a halt. I was still attending church, and the Spirit began working in me on Sundays and during service projects for neighbors. Soon, I started to forget my anger towards my brother. Sunday school and priesthood lessons seemed to be speaking directly to me. I remember thinking, 'How do they know?' I eventually realized I *was* sorry for my actions', and I needed to forgive, ask forgiveness, and allow the love of God back into my heart.

These words seemed to whisper to me, "If you can't forgive your brother, then I can't forgive you."

My baby brother was born, and the baby blessing would be in one month. The Holy Ghost softened my heart. I had fasted for two days and called upon my Heavenly Father for mercy. I stopped asking for justice, and instead asked for forgiveness for falling prey to the evil enticing of the natural man. I felt godly sorrow and prayed that Sam would forgive me for the hate and anger I had shown him.

The day came for the blessing. I wanted to be with my brother Sam, and stand in the baby blessing circle with all my brothers and uncles. This Priesthood Ordinance (for me) needed to be a circle of love, forgiveness and harmony towards each other. Sam and his family sat four or five rows behind Cassie and our small family. As the bishop announced the blessing, I arose and met Sam in the aisle. We embraced and begged for forgiveness of each other, and expressed our love for one another. He had been going through the same turmoil and depression as me. In our pride, we couldn't comprehend what the other might be feeling. We stood in that baby blessing, side-by-side as brothers should; and from that day forward were best friends again; the way brothers should be."

Words can't describe the feeling of total peace and serenity that all the members of our family felt that day. I testify that my life began again to make spiritual progress toward eternal life. That day in the shop, the Christ-like thing would have been to 'turn the other cheek', and pay him the money I owed. The Lord would have blessed me in return. I know our parents and other family members offered a lot of prayers in our behalf. For me, removing pride from my life is one of my greatest challenges and weakness of the flesh. I'm not perfect, and indeed am (as are we all) a constant work in progress.

Over the next five years I was called to many church leadership assignments, including that of LDS Bishop at the age of twenty-five. I know these callings would never have come to me, had I not been working to overcome the natural man; and gone through the steps of repentance. Later, Sam was also called as a Bishop in his ward.

The key to this type of transformation is for us to first look inwardly (to ourselves) for the cause of our halted progression; not outwardly (blaming others). What I'm trying to say is we need to get rid of the blame game of, 'Satan (or some other outside influence) made me do it.' And instead, accept full responsibility and replace it with, 'I did it; I gave into the enticements of the natural man.' Most of our imperfections and sins are committed by the natural man; our appetites of the flesh. Satan works on the imperfect natural man because the spirit (within each of us) is perfect. He attacks our weaknesses of the flesh. If he can get us to allow the natural man to take control, he knows our perfect spirits can weaken; then <u>he</u> can take control.

Every day when you wake up and look in the mirror, picture two of you: one is your spiritual self; and the other the natural man. Ask yourself, "Which one am I going to be today? The goal of this life is for the spirit body to learn how to control the appetites and passions of the natural body [man]. Remember, the natural man is an enemy to God. When we allow the appetites of the flesh [natural man] to control our lives, we are giving Satan the opportunity to enter into our physical bodies and suppress our perfect spirit body. Then, over time, he will extinguish the perfect light that shines within us.

Not too long ago I was in charge of a Family Home Evening. The subject I chose was the natural man. Here's how I presented the lesson:

"Someone broke into our house last night! As I went into the bathroom this morning, I ran right into him face-to-face as I looked into the mirror. Yesterday when I went to work at 2:30 a.m., there was two inches of snow on the ground. I was the first one to arrive at work in my department. After about one hour, I looked outside and I thought I could see two sets of footprints entering the building. Who had entered the building with me? Was it the one of me which says, 'I want to be disrespectful, show hate, be unhelpful, and (instead of working) surf the internet.' Or, was it one of me that, 'Respects his coworkers, is compassionate and helpful; and turns on soft background music while diligently doing constructive work?' At home I found there was one of me that said, 'Let's start a fast today to show gratitude for our blessings and to get help with our needs.' But wait says the other me, 'I love food, chocolate and candy! It's okay to put on a little weight; I've earned every pound. I'm too tired to exercise'. And then there was the one of me that said,

'This movie isn't so bad, it has some historical value and I can ignore the bad language; it won't affect me.' But there also was the one of me that said, 'If we're careful about our media choices, our home will have a greater spirit of peace and harmony.' Which 'me' is in charge: the natural man me; or the perfect spirit me? We each have choices every day. Which choice will you make?"

This family night really impressed my oldest daughter Emily, who struggles just like you and me with the weaknesses of the flesh.

This is a personal story of a 10-year-old fourth grade boy, many years ago. Yes, even then the other 'me' was there. I had a good friend whose father was someone who had allowed the natural man to take charge of his life. He had a subscription to a pornographic magazine. My friend said, "You can look and it won't hurt you." I took some of the pictures home, but my mom soon found them; and I received a lesson about Satan's plan to destroy me. It's one of Satan's lies that pornography won't hurt you. Even after all these years, I can still see some of those images in my mind, even after sincere repentance. I cringe when I see guys with these images in their toolboxes, and cringe even more at how accessible it is to men and women now some fifty years later. I'm grateful that I've never fallen into this trap again. It is liberating to live my life with good thoughts; and never worry about doing something that could destroy my marriage and family.

Cassie and I had the experience two years ago of being a 'Pa' and 'Ma' for a 'family' of youth at our Stake Pioneer Trek reenactment. We listened to the Spirit as we prepared and participated in this event. We got to know each of the young men and women assigned to our family. Because of our dependency on and guidance from the Spirit, we were able to show unconditional love for each of these ten youths; and because of that love, it was expressed back to us in kind. During the challenging three days of pulling handcarts and living in primitive conditions, there wasn't a single angry moment to interrupt the spiritual and challenging experience.

Listening to the Spirit and obeying its promptings, is an essential skill that needs to be honed. One day I came across a man hitchhiking near Echo, Utah. I had just come from a job interview in Park City, and I noticed this elderly man alongside the freeway. I didn't think much of it, but the Spirit whispered to my spirit, 'When you have done it unto the least of these, my brethren, you have done it unto me.' I drove down the road five miles to the next exit and returned to the hitchhiker. I picked him up and let him off twenty-five miles later in Ogden, which was his destination. When I picked him up, he was freezing cold and dripping wet from the rain and snow. Of course my car became wet as well, but he was very grateful that someone would pick him up in that condition and help him on his way.

He thanked me all the way to Ogden and as he got out of the car he couldn't stop thanking me. I felt good for the service I had rendered to someone in need. The next day, the company that I had interviewed with, called me and offered me the job. I know I was blessed with that job opportunity because I had listened to the spirit. I had helped someone in a challenging situation, get to his destination. The 'natural man' had said, 'You don't have time for this; and you're already past him.'

It would be wonderful if each of us had some method to remind ourselves who we really are each day before we go out into the world. Perhaps a simple little sign or note that we could put in a conspicuous place would do the trick:

"I am not the natural man. I'm a son [or daughter] of God. I carry the light of Christ within me. I will not allow the natural man to dim that light in any way. Today, my words and deeds will be Christ-like in every way."

Many years ago, at the company where I worked, eight men were transferred from the main plant in Michigan; and brought their families to Utah. In working with these men, it became very apparent that religion wasn't a part of their life or of their families. One of the men was my foreman. He had a 14-year-old daughter in Junior High School who had been sent home (now for the third time) for wearing immodest clothing to school. He expressed to me one day how, 'Unhappy' he was with the school; and specifically with the LDS Church. He felt that church dress standards were being forced upon his daughter at school.

I asked him for a picture of his daughter so I could get an idea of what she looked like; and asked him what type of clothes she had worn that the school felt was inappropriate. He said she had been wearing tank tops and spaghetti strap, short dresses. I told him that his daughter was very beautiful and looked more like 16 or 17. I suggested that her beauty, along with the skimpy clothing might tend to bring out the worst in the teenage boys with whom she associated at school. I told him (as a father of girls myself) I would be concerned that she was putting herself in a potentially dangerous situation. Boys could easily have unclean thoughts when looking at his daughter; those thoughts could turn into actions, and she might have her morals compromised; or even become pregnant as a result.

I was surprised and shocked by his angry reply. He said, "It's none of the school's business to tell my daughter what to wear." And he wasn't worried about his daughter becoming pregnant because she had been using birth control measures since the age of 12. So, I asked him, "Kevin does that pill solve the problem?" His answer was a resounding, "Yes." In the coming months and years following this experience, Kevin had to deal with many problems with his daughter. By the age of 17, she had left home and was married.

This is a good demonstration how the natural man becomes an enemy not only to God, but also to his fellow humans. In this example, it was the God-given gift of having feelings of attraction between males and females that was exploited by Satan. Until the time is right (based on age and maturity) our spirits must be able to control the appetites and passions of the physical body. These feelings are strong to draw men and women together in marriage relationships. Satan knows this and capitalizes on these weaknesses to encourage early use of these passions; and he turns good into a tool of evil. In this girl's case, she was exposing parts of her body that were enticing to every teenage boy that laid eyes on her. She became sexually active at an inappropriate age and time in her life. This beautiful girl had her youth cut short because her outward immodest actions overshadowed and overcame her inward spiritual beauty. Below are some scriptures from *The Book of Mormon* and *The Doctrine and Covenants* that speak to this:

"Therefore, as they had become carnal, sensual, and devilish, by nature, this probationary state became a state for them to prepare; it became a preparatory state." (Alma 42:10)

"O Lord, thou hast said that we must encompass about by the floods. Now behold, O Lord, and do not be angry with thy servant because of his weakness before thee; for we know that thou art holy and dwellest in the heavens, and that we are unworthy before thee; because of the fall are natures have become evil continually; nevertheless, O Lord, thou hast given us a commandment that we must call upon thee, that from thee we may receive according to our desires." (Ether 3:2)

"O Lord, I have trusted in thee, and I will trust in thee forever. I will not put my trust in the arm of flesh; for I know that cursed is he that putteth his trust in the arm of flesh. Yea, cursed is he that putteth his trust in man or maketh flesh his arm." (2 Nephi 4:34)

When we exercise these behaviors or characteristics, we are actually allowing the natural man to be in charge of our spirit. Remember, the spirit is a perfect being; and that spirit is made of pure spirit matter or element, created by our Eternal Parents in the pre-earth realm.

"Adam fell that men might be; and men are, that they might have joy." (2 Nephi 2:25)

This joy, of which Lehi speaks, is eternal and spiritual. When you have that moment of epiphany, and are able to embrace a concept such as this; it is a moment in time you will always remember; albeit sometimes that moment is fleeting.

"And the Messiah cometh in the fulness of time, that he may redeem the children of men from the fall. And because that they are redeemed from the fall they have become free forever, knowing good from evil; to act for themselves and not to be acted upon, save it be by the punishment of the law at the great and last day, according to the commandments which God hath given.

Wherefore, men are free according to the flesh; and all things are given them which are expedient unto man. And they are free to choose liberty and eternal life, through the great Mediator of all

men, or to choose captivity and death, according to the captivity and power of the devil; for he seeketh that all men might be miserable like unto himself.

And now, my sons, I would that ye should look to the great Mediator, and hearken unto his great commandments; and be faithful unto his words, and choose eternal life, according to the will of his Holy Spirit;

And not choose eternal death, according to the will of the flesh and the evil which is therein, which giveth the spirit of the devil power to captivate, to bring you down to hell, that he may reign over you in his own kingdom." (2 Nephi 2:26-29)

The main purpose of this chapter is to help us understand that our spirit bodies must be in charge of the physical, throughout this earthly life. We must look inward first, and cast off the natural man (the appetites of the flesh). We must always remember that the act is always preceded by the thought; whether it is a good thing or a bad thing, we'll always think about it before we do it.

> "For our words will condemn us, yea, all our works will condemn us; we shall not be found spotless; and our thoughts will also condemn us; and in this awful state we shall not dare to look up to our God; and we would fain be glad if we could command the rocks and the mountains to fall upon us to hide us from his presence." (Alma12:14)

When an idle thought that is evil, enters our mind; we need to replace it with something good. For example: a Primary song, special music, thoughts of your marriage day, start to sing a church hymn, remember a special moment with a family member; anything that can replace that errant though that could turn into an evil action. The human mind can only accommodate one thought at a time.

More and more I am noticing people listening to scriptures or uplifting music to and from work; and humming or singing along; or, they are reading scriptures or books of faith while on work breaks. They've all testified to me that it has given them added strength against the 'unseen enemies'; and their desires are turning to good rather than allowing themselves to play into the hands of Satan.

> "Remember the great and last promise which I have made unto you; cast away your idle thoughts and your excess of laughter far from you." (D&C 88:69)

> "Let thy bowels also be full of charity towards all men, and to the household of faith, and let virtue garnish thy thoughts unceasingly; then shall thy confidence wax strong in the presence of God; and the doctrine of the priesthood shall distil upon thy soul as the dews from heaven." (D&C 121:45)

I would like to refer to the book *Return from Tomorrow* that illustrates some of the things that I'm trying to explain. The author recounts a death experience where for nine minutes he was clinically dead. He describes what he saw (in the spirit) on the other side of the veil.

Here are two examples of what he witnessed. He saw a person who had a tobacco habit (while alive) and now as a disembodied spirit, still had the same need or desire to put a cigarette to his lips, yet his earthly urge could not be satisfied. The second example is one that I encourage you to ponder. He observed a living person walk into a bar and begin drinking. When the drinker got to the point of drunkenness (where he was no longer in control of his physical body), a demon (that seemed to be resting on his shoulder just waiting for that moment); literally dove into this inebriated man's body, and took control.

This shows that these devils, demons and evil spirits (the followers of Satan) are just waiting for that window of opportunity when we are not fully in control, to slide in and possess our bodies. First the natural man is ensnared by whatever is that person's weakness; and in time, when we are no longer in control of the physical body, the chance comes for Satan to get an even stronger foothold; to enter and stay for as long as the possession is allowed. At this point, he suppresses our spiritual being, and freeing the person requires Priesthood Authority.

Let's turn again to the scriptures and read the words of Nephi, one of the great Prophets of *The Book of Mormon*. In these verses, he is humbly describing his weaknesses of the flesh:

> "Nevertheless, notwithstanding the great goodness of the Lord, in showing me his great and marvelous work, my heart exclaimeth: O wretched man that I am! Yea, my heart sorroweth because of my flesh; my soul grieveth because of mine iniquities.

> I am encompassed about, because of the temptations and the sins; which do so easily beset me." (2 Nephi 4:17-18)

> (And then this great prophet tells us where he gets his support)

> "My God hath been my support; he hath led me through mine afflictions in the wilderness; and he hath preserved me upon the waters of the great deep.

> He had filled me with his love, even unto the consuming of my flesh." (2 Nephi 4:20-21)

By accepting God's plan, we earned the opportunity to come to the Earth, get a body, and gain experience in this probationary state. Given our Moral Agency, we're supposed to learn to become 'one' like the Father and the Son are 'one'; and strive to become perfect in every way. Our goal is to 'overcome the natural man' and follow the teachings of Jesus Christ. The flesh is weak, but if we call upon our Heavenly Father in the name of Jesus Christ we can have the strength (through prayer, through service, and the love of God and all men) to overcome all things.

When we actually take control of ourselves, our light can be as a beacon, to bless and bring along those that we love. Those that know and see us will trust us, love us, and want to be more like us. Does this mean we have to be perfect? No; it means we must keep trying to be better, one day at a time. Sincerely following after the Savior Jesus Christ, and having him be in our thoughts always, we will have the privilege of the Ministering of Angels help us in the work of salvation.

"And by day have I waxed bold in mighty prayer before him; yea, my voice have I sent up on high; and Angels came down and ministered unto me." (2 Nephi 4:24)

May I suggest the following experiment? By seeing, hearing, and speaking (literally living) the things of the spirit (rather than the passions and desires of the flesh); we can realize, not only more unity with Christ and His teachings; but also experience renewed strength to overcome the natural man. This must be a gradual process and it eventually becomes a life-long endeavor. First, try it for one day, then two days, then a week, and then three weeks and longer. You will see yourself becoming a better person; someone who is a joy to be around. May our light so shine that others can see our light and give them hope for a better day.

1. Wake up unto the Lord by kneeling in prayer and calling upon him for strength and support for your day.

2. Read the Scriptures for 5 to 30 minutes daily

3. Exercise for 15 to 30 minutes

4. Eat breakfast, lunch and dinner

5. Listen to uplifting or inspirational music or talks whenever possible throughout the day.

6. Eliminate the following: swearing, taking the Lord's name in vain, anger in any form (including raising your voice against a loved one or anyone else), negative comments, idle time (including watching TV where much evil is shown - replacing that time with something more positive), remove any other thing that is downgrading or depressing to your senses.

7. Show love to everyone, including you. Lift up the depressed, look for ways to serve others (look around, they are there), and be Christ-like in everything you say and do.

8. Close the day in prayer unto the Lord giving him thanks for all things and express love to him for the beautiful day.

Doing these things, you will become a better person day-by-day. Your spirit will be in charge of yourself. You will progress toward perfection; and be especially closer to your Heavenly Father and his Son Jesus Christ. Studies have shown that it takes an average of 21 days to replace a bad habit with a good one. Does this mean that the natural man and Satan will leave you alone during this experiment? Think again, they will unleash the appetites of the flesh; and try to expose you to even greater temptations.

When those moments come, and you feel you're going to fall; fill your mind with goodness, and think of something that has been positive in your life. This is why repetition is so much a part of learning in this probationary state. When you literally bombard yourself with good and wholesome things, they eventually become a permanent part of your life.

By encircling ourselves with good things, our thoughts and feelings will be Christ-like. We will overcome the temptations of Satan; bind him and cast him aside, forever. This can only be done by 'standing in Holy places' and being 'not moved'. By enduring to the end, keeping our hope alive, and deepening our faith in the Lord Jesus Christ, we will realize the promise of the Savior given at the Sermon on the Mount: ". . . the pure in heart shall see God".

Here are some examples that might indicate that the natural man is in control:

- ✓ At work you are jealous because a friend got a promotion.
- ✓ A married man tries to sleep with as many women as he can at work, thinking his wife will never know.
- ✓ I can speed as long I'm not caught; everyone else speeds.
- ✓ I'll only take ecstasy to go to this concert.
- ✓ I'll tell my wife that it was my friends smoking not me.
- ✓ I can tell the doctor she fell down the stairs, I didn't lose control.
- ✓ My wife is asleep; she will never know I'm tired because I got up during the night to view porn.
- ✓ When I read my romance novels I forget what a jerk my husband is and pretend to think the main character is my spouse.
- ✓ I have to borrow some money so my husband will not know I spent our entire check on a shopping spree.
- ✓ I'm the father of this home; I don't need to ask my wife's opinion, only mine matters.
- ✓ I don't want to go to church; I need a day of rest.
- ✓ Because I go to church, I can sin all week long and repent on Sunday.
- ✓ I'm the boss I'm better than my workers; I'll hold down their wages because I need more material things.
- ✓ I'm educated so I will never associate with undereducated people.
- ✓ I won't be seen around some of my family because they are trailer trash.
- ✓ I can't be your friend because my mom says you don't live in a good enough area.
- ✓ I don't care if my kids go without; I'm going to have my nails and hair done and wear the latest fashions.
- ✓ I opened up a secret account that my spouse will never know about.
- ✓ I earn more money than you, for that reason I'm the boss.
- ✓ My husband is happy with his low paying job and I'm embarrassed.
- ✓ My brother is so stupid; I don't claim him as a relative.
- ✓ She has rotten teeth don't talk to her.
- ✓ She has to walk everywhere because she can't manage her money.
- ✓ My sister offended me so I won't talk to her ever again.
- ✓ It's okay to steal from my employer, they have money.

- ✓ My mom will not ask where I'm spending the money she needed for some expensive repairs.
- ✓ This music can't have any influence over me.
- ✓ I'm proud of being a bully; it shows my toughness.

If we can identify with any of these, we are feeding the natural man and we have some work to do. Some of these if allowed to be built upon, can allow Satan that the window of opportunity to enter in. It isn't just the big sins; but the little ones as well. Little sins, left unresolved, lead to more serious sins. So ask yourself, "Who am I feeding; the spirit or the natural man?" Short phrases our natural man uses:

- The Devil made me do it.
- My sister made me want to do it.
- Just this once won't matter.
- I'm the only one that will know.
- I only have Saturday and Sunday to hunt, God will understand.
- It's OK I can always repent tomorrow.
- I'm over weight but that cake tastes so good.
- I don't get enough sleep so I can rely on harmful things to sleep or stay awake.
- It's only a BAD Thought she's so beautiful and I didn't even touch her.
- Everyone is doing it; it's just a little lie.
- The police won't catch me, I'll watch out for them.
- It's only 15 minutes before the end of the shift and I've worked thru break so I'm justified in leaving early.
- Being out here with my good friends we've agreed to never tell our wives.
- I'm not worth anything.
- I'm an unforgiving person.
- No one will ever love me I'm just too ugly.
- That guy is just so much better than my husband I wish he was with me.
- I hate you Mom!!! I hate you Dad!!!
- You're so stupid Mom you don't have any education.
- That person takes Drugs and look how special they are to everyone.
- You're my girlfriend and I love you, no one else so show me how much you love me.
- No more double dating we can prove to everyone including our Parents that we can handle it.

- Don't you trust us?
- The movie has only one bad sex scene.
- Tattoos show how strong we are.
- I don't listen to the lyrics, just the sound of the music.
- Just because he uses the "F" word a lot doesn't make him bad, I can always change him later.
- I'm better than you, you're the problem.
- I don't need to repent until I'm on the other side.

Wouldn't it be better to make the necessary changes while we are here [on Earth]? When you get up in the morning and look in the mirror, there will always be two of you. Every one of God's children on this earth is two individuals in one.

They are different and yet together wherever they go, in whatever situation including trials, pain, good times, and bad times they are you. Does your image reflect which one you feed and who is your master?

1. The Natural Man (Flesh) has desires and passions basically all five of the senses given from God.

2. The perfect spirit (created by God) within each of us.

Every one of the statements I sited above involves the five senses. These come only from the Natural Man; and not from the Perfect Spirit. From the very moment of our birth, these two together, affect our destiny and future.

After reading this chapter I pray you'll look at that special person in the mirror and feel God's unconditional love as a son or daughter of God.

(References: *The Book of Mormon*, and *The Doctrine and Covenants*)

CHAPTER 8

Depression

What is this thing called depression? The simple dictionary definition includes: being in a hollow or low place, low spirits, and dejection. Symptoms may also include: mood swings, behavior changes, loss of interest in normal activities, stress, emotional extremes, fatigue, feelings of worthlessness, feelings of guilt, difficulty concentrating, difficulty making decisions, helplessness, outbursts of anger, weight gain, eating disorders, crying spells, frequent headaches, heart palpitation, unhappiness, persistent sadness, substance use or abuse; the list goes on and on. Simply from the sheer number of indicators and symptoms, 'depression' seems to be one of the worst (if not the most prolific) weaknesses of the natural man. And sadly, depression is often linked with thoughts of death, attempted and successful suicide.

Every one of these symptoms can be attributed to the natural man. I would even venture to speculate that every person on Earth has, at one time or another, experienced one or more of these symptoms. Why? These are all descriptive of the weaknesses of the flesh or the natural man. In this era recognized as the Last Days of the Earth's temporal existence, depression has become one of Satan's most effective tools. We are bombarded every waking minute with the pressures and challenges of life. Satan works overtime, and persistently strives to weaken the natural man until he can enter and succeed in taking possession of the mortal body. In this chapter, we'll discuss the possible causes of depression; and consider what we can do to prevent and cure this bane to humanity.

Let's turn to the scriptures of the *Doctrine and Covenants* and read what the Lord says about our day:

"And in that day shall be heard of wars and rumors of wars, and the whole earth shall be in commotion, and men's hearts shall fail them, and they shall say that Christ delayeth his coming until the end of the earth.

And the love of men shall wax cold, and iniquity shall abound.

And when the times of the Gentiles is come in, a light shall break forth among them that sit in darkness, and it shall be the fulness of my gospel;

But they receive it not; for they perceive not the light, and they turn their hearts from me because of the precepts of men.

And in that generation shall the times of the Gentiles be fulfilled.

And there shall be me men standing in that generation, that shall not pass until they shall see an overflowing scourge; for desolating sickness shall cover the land.

But my disciples shall stand in holy places, and shall not be moved; but among the wicked, men shall lift up their voices and curse God and die." (D&C 45:26-32)

From my personal experience, I believe this 'desolating sickness' is this thing called depression. Depressions worst outcome is suicide. When someone loses all hope, they 'curse God' and want to 'die.' Another key phrase from the verses above is what I believe to be true and prophetic: 'the love of men shall wax cold'. To me this means the normal human feelings of love (for self, family and fellow man) will be dimmed and extinguished. Without love, life seems without value; and persons who feel no love in their life, may not want to go on with life. Satan has taken over, and the walls close in. Depression becomes a black hole of despair and hopelessness. They feel worthless, life isn't worth continuing, and other people (including family) mean nothing to them. They've come to an overwhelming low in their lives and Satan pounces on that opportunity to take possession of those suffering this condition.

In the conventional wisdom of today, why (in the past two decades) has suicide increased to epidemic proportion in the world; and why do the numbers continue to rise at alarming rates?

Suicides now average over 1 million per year in the world. In the United States alone, the average is over 33,000 each year. In Utah where I live, there are nearly daily reports of suicide. We hear of steady increases in suicide rates among the military. Two years ago, the cover of *TIME* magazine proclaimed: "One a day" displaying a photo of one of our military personnel. Today the suicide rate in the military has increased to twenty-two each and every day of the year. That's over 8,000 of our valiant and heroic men and women per year; lost to this scourge. Society at large is baffled at how to quell this rapidly increasing suicide epidemic.

Countries like France are declaring pandemic numbers of suicides and wanting answers. It's getting to the point where every family in the world has been touched by suicide.

Depression is a disease. I just read a statistic that indicates there are nearly 20 million adults in the USA who are afflicted with chronic depression. In other words, depression has taken over the lives of nearly eight per cent of the adult population; or one person in every twelve! To a greater and greater extent; depression (this affliction of the natural man), is taking control of the perfect spirits of men and women. As Satan takes the opportunity to influence those whose resistance has weakened due to depression, more and more will be convinced the body is just not worth all the pain, sorrow and suffering. Statistically, a significant number will take the tragic option of suicide. Two-tenths of one per cent of depressed adults ending their lives may not be too remarkable, until you realize that represents 33,000 men and women, fathers and mothers, brothers and sisters and adult children who belong to *families*. As of 2013 the Centers for Disease Control (CDC), reported that suicide ranks as the second most common cause of death among those between the ages of 15 and 34. The numbers are increasing to the point that it could eventually rise to the number one ranking. In 2013, there were twice as many teenage suicides as there were teenagers killed in automobile accidents.

Some of the many reasons people can be or become depressed (some of which may hit particularly close to home) include or involve relationships, money, loss of a loved one, loneliness, injury, health changes, disappointments, failure, and sin.

Depression can be brought on by any event or situation that causes fear or being afraid; and involves overload of one or more of the five senses. Russell M. Nelson, a renowned heart surgeon and current leader in the LDS Church, once described an experience he had while flying on a commercial airliner. During the flight, he witnessed one of the plane's engines catch fire. The passengers began to fear for their lives and became extremely emotional as the plane began to descend; yet he remained completely calm. He said this of the experience, "When you become so afraid that fear takes over your body [sensory overload] you lose two very important things that keep hope alive. They are: *identity as a son or daughter of God;* and [the understanding of] *the purpose of life itself*. Fear is the opposite of faith, and is part and parcel the weakness of the flesh or the natural man; fear suppresses the perfect spirit within each child of God.

At this point I would like relate some brief stories of the past few years of my life. The reason I do this is to show that even in a 'normal' person's life, there are many trials, tests and tribulations that could contribute to depressive tendencies. Thankfully, with the application of principles of faith, I have largely avoided that consequence.

Let's start with the time when my oldest daughter Emily and her two daughters lived with us. They stayed with us for two years after her difficult divorce; and while she finished her degree. After graduation, she met a young man from California, and they soon were talking of marriage. Scott and Emily decided she and the girls should move to California a couple of months before the wedding date. As you can imagine, over that time we had become very attached to having her and our two beautiful granddaughters in our home. That close relationship and emotional connection as grandparents, made it very difficult to part with the girls.

At this time, I had been working for a year as a dimensional inspector for a company in Ogden, Utah. On the day of the departure of my three 'little girls' (with their future husband and step-father), I went to work and had what could have been, a life-threatening accident. I had just hooked up the crane to a 300-pound, 12-foot long stainless steel bar. The bar was at eye-level as I slowly moved it to my inspection bench. At that moment, I heard the warning tone of my manufacturing supervisor backing up his golf cart. Unfortunately there was a blind spot between us that made it impossible for us to see each other momentarily. As he approached my position, he didn't see the bar protruding into the aisle; and the top of the golf cart struck the bar. This impact spun the bar around its pivot-point, striking me in the head. I was violently knocked off my feet, and fell onto the concrete floor, unconscious.

After less than a minute, I regained consciousness. It happened so fast, and in the matter of a few seconds I should've been killed. The supervisor stopped the cart, and other coworkers came running to help. I was sitting up wondering how much blood I had lost, and if I was still alive. To everyone's amazement, I didn't have a scratch, and I was awake and alert. I *was* taken to the hospital to be checked for a concussion.

On the way to the hospital with my supervisor, many things went through my mind. Why this? Why today? With the departure of the girls that morning, it had already been a day of many tears; but I felt very blessed. The hospital found no concussion, so I was cleared to leave. I made a phone call to Cassie and she picked me up at the hospital. She notified our family of the incident and assured them I was fine. When she talked to Emily (who was en route to California), little Violet became overwhelmed with emotion said to Scott (her soon to be step-dad), "Why did you take me away from my grandpa?!" These types of experiences are all of a highly emotional nature, and could make anyone depressed. Instead, we all made it through. It could've been worse. I could have lost my life, and my little Violet could have become depressed over her significant family and home changes.

The next of my life's challenges began in the winter of 2011, and is still not resolved today. I love snowmobiling and in the course of fine-tuning my own sleds, I came up with a patent pending process that improved speed and fuel economy. I was working so many hours getting my business going, *and* working the late shift at my job as an inspector; that there were times when it was almost impossible to make it home without falling asleep at the wheel, before I could make it to my destination. It got to the point that it became a life and death situation almost every night as I drove home. There were times when I drove off the road and awakened just in time to avoid a crash. I became so overwhelmed with the lack of sleep, I decided to make the high-risk decision to quit my full-time job; and focus on building the snowmobile engine business.

For the period of four years, we had a repeated water problem in our home. The action that precipitated the problem was a city road that had been improved up-hill from our home. This resulted in changing the natural springs in the area, and we had a series of ten different floods in our basement. We had replaced the carpet twice in three different rooms, and installed water pumps to hopefully mitigate the problem. Many times our friends, family, and neighbors helped us clean up the mess. Then I got a phone call from the insurance company saying that our home insurance was being cancelled. At one point, Cassie and I couldn't even sleep a full night without worrying about a basement full of water, or the pumps failing.

My business was going well. Then a phone call came from one of my customers in Washington State. He reported that one of my aluminum rotor engine products had disintegrated in his snowmobile. Then, a few more phone calls saying they too were experiencing failures of the parts I had sold them. I was facing a complete recall of all the aluminum rotors. It was a great blessing that the winter storms that year had been so mild across North America and Canada, that people hadn't extensively used my product; effectively reducing the possible liability. I thanked my Heavenly Father for this. However, it soon became a devastating situation since the business was my only source of income. Cassie was still working, but her income could only cover our monthly utility costs; we didn't have the funds to keep our mortgage current. The stress became overwhelming for both Cassie and me. I began receiving ten to twenty phone calls a day, seeking answers to the rotor issues. Then to add insult to injury, another problem cropped up involving breakage of a related snowmobile system. I started to receive threatening phone calls from those customers requesting refunds and making demands for replacement parts. My small startup business was becoming a financial disaster.

My machinist needed to be paid, my patent attorneys needed to be paid; the business was facing extensive warranty costs and possible lawsuits. Family members who had invested were becoming discouraged, and I couldn't pay a friend that I had employed; need I go on? You get the picture. Even with all this, I was optimistic that I could make things right, and save the business.

Then, one of my unhappy customers posted a YouTube video (that was linked to my website) containing false information and slanderous accusations that was totally devastating to the business, and my personal integrity. The video had over 13,000 hits, which immediately decimated my customer base. Comments on the video further exacerbated the image of the company, and the possibility for future business was instantly gone. His attorney send me a letter threatening court action if I didn't pay refunds and make good on parts replacements. We were placed in a financial situation from which it would be almost impossible to recover.

During this same time-frame, my oldest brother Sam became very ill with Melanoma cancer and suddenly (after a family fast), passed away. Several times during those days, I would pray to Heavenly Father, "I can't handle any more!" Life can be challenging and overwhelming for anyone, but the knowledge that God loves us sustained me and my family during this difficult time, was reassuring. Knowing He loves us so much that he allowed his only begotten Son to Atone, suffer, and be crucified for us. He wants you and I to return home to him; and no earthly circumstance can change that fact.

I would be lying if I said I didn't become depressed several times a day while fielding calls from angry customers, telling me how 'worthless' I was; or how I didn't 'know what I was doing'. You and I live in difficult times; we live in the Last Days. As we stand by each other, and work together, even in our extremity we can be positive and uplifting. The love I have received from my Heavenly Father through His Spirit, along with the love of my companion Cassie, and the love of my children, has sustained me in these trying times. In addition to this love; I have felt a great 'depression-smashing' joy by looking beyond myself and serving others in the duties of my church.

That's the formula to keep depression away: Love someone else, help someone else, and especially acknowledge the presence of God in our lives through sincere, prayerful expressions of thanksgiving. Acknowledge the pain, and turn discouragement over to God. Give yourself time to heal. Look at the beautiful things of the world all around. Laugh; ask what can be learned from the experience; and how your experience might help others who are facing similar challenges and crisis. As the song goes, 'Smile though your heart is aching'; and 'Help someone else in need'.

During all of these trials, our youngest son went through tests for possible prostate cancer and was detected with a hernia. He also got into a snowmobile accident where he was thrown thirty-feet and hit a tree. Thankfully he was wearing his protective gear; and walked away with a concussion, chipped teeth and a badly bruised knee. Then his son, who was two years old, nearly severed a finger the next day playing in the yard. Another phone call the following day, revealed a near poisoning (with possible liver damage) when Lilly's youngest son Ryan, drank a nearly full bottle of liquid Tylenol. As you can imagine, the good people at the hospital and emergency room were wondering if we are going to take up residency!

Each of these events singularly (let alone collectively) could cause feelings of, "I don't want to go on - why me? Enough is enough". Still, our faith was bolstered and renewed as we witnessed several family miracles during this time; and at the conclusion of, several of these trials. One such miracle was Lilly's little boy who drank the Tylenol. They didn't have health insurance at the time; so the first thing Lilly did was bring him to my house for a Priesthood Blessing. At the time he was unconscious. After the blessing, he awoke and we were able to get him drink a lot of water to help dilute the medicine in his system. We took him to the hospital where they performed tests to determine if he was in liver failure or had severe liver damage. After four hours of waiting for the test results, the doctor said he couldn't believe it, but his liver function was completely normal.

We ended up losing our business, and our home. This required us to depend on our family even more. We moved to our daughter Lilly's basement for a period of time. I was unable to find employment for months. Humbled, but still strong in the faith, we put our trust in the Lord. We know the outcome will be in the Lord's hands, which to us, means 'it will be okay'. Do I think I have more trials than anyone else? Absolutely not! I *do* know that Satan doesn't like me very much, and he's going to put every obstacle he can before me and my family. Because I know this, I will never allow the natural man and the weaknesses of the flesh to dictate my future. For all of us (God's children), when those feelings of depression come along; they must be suppressed. Feelings of worthlessness have no place in a life with Godly identity and purpose. We don't have to look very far to see another in a worse position; or one who has totally given up on hope or life itself. Let's go and help! When you help another in need, you somehow forget about your own problems. In fact in my case, the problems literally seemed to disappear; and we were able to bear the burden.

Find hope in something, have faith in yourself, and in Jesus Christ. Go to your knees in prayer and serve others. Don't turn to substances that may seemingly give you temporary relief; but in the long-run possibly produce spiritual side-effects or even death. Remember that depression is an opportunity that Satan looks for; that tiny chink that may weaken the natural man for a complete take-over; allowing Satan to be the mastermind of your demise.

Depression is a disease that's growing at alarming rates. It's all part of Satan's plan to destroy the souls of men. Depression is the biggest weakness of the natural man in these 'last days'. When 'hope' diminishes, then life becomes darkness and pain. Thoughts of suicide come from Satan; and he wants us to be miserable just like him, until we give up on ourselves.

If or when you hear voices saying, 'the pain isn't worth it, Just take your life; you are no good to anyone.' Maybe it's a 'familiar voice' like you talking to yourself. Believe me, it's Satan the imposter, the father of lies. Heavenly Father loves you more than you will ever love yourself; it is a 'total' and 'perfect' love. It's 'unconditional' love; no matter what you've done, He will NEVER direct you to harm or kill anyone, including yourself.

God's goal is to 'bring to pass the immortality of man' and for us to receive a 'fullness of joy'. He wants all of his spirit children to return to his presence so he can give us 'all he has', including Eternal Life.

Maybe you're one of those individuals who have never been taught how to pray. First and foremost you must have a genuine heartfelt desire to get help. Second, you must have hope in a better life. Then third, you must have faith in Jesus Christ. You must believe in Him who paid the ultimate price for you; making it possible to overcome all things. Wanting to become whole again, happy, full of life, and back on the path towards the light; is a natural desire of all people.

Then, with a sincere heart, with real intent, and a contrite spirit; humbly go to your knees. The following is one suggestion to help generate ideas for your prayer. The key is to talk to your Heavenly Father in a way that is comfortable and natural for you.

"Heavenly Father I love you. I give you thanks for all that I have. I believe all good things come from you. I know you love me; and I love you. My heart is heavy, and my spirit depressed. I ask you with all my heart and soul, to please listen to my plea. Help me, I can't go on. I know the Savior can lift my burdens and lighten my load through his Atoning Sacrifice. Bless me to listen to the voice of your Spirit giving the answers I need to move forward from here. I ask for strength beyond my own. I can't go on, the adversary has taken control. His bitter chains are so tight and his darkness has blinded my eyes and closed my ears. Father I plead for help. I'm so alone, and feel I have nowhere to turn. I ask for forgiveness for my sins. I'm so sorry; I ask forgiveness Father, I will never do it again. Show me the way back, I know all things are possible through you and your love. I pray for continued guidance from the Holy Spirit. May I be worthy of your blessings? I pray and ask for these things in the name of Jesus Christ; Amen."

The basic components of every prayer are:

- o Address God the Father in a way that is natural to you;
- o Thank Him for the blessings you have received;
- o Ask Him to help you with your needs;
- o End in the name of Jesus Christ.

I testify if you pour out your soul, with real intent, humbly asking Heavenly Father for help and guidance, it will come; but only in *His* time. Why? Because he knows what's best for you. He also knows when it will help you the most. I testify he listens to every prayer and knows our needs, *before* even we know what we need. He only requires that we ask; and acknowledge him in all things. Giving Him thanks (even for the trials and tests of life) shows Him we are sincere, humble and willing to endure

Some of us need to first swallow our pride. Humbly acknowledging we can't get through this life without help from God. So, the first step in eliminating depression is prayer; and the second is losing one's self in the service of others.

The Savior said, 'If you lose yourself, you will find yourself'. Get out of your comfort zone. Seek out the 'one' by getting off the couch or out of bed. Find someone else who's worse off than you. You'll be surprised; they're out there, and possibly even in your own home and family. Maybe it's a neighbor, close friend, or a complete stranger. Be the angel someone is praying for. You in turn will find yourself. Remember the first step, prayer. Ask your Heavenly Father to put that person in your path so that you can personally help. You could be the hero like the boy in the following story:

'A young boy who felt like he had no friends in his high school; had just emptied his school locker of all his personal items for the last time. He was headed home where he intended to end his life. Another boy from the same part of town, noticed him from across the street. He crossed to the other side and offered to help him. As the boys walked, they talked, listened to each other, and found common ground; that blossomed into a friendship that would last a lifetime. What the boy needed was a friend. The boy returned to school and excelled; eventually becoming the school valedictorian. At graduation he gave the commencement speech and revealed the story of how a simple act of service had saved his life.'

'When you are in the service of others, you are only in the service of your God.' I believe there are only five steps in curing depression. The first two come from commandments number one and two of the Ten Commandments:

Step 1: Love God your eternal Father and his Son Jesus Christ.
Step 2: Love your neighbor.
Step 3: Love yourself.
Step 4: Pray to Heavenly Father in the name of Jesus Christ.
Step 5: Lose yourself in the service of others.

These are the basic steps, but you could add many others to motivate and lift the down-trodden. I love music, gospel hymns are a form of worship. Good music draws on the Holy Spirit and the light around you increases. Surround yourself with goodness; and God fearing people. Many times in my life, after prayer, I've picked up the Holy Scriptures, and randomly turning to a page, read the divine counsel from God that I needed in that moment.

I know without a shadow of doubt these things are true. Your problems, whether they are feelings of depression or other trials, will pass if these steps are followed. The challenge is enduring the test or trial to the end. The blessings come, *if* we endure the trial well. The Lord says, 'To be called my people, you will be tried in all things.' That's a formidable statement; but the Savior also offers hope, 'I will not test you beyond your strength and ability to overcome such trials'. No matter whom you are, or what you've done, you can make yourself whole and right again.

(References: the *Doctrine and Covenants*)

CHAPTER 9

Satan/Lucifer/The Devil:
The Enemy to all Righteousness

His titles are many: Perdition, son of the morning, evil one, the beast, father of lies, outer darkness, fallen angel, opposition, adversity, demons, false spirits, evil spirits, prince of devils, antichrist, sons of Baal, angel of the bottomless pit, destroyer, Abaddon, Beelzebub, Apollyon, common enemy, dragon, prince of power of the air, master Mahan, tempter, hell, god of this world, serpent, spiritual death, to name a few. The 'devil' (literal meaning slanderer), is a spirit son of God born in the morning of the pre-existence. It is difficult to talk about, but it's necessary in order to expose him to the world. We must gain knowledge of him to be able to detect his evil works and his presence around us in this, 'his world'; he and the billions who've sworn duty and allegiance to him.

First, here are some common questions that might be asked about Satan:

> ➤ Who is Satan?
> ➤ Is he alive today?
> ➤ What's his main purpose?
> ➤ What's his number one goal?
> ➤ Does he have power?
> ➤ Where does he get his authority?
> ➤ How many followers does he have?
> ➤ Where does he live?
> ➤ Who does he affect?
> ➤ When will he have no effect upon the people of Earth?
> ➤ Has he ever personally appeared to anyone on Earth?
> ➤ Will he ever have a physical body of flesh and bones?
> ➤ Can he ever take over our body?

Let's take a look at the scriptures and the words of modern day Prophets and Apostles, which have described this being known as the Devil. Elder Bednar spoke at a Church Education System (CES) Fireside at Brigham Young University Idaho on this subject. First he speaks to the question of Satan's physical status:

"Satan does not have a body, and his eternal progress has been halted. Just as water flowing into a riverbed is stopped by a dam, so the adversary's eternal progress is thwarted because he does not have a physical body. Because of his rebellion, Lucifer has denied himself all of the mortal blessings and experiences made possible through a tabernacle of flesh and bones. He cannot learn the lessons that only an embodied spirit can learn. He cannot marry or enjoy the blessings of procreation and family life. He cannot abide the reality of literal and universal resurrection of all mankind. One of the potent scriptural meanings of the word damned is illustrated in his inability to continue developing and becoming like our Heavenly Father. Because a physical body is so central to the Father's plan of happiness and our spiritual development, we should not be surprised that Lucifer seeks to frustrate our progression by tempting us to use our bodies improperly. One of the ultimate ironies of eternity is that the adversary, who is miserable precisely because he has no physical body, invites and entices us to share in his misery through the improper use of our bodies. The very tool he doesn't have, and cannot use, is thus the primary target of his attempts to lure us to physical and spiritual destruction."

Next, he addresses the importance of this body that Satan cannot have:

"We came to this earth that we might have a body and present it pure before God in the celestial kingdom. The great principle of happiness consists in having a body. The devil has no body, and herein is his punishment. He's pleased when he can obtain the tabernacle of man, and when cast out by the Savior he asked to go into the herd of swine, showing that he would prefer a swine's body to having none. All beings that have bodies have power over those who have not. The devil has no power over us only as we permit him; the moment we revolt at anything which comes from God, the devil takes power. Our physical bodies make possible a breadth, a depth, and intensity of experience that simply couldn't be obtained in our pre-mortal estate."

We must have this physical, mortal body to exercise all the freedoms of agency. Boyd K. Packer said this:

"Our spirit and our body are combined in such a way that our body becomes an instrument of our mind and the foundation of our character. Thus, our relationships with other people, our capacity to recognize and act in accordance with truth, and our ability to obey the principles and ordinances of the Gospel of Jesus Christ are amplified through our physical bodies. In the classroom of mortality, we experience tenderness, love, kindness, happiness, sorrow, disappointment, pain, and even the challenges of physical limitations in ways that prepare us for eternity. Simply stated, there are lessons we must learn and experiences we must have, as the scriptures describe, 'according to the flesh'."

Now, let's discover some of Satan's background and history. We must go back to the pre-existence realm and the war in heaven; in which Lucifer convinced one-third of all his spirit brothers and sisters to follow him. I'll be quoting from the *Doctrine and Covenants* and *Pearl of Great Price*.

First, think about this: How important is our short earthly life in relation to an eternal time span; eighty-five years compared to infinity? Consider this; in the short span of a human lifetime, Satan and his followers must entice us to embrace his ways and forsake the birthright we have earned: the possibility to become like God and share in all that He has. Satan has all this earth's temporal time (roughly) 6000 years, and then, at the Savior's Second Coming, he will be bound for 1000 years. He will have a 'short season' at the end of the millennium, and then be cast into 'Outer Darkness' as a spirit, never being able to grow, gain experience through trials, feelings of love, eternal joy, happiness or the great blessings of companionship; never realizing the power of faith and the Atonement of Jesus Christ. He (and his followers) has lost all of this, because of open rebellion in the preexistence, against Heavenly Father and the Plan of Salvation.

"And this we saw also, and bear record, then an angel of God who was in authority in the presence of God, who rebelled against the Only Begotten Son whom the Father loved and who was in the bosom of the Father, was thrust down from the presence of God and the Son,

And was called Perdition, for the heavens wept over him - he was Lucifer, a son of the morning.

And we beheld, and lo, he is fallen! is fallen, even a son of the morning!

And while we were yet in the Spirit, the Lord commanded us that we should write the vision; for we beheld Satan, that old serpent, even the devil, who rebelled against God, and sought to take the kingdom of our God and his Christ-

Wherefore, he maketh war with the saints of God, and encompasseth them round about.

And we saw the vision of the sufferings of those with whom he made war and overcame, for thus came the voice of the Lord unto us:

Thus saith the Lord concerning all those who know my power, and have been made particulars thereof, and suffered themselves through the power of the devil to be overcome, and to deny the truth and defy my power-

They are they who are the sons of perdition, of whom I say that it had been better for them never to have been born;

For they are vessels of wrath, doomed to suffer the wrath of God, with the devil and his angels in eternity;

Concerning whom I had said there is no forgiveness in this world nor in the world to come-

Having denied the Holy Spirit after having received it, and having denied the Only Begotten Son of the Father, having crucified him unto themselves and put him to an open shame." (*Doctrine and Covenants* 76:25-35)

What we understand from this is, by the same moral agency, the free power of choice received by all the spirits of God, Lucifer freely chose rebellion, placing himself and a third of all of God's children in eternal *opposition* to God's plan of happiness.

"And I, the Lord God, spake unto Moses, saying: That Satan, whom thou hast commanded in the name of mine Only Begotten, is the same which was from the beginning, and he came before me, saying - Behold, here am I, send me, I will be thy son, and I will redeem all mankind, that one soul shall not be lost, and surely I will do it; wherefore give me thine honor.

But, behold, my Beloved Son, which was my Beloved and Chosen from the beginning, said unto me Father, thy will be done, and the glory be thine forever.

Wherefore, because that Satan rebelled against me, and sought to destroy the agency of man, which I, the Lord God, had given him, and also, that I should give unto him mine own power; by the power of mine Only Begotten, I cause that he should be cast down;

And he became Satan, yea, even the devil, the father of all lies, to deceive and to blind men, and to lead them captive at his will, even as many as would not hearken unto my voice." (Moses 4: 1-4)

Satan was one who stood before God the Father, and using his agency, gave up his birthright; never being able to progress with a physical body as a son of God. He wanted all the glory and power that God had; his desire was to force us back to the presence of God effectively eliminating the agency of man.

The following is the scriptural account of Moses on Mount Sinai. Moses describes seeing the face of God (Jehovah) and then, how Satan appeared. In this description, Moses describes his feelings towards these two personages. His description is important because it helps us to recognize the nothingness of Satan, and state of man in comparison to God.

"And he saw God face-to-face and he talked with him, and the glory of God was upon Moses; therefore Moses could endure his presence.

And God spake unto Moses, saying: Behold, I am the Lord God Almighty, and Endless is my name; for I am without beginning of days or end of years; and is not this endless?

And, behold, thou art my son; wherefore look, and I will show thee the workmanship of mine hands; but not all, for my works are without end, and also my words, for they never cease.

Wherefore, no man can behold all my works, except he behold all my glory; and no man can behold all my glory, and afterwards remain in the flesh on the earth.

And I have a work for thee, Moses, my son; and thou art in the similitude of mine Only Begotten; and mine Only Begotten is and shall be the Savior, for he is full of grace and truth; but there is no God beside me, and all things are present with me, for I know them all.

And now, behold, this one thing I show unto thee, Moses, my son, for thou art in the world, and now I show it unto thee.

And it came to pass that Moses looked, and beheld the world upon which he was created; and Moses beheld the world and the ends thereof, and all the children man which are, and which were created; of the same he greatly marveled and wondered.

And the presence of God withdrew from Moses, that his glory was not upon Moses; and Moses was left unto himself. And as he was left unto himself, he fell unto the earth.

And it came to pass that it was for the space of many hours before Moses did again receive his natural strength like unto man; and he said unto himself: Now, for this cause I know that man is nothing, which thing I never had supposed.

But now mine own eyes have beheld God; but not my natural, but my spiritual eyes, for my natural eyes could not have beheld; for I should have withered and died in his presence; but his glory was upon me; and I beheld his face, for I was transfigured before him.

And it came to pass that when Moses had said these words, behold, Satan came tempting him, saying: Moses, son of man, worship me.

And came to pass that Moses looked upon Satan and said: Who are thou? For behold, I am a son of God, in the similitude of his Only Begotten; and where is thy glory, that I should worship thee?

For behold, I could not look upon God, except his glory should come upon me, and I were transfigured before him. But I can look upon thee in the natural man. Is it not so, surely?

Blessed be the name of my God, for his spirit hath not altogether withdrawn from me, or else where is thy glory, for it is darkness unto me? And I can judge between thee and God; for God said unto me: Worship God, for him only shalt thou serve.

Get thee hence, Satan; deceive me not; for God said unto me: Thou art after the similitude of mine Only Begotten.

And he also gave me commandments when he called unto me out of the burning bush, saying: Call upon God in the name of mine Only Begotten, and worship me.

And again Moses said: I will not cease to call upon God, I have other things to inquire of him: for his glory has been upon me, wherefore I can judge between him and thee. Depart hence, Satan.

And now, when Moses had said these words, Satan cried with a loud voice, and ranted upon the earth, and commanded, saying: I am the Only Begotten, worship me.

And it came to pass that Moses began to fear exceedingly; and as he began to fear, he saw the bitterness of hell. Nevertheless, calling upon God, he received strength, and he commanded, saying: Depart from me, Satan, for this one God only will I worship, which is the God of glory.

And now Satan began to tremble, and the earth shook; and Moses received strength, and called upon God, saying: In the name of the Only Begotten, depart hence, Satan.

And it came to pass that Satan cried with a loud voice, with weeping, and wailing, and gnashing of teeth; and he departed hence, even from the presence of Moses, that he beheld him not." (Moses 1: 2- 22)

We see here that Moses tried two or three times to get rid of Satan, but he couldn't, until he commanded him to leave in the name of the Only Begotten (Jesus Christ); then, and only then, did Satan leave immediately.

Moses also describes the power and the brightness of God, and that he had to be 'transfigured' in order to stand in Christ's presence; and see him with his 'spiritual' eyes. In contrast, Moses (in his natural state and seeing the lack of glory); practically laughed at Satan when asked to worship him. As he stated' 'where is thy glory, that I should worship thee?' And, 'But I can look upon thee in the natural man.'

This chapter should illuminate our minds, to the reality that Satan and his followers *don't have any power or glory*. We hold the power to put these true enemies in their rightful, lowly place. This is done simply by exercising our agency in choosing 'good' over 'evil'. There is no 'middle ground' upon which to stand; we can't 'serve two masters'; and *our* master is the Lord Jesus Christ. Becoming and being clean, and pure of heart (in every thought and deed), will bind Satan so he can't have any influence upon us.

That being said, Satan (and his influence) is essential in this world so we can know both good and evil; and exercise our agency and freely make our choice. Satan knows our weakness; he exerts every influence possible to get us to embrace those weaknesses so he can get access to our bodies. He knows us; he is at the ready to change the outcome of our life's journey; *if* we allow him to become our master. He and his followers will stop at nothing to prevent the learning and growth that brings us closer to God.

Satan is so sly in his approach. If he can get us to the point where there is no hope; where we feel worthless; where we experience doubt; then he has us where he wants us. In that state, we may blame others for our mistakes, and even express hate toward God for our troubles. When get to the point that we cast Heavenly Father aside; Satan becomes the master. He'll exploit the cracks in our character, enter into our body, and ultimately work to control our every move. He is relentless until he finally convinces us to hurt others and eventually take our own life.

The following story is true, and the people involved are good people. The influence that Satan has tried to exert on them is real. That evil influence ruined plans, broke relationships, nearly resulted in suicide, and has significantly disrupted their lives.

'Steve' is a 19-year-old young adult who belongs to my same faith. At the time of this story, he was thinking about serving an LDS mission; but wanted to 'have a good time' before he made any serious decisions concerning the direction of his life. Basically, he wanted to 'eat, drink and be merry', 'one more time'. But seemingly safe or innocuous events in life have a tendency to turn out much differently than we expect. Satan and his followers never sleep; he is always waiting in the wings, patiently biding his time until he can seize the right moment for his attack. It's also interesting (as a side-note) that often when someone is trying to change, or do something good, or gain knowledge, or growth through special righteous experiences in life; that is when Satan intensifies his attacks on the natural man (notice Steve was considering going on a mission).

Steve moved far away from home, and his familial support group, so he could 'be on his own and really experience what life is all about'. He met a beautiful girl named 'Laura'. She soon started to 'win over his heart'; and he began to have normal and natural feelings of love for her. His mother (always concerned for her son) received a prompting of the Spirit' to immediately call Steve in that faraway place. As they talked, she told him that she was 'impressed' that he should 'come home now'. His response: "Oh mom, don't worry, I'm all right; I'll be home in a couple of weeks."

Life can change very quickly in a 19-year-old's life. The same night of his mother's phone call, he had sex with Laura, and she became pregnant. Steve wanted to do the honorable thing (and after all, he loved her). Her parents were of another religion, and didn't approve of them getting married. He tried everything imaginable to get her parents to give their consent. He went to Laura's church, and even talked about converting; but it didn't get any better. Steve's life had become a mess. He finally went home to his family; and left Laura and the baby behind. Depression started to creep in and take over his life. Things got worse as he struggled to get along with his step-father. Things got so bad, that he decided to move out (even though he didn't have the finances for an apartment). The financial problems increased, and he felt the weight of the world upon his shoulders. He stopped praying because he felt the prayers were falling upon deaf ears. Thoughts of, 'life isn't worth it' started to enter his mind.

In desperation, Steve actually began to pray to Satan for help with his money problems. Within a day, Satan came through and Steve came into a large sum of money. Realizing that nobody would ever believe how he came by the funds, he decided to secretly spread the ill-gotten gains around among his friends and neighbors. His intentions were good, but this was Satan's money, and nothing good could come by it. Steve mistakenly convinced himself that somehow the Lord would understand and make it right.

Steve's thinking had become so distorted by his relationship with Satan that nothing could be further from the truth. His intended generous actions were simply promoting Satan, who will always give freely of his evil gains. As he shared the filthy lucre, he had a false sense of security that everything would be alright. He didn't understand that Satan had something else in mind. Satan is never satisfied until he has 'all of you'; he doesn't stop until you're completely bound in his chains.

With the money in hand, Steve left his apartment. Getting into his car, he looked into the rearview mirror, and was horrified to see his face and head appear to become distorted and disfigured right before his eyes. He quickly turned away and began backing out of the driveway. As he drove away, he glanced at the side mirror and was shocked to see his entire apartment complex engulfed in flames. He slammed on his brakes, put the car in reverse, and stopped in front of his building. His car started to go crazy; the windows began going up and down, lights going on and off, the engine starting and stopping, and the car began bouncing and shaking violently; everything was out of control. Out of his mind with fear, Steve grabbed his cell phone and called his friend 'David' that lived nearby.

David was his friend from school and was a faithful priesthood holder and active member of the church. When he arrived he got into Steve's car, and heard the details of what he had experienced. David was instantly overcome with fear, because he knew the source of the evil that his friend was experiencing. He picked up his phone and dialed their priesthood leader, Bishop Sorenson. The Bishop soon arrived at Steve's apartment and assessed the situation. He too knew the source of the evil, and offered to help. Bishop Sorenson laid his hands on Steve's head and cast the evil spirits out in the name of Jesus Christ; and gave him a priesthood blessing. Then he cast the evil from his apartment, gave it a blessing that it would remain free of Satan and the evil ones. Steve was the only one that could see the flaming apartment, the car going crazy, and the distortion of his face and head. Satan had taken over Steve's body and created those images and sensations in his mind. If he hadn't received this help when he did, who knows what evil Satan's influence would have caused him to do? When a person is overcome by a demonic presence, they can be convinced to do any evil, up to and including murder. Steve's story doesn't end here. He moved back with his mother and step-father. Even though he was a large, muscular, twenty-one year old; he was so traumatized by the experience, he slept at the foot of their bed for several months.

Did Satan go away and give up on Steve? The answer is a resounding "NO." He never gives up on any man, woman or child. In the New Testament we read this about Satan and his evil followers:

"When the unclean spirit is gone out of a man, he walketh through dry places, seeking rest; and finding none, he saith, I will return unto my house whence I came out.

And when he cometh, he findeth it swept and garnished.

Then goeth he, *and taketh to him seven other spirits more wicked than himself;* and they enter in, and dwell there; and the last state of that man is worse than the first." (Luke 11:24-26 – *emphasis added*)

We will never be free of Satan's influence until the Millennial Reign of Christ, when Satan and his followers will be bound for a thousand years. I look forward to that day of freedom from his influence, and pray every day for the Second Coming of the Lord and Savior of all mankind.

Steve's life had gone on, and taken a better course; he had a nice home, a wonderful wife and three beautiful children. Recently, though he experienced another brush with the evil of this world in the form of demon spirits. From his previous experience, he knew what to do. He called on a worthy priesthood holder, his step-father. When his step-father arrived at their home, he raised his right arm to the square and commanded the evil ones to depart in the name of Jesus Christ. He gave Steve, his wife, and his children priesthood blessings and blessed and dedicated their home. Steve and his family were so affected by this evil encounter that they haven't been able to live in the home since. It's currently up for sale and being rented at the time of this writing. Steve and his little family have become emotional wrecks, and have again seen demons in their current home. So what went wrong in Steve's life? It goes back to the time in his youth that he prayed to the adversary. As the scripture sited above indicates, once Satan has been embraced, it becomes a lifetime, literal all-out-battle, to keep his influence from returning. Guard can never be dropped, and efforts must double and tripled to thwart him by sheer righteousness. The moral of the story: avoid the very appearance of evil; Satan doesn't need an invitation.

In this evil world, there is a chance that we'll run into a situation where we need to defend ourselves from Satan or his followers. What if there's not a righteous priesthood holder available at that moment? Whether you're an innocent child, a woman, or a man (that doesn't hold the priesthood of God), you can call upon the powers of heaven; and in the name of Jesus Christ, stop evil from harming you. By using the Light of Christ within you and by the power of the name of Jesus Christ, Satan (or those within evil persons) can be stopped; and you will be protected from being assaulted, raped, murdered, or any other evil act or influence.

This is how it is done: With faith in the Lord Jesus Christ, raise your right arm to the square and say, "I command you to leave in the name of Jesus Christ my Master." When the Son of God's name is invoked they have to obey, and those persons (and the evil controlling them), must leave. This is power of the creator of this earth, over entities that are forever less, because they have no body. Remember: Priesthood Authority is required to cast evil out of the host body; and unless ordained to that required authority, you cannot cast the evil out of the person. But by following this instruction, you can save yourself or others from an evil outcome.

Paul illustrates that 'authority' is required in this scripture from The Book of Acts:

> "And God wrought special miracles by the hands of Paul:
> So that from his body were brought unto the sick handkerchiefs or aprons, and the diseases departed from them, and the evil spirits went out of them.
>
> Then certain of the vagabond Jews, *exorcists*, took upon them to call over them which had evil spirits the name of the Lord Jesus, saying, We a adjure you by Jesus whom Paul preacheth.
>
> And there were seven sons of one Sceva, a Jew, and chief of the priests, which did so.
>
> And the evil spirit answered and said, Jesus I know, and Paul I know; but who are ye?
>
> And the man in whom the evil spirit was leaped on them, and overcame them, and prevailed against them, so that they fled out of that house naked and wounded." (Acts 19: 11-16 – *emphasis* added)

From this we learn that the chief priest of the Jews in that area, performed exorcisms or the casting out of evil spirits. We also discover that his seven sons were not righteous priesthood holders and had no power over the demons. The evil ones knew they were nothing, so they leaped into the bodies of the seven sons.

Hopefully, you can see that Satan is pure evil, and something not to be trifled with. He will take you down by whatever deceit possible, if you allow him. Suppose you've had a vision or dream, and a 'spirit' appears; asking you to do something. How would you detect whether he or she is from God or Satan? The Prophet Joseph Smith explained the essential answer to this question in the Doctrine Covenants section 129:

> "There are two kinds of beings in heaven, namely: Angels, who are resurrected personages, having bodies of flesh and bones—
>
> For instance, Jesus said: *Handle me and see, for a spirit hath not flesh and bones, as ye see me have.*
>
> Secondly: the spirits of just men made perfect, they who are not resurrected, but inherit the same glory.
>
> When a messenger comes saying he has a message from God, offer him your hand and request him to shake hands with you.
>
> If he be an angel he will do so, and you will feel his hand.
>
> If he be the spirit of a just man made perfect he will come in his glory; for that is the only way he can appear—
>
> Ask him to shake hands with you, but he will not move, because it is contrary to the order of heaven for a just man to deceive; but he will still deliver his message.
>
> If it be the devil as an angel of light, when you ask him to shake hands he will offer you his hand, and you will not feel anything; you may therefore detect him.
>
> These are three grand keys whereby you may know whether any administration is from God." (Doctrine and Covenants 129: 1-9)

If you know anything of Joseph Smith's life history, you know these verses come from personal experience; and the process is true. Extend your hand to the being, and if you feel nothing, raise your right arm to the square and command it to leave (as previously described above). The impostor has to leave.

What if you hear a voice, but don't see a spirit being; and they ask you to do something? This is the most common method evil spirits use when dealing with people. The above test won't help; but it is very easy to tell the source. If you are asked to do something or given information from God or one of His servants; that action or information will always be in harmony with the Gospel and the light of Christ. The action or the information will literally 'testify of Christ'. If on the other hand, you are asked to do anything evil, to someone else or yourself; it's from Satan.

On many occasions, I've felt evil around me (yet seeing no one), and raised my right arm to the square and pronounced the words I have described. I testify I've felt the evil leave immediately. I always follow up with a prayerful thanks to Heavenly Father for delivering me from the demon. Something important to know is that neither Satan (nor his followers) has the power to read minds.

When you're going to try to accomplish some righteous endeavor, it's sometimes a good thing to talk about it only in holy places such as your dedicated home or church building. There are many stories of the early Saints following this pattern. I know if I'm going to go to the temple, I don't broadcast it out loud. I get ready and go before Satan has an opportunity to put road blocks in my way. I've seen enough of Satan's pattern of behavior that I can almost guarantee; if a special spiritual event of any kind is announced, Satan and his army will do everything in their power to stop that event.

Let's review the story about the antichrist Korihor in the *Book of Mormon*. For context as we begin, Alma the chief judge is talking to Korihor:

> "Behold, I know that thou believest, but thou art possessed with a lying spirit, and ye have put off the Spirit of God that it may have no place in you; but the devil has power over you, and he doth carry you about, working devices that he may destroy the children of God." (Alma 30: 42)

Korihor was so hard-hearted that he demanded a sign from God, and by the power in Alma, Korihor was struck dumb. The record states what happened next:

> "And Korihor put forth his hand and wrote, saying: I know that I am dumb, for I cannot speak; and I know that nothing save it were the power of God could bring this upon me; yea, and I always knew that there was a God.

> But behold, the devil hath deceived me; for he appeared unto me in the form of an angel, and said unto me: Go and reclaim this people, for they have all gone astray after an unknown God. And he said unto me: There is no God; yea, and he taught me that which I should say. And I have taught his words; and I have taught them because they were pleasing unto the carnal mind; and I taught them, even until I had much success, insomuch that

I verily believed that they were true; and for this cause I withstood the truth, even until I have brought this great curse upon me." (Alma 30: 52-53)

In a very short time, Korihor was destroyed. We see that Satan cannot prevail when facing a disciple of Christ.

"And it came to pass that as he went forth among the people, yea, among a people who had separated themselves from the Nephites and called themselves Zoramites, being led by a man whose name was Zoram—and as he went forth amongst them, behold, he was run upon and trodden down, even until he was dead.

And thus we see the end of him who perverteth the ways of the Lord; and thus we see that the devil will not support his children at the last day, but doth speedily drag them down to hell." (Alma 30: 59-60)

Korihor and countless sons and daughters of God have fallen prey to the controlling chains of Satan from the beginning of time; and will continue to fall until the millennial reign of Jesus Christ.

In the Church of Jesus Christ of Latter-day Saints, we have been privileged to have living Prophets in our day. Thanks to these Prophets, we've been given a significant amount of knowledge about what is known as man's 'preexistent' (pre-earth) spirit life; also known as our 'first estate'. In this place, we lived with God, our Eternal Father. God wanted to share everything he had with us, his spirit children. We could see that we were different than our Heavenly Father who had a glorified body of flesh and bone. God the Father commissioned an earth to be created. This would be a place we could be sent to receive a physical body and to be tested; to see if we would follow God's commandments – even when no longer in His presence. It came time for the 'Plan' to be discussed, and decisions made on how it was to be accomplished. God asked for proposals, and two of God's eldest spirit children stepped forward with ideas. Simply put, Lucifer's plan was to take choice (agency) out of the equation; and insure that all God's children would return to Him after the test. And, oh yes: the glory would be on him [Lucifer]. Jehovah's plan was just the opposite; preserve man's agency, even if that meant not all of God's children would return. And the glory would be God's.

A polarizing 'discussion' ensued known as the War in Heaven. Eventually the factions separated. When the count was tallied, one-third of all of God's spirit children followed Lucifer (who would become known as Satan). The balance (two-thirds) counted their allegiance with Jehovah (who would become the Christ). At the close of the conflict, penalty and reward was to be meted out. Those spirit children who chose freely (by their God-given agency) to follow Jehovah and accept God the Father's 'Plan of Happiness', earned the right to go to Earth at their appointed time, and receive a physical body of flesh and bones. Those who chose to side with Lucifer, would go to the Earth but without the opportunity for a physical body. With Lucifer at their lead, they would not be added upon or ever be able to become as God.

Certainly great tears of sadness swelled up in the eyes of God the Father and God the Mother, for the loss of one-third of their spirit children. I'm sure too, that tears also flowed from the other two-thirds who would be losing their spirit brothers and sisters I believe that we felt, for the first time, Godly sorrow. As I write, the tears are flowing now because God the Father has allowed me to feel, even though a small portion, his pain and Godly sorrow. I can picture his out stretched arms of love for all his children. I picture the billions of loving spirits falling to their knees, overwhelmed at the loss of their spirit brothers and sisters. I imagine the eons of memories they must have shared flashing before their spiritual eyes.

I'm sure we were baffled at how they could have thrown away the opportunity for Immortality (the union of our spirit bodies and resurrected physical body) and Life Eternal (endless life in the presence of our Heavenly Parents). How could they have hated God and us, their spirit brothers and sisters, so much?

Lucifer and the one-third gave up their birthright. That moment would be the last time they would ever stand in the presence of the Mother and Father of their spirits. I can imagine the last exchange of words between God the Father and Lucifer may have gone something like this: You will be 'OPPOSITION', for there needs to be opposition in all things." This is very important to know and understand; and, the *main reason for the creation of this book*.

God the Father, knowing all things from the beginning to the end; certainly laid out how the process would proceed on the Earth; and pronounced Lucifer and his followers' earthly 'mission'. It may have gone something like this: 'my faithful spirit children cannot create darkness and evil, for they are pure light and truth. After I cast you out of heaven and down to earth, I will place Adam and Eve in the Garden of Eden. I will command Adam and Eve to multiple and replenish the earth. I will also command Adam and Eve *not* to partake of the tree of knowledge of good and evil'. Satan could do nothing about the first commandment given to Adam and Eve. So he probably thought he could challenge their agency on the second commandment.

Satan has no wisdom; he didn't realize that by partaking of the fruit, man would be able to come to this earth. Had they not partaken of the fruit, they alone would have remained in the garden; having no children. Satan has no understanding of God's ways; and naturally will do the opposite of the will of God in all things. Adam and Eve had to transgress one law in order to fulfill the other. We all should be eternally grateful to Eve who partook first; and Adam for seeing that by also partaking, the Plan would be initiated; making it possible for each of us to come to earth.

Satan's response to the 'mission statement' was undoubtedly full of hate, gnashing of teeth, and anger. He shouted out, 'My spirits will take possession of all the mortal bodies of the children born to this earth'. He declared his solemn decree in the presence of God and all his spirit children. That is his ultimate goal even though he knows it will be temporary. Before God cast Satan and his followers down to earth, He surely announced the great blessing he will bestow on all his faithful spirits, 'The Light of Christ will be within every child born to the Earth.' This great gift is protection against the fiery darts of the adversary.

Satan is an entity of spirit. Spirit matter is normally unseen by the eye of man; but once Satan has possessed a body; he becomes visible in doing the evil actions of those who do his bidding. That person now serves his new master; who controls his every move. Satan becomes invisible and un-detected by the person he has possessed. He is, 'opposition' and has no godly attributes; never to have a body of flesh and bones, or the sensations of smell, taste and touch. Satan and his followers only have sight and hearing; it's almost impossible to imagine existence without the touch of a loved one, the smell of lilacs in the spring, or the taste of fresh strawberries.

The mission of the Holy Ghost is to testify of the reality of God the Eternal Father, and his Son Jesus Christ. Being the third member of the Godhead, he testifies of the truth of all things. Because he is spirit, he can dwell within us as the comforter. Through our righteous living he can be with us always guiding and directing our every step back to our Heavenly Father.

I boldly testify that Heavenly Father has a resurrected immortal body of perfected flesh and bones, and a perfect, eternal spirit. If this were not so, Jesus Christ could not have been conceived in Mary's womb (she being mortal) by God. God the Father planted his seed in Mary as her mortal body was carried away 'in the spirit'. I testify that Jesus Christ is the only literal begotten son of God in the flesh. The truth of His Divine conception and birth is essential to our understanding. This knowledge bears testimony to us of the great blessing that is mortality and this probationary state; allowing us to gain a body and experience life on earth.

To demonstrate how Lucifer may have 'campaigned' for the preexistent spirits' allegiance, let's imagine the argument he may have used. Satan's final plea for loyalty would have had everything to do with the mortal body. He probably said something such as:

'My special brothers and sisters, if you come join ranks with me; you may praise me and give me the glory as your true god. I can promise that when God sends his children to the earth, we will possess their bodies. Under my direction, all the blessings of mortality which they received will be yours for the taking. You won't need to worry about physical death, for you will never die; with no death, there is no need for an atonement or resurrection. Earthly life will be filled with ease: no laws, no commandments, no such thing as sin, no such thing as a God; you will be able to do anything you desire, for anything will be possible on my world. You will be able to indulge in carnal and devilish acts, having sex with anyone or anything; whatever you desire. And by the way, because there is no devil, there is no opposition. Embodied in one of God's followers, you may eat, drink, and be merry; you won't have to worry if your influence kills your host; there will always be plenty more. Just chose another living mortal and possess their body. All the appetites and feelings of the flesh will be yours. You will have their personal identity. All the power and riches you desire. If you don't like the mortal you're controlling, just convince them to commit suicide. If you really want to create a stir, get your host to eliminate one or many through murder or terrorism. Man will create many and varied weapons; you can even incite wars and bloodshed of every kind. Heavenly Father's plan only offers pain, sorrow, trials, tribulations, disease, failure, disappointment, depression, disobedient children, and sicknesses of all kinds, cancer, old age, and then death. I offer you the world and everything in it! You would be very unwise to choose Father's Plan; there are no guarantees. All of Gods promises are either lies, or too difficult for you to be successful. With me, you'll have it 'easy''.

Satan wanted all of us to be like his evil spirits, and mindlessly follow him. In the imaginary campaign speech above, there *is* one true statement; Heavenly Father's Plan *does* offer trials, tribulation, pain and sorrow. Yet, we freely chose that plan. We knew that these trials would give us experience; which in turn, would help us become like God. Only beings such as us can experience the blessings of the atonement and resurrection.

To close this chapter, I want to discuss 'Love'. That may sound like a strange way to end a chapter on Satan; but my comments will be directed at Satan, the father of all lies; and the 30 billion plus followers at his command. I believe he will read or hear these words, and his hate and anger within him will explode, towards me and my family. If you are the least bit intrigued, read on.

Satan, I want to tell you in a real and personal way about the relationship that Cassie and I have with each other. I cherish our love. She's my best friend. I love her laugh, her smile, her scent, her touch and how we have worked side-by-side in building our life and our family. She's the mother of our children. Together we have tried to teach each of them about God's Plan of Happiness. Every night, as we kissed them goodnight, our love for them was real. Each of them has been a blessing to us, and we have learned a lot from them. We've made mistakes like every parent does; but we will never give up on any of them because we are a 'Forever Family'. What God offers is real; not imitation.

You only offer pain and misery like unto yourself. I'm sure you laughed as you watched the soldiers beat my Savior. I know the blood from the crown of thorns made you feel happy. I'm positive you had sheer delight as you saw the nails go through his flesh and into the cross. With every pain he experienced you felt better about your ruthless plan.

I know that when you convinced my son he wasn't good enough, that it gave you great pleasure to see the rifle placed in his mouth, and the trigger pulled. I know it brings you even greater pleasure to see suicide and death cover the earth. Death is real; but it is also reality that we will literally embrace our Brother Jehovah; the 'One' who was willing to give His life for us, and atoned for our sins, if we but repent. His power is just like our Father. It is the power of love; something you will never experience. You have no light, and no glory; your nothingness is witnessed everyday throughout this world.

There is a line of demarcation that divides what the Savior has to offer, compared to what you offer. Those of the world, who are pure of heart and truly seek after Christ and His Gospel, can see the difference. You cannot deceive the true believer. I testify of the truth of these things. My testimony of Jesus Christ is that he lives. I testify the Opposition lives as well. I say this in the name of Jesus Christ; Amen.

(References: *King James Version of the Holy Bible, Book of Mormon, Doctrine and Covenants, Pearl of Great Price*, CES Fireside at Brigham Young University Idaho by Elder David A. Bednar, and LDS Conference address by Elder Boyd K. Packer)

Chapter 10

Satan's Tools and Games of Destruction

When you are playing against an opposing team, it's always best to know their tools, tactics and weapons. For us, we need to be able to recognize the methods Satan uses to entice; ensnare and blind the children of God. Not surprisingly, his plan is the same as it's always been. However, the apparatus has been disguised with new packaging, to keep us off guard. His vicious attacks are directed at the natural man within us, through the appetites of the flesh. 'Opposition in all things' is necessary for salvation. This may seem counterintuitive, but we must be able to exercise our agency in the choice between good and bad. Heavenly Father wants all his spirit children to return to him; but they must choose for themselves the path that takes them there.

Satan knows your weaknesses; and he will be relentless in bringing you down. We live in the Last Days; Satan knows his time is short, and will show no mercy. He has no compassion, no light and only darkness; he wants what he thinks is his; even though he knows he can NEVER have it. He's knows that the pleasures man seeks are only temporary; yet the natural man will easily be enticed to return to them again and again, just like a 'dog to its vomit'. For the natural man is an enemy of God. The appetites of the flesh are carnal and devilish and always will be. Freedom, satisfaction and happiness never come by way of sin. And yet, when we choose Satan's 'game plan' we may feel (at least temporarily) the elation of being on the 'winning team'. Satan will never support his followers in the end. Sooner or later, they come to know the chains that bind them.

The statement, 'Men are that they might have joy', came from God, not Satan. In that simple phrase, Heavenly Father is talking about the Eternal Joy that comes by following the teachings of Jesus Christ.

We are each a spirit child of a Heavenly Father who created us in his image, male and female. Then, through agency, we chose Heavenly Father's Plan of Happiness. This choice was made in what is known as our 'First Estate' or Preexistence. Because we were faithful, we received the assurance and blessing that we would have a mortal body of flesh and bone. As a result of this one choice, we received the privilege of coming to Earth (our 'second estate') to be 'added upon'. Thus, we entered the time of our earthly 'probation'; a time to gain experience and knowledge; and to prove our obedience, so we might return to God's presence. We all agreed that this life would not be easy; and we knew that a 'veil of forgetfulness' would cover our 'eyes'. This would require us, 'by faith alone' to use our 'agency' to individually choose good over evil. In that pre-earth realm, we certainly witnessed Satan and his followers being cast to the Earth. We understood that they wouldn't have the veil cover their eyes; Satan and his billions, would know each of us personally when we came to Earth. Our choice to follow Gods Plan of Salvation would cause him to hate and loathe each one of us; because we had a body, something he would never have. Because he knew us before, he would have knowledge of our weaknesses, and would be able to identify those who were foreordained as the 'noble and great ones'. It would be they, on whom he would concentrate his efforts! As followers of Jesus Christ and His Gospel, we are in his sights.

Job was a 'perfect' and 'upright' man. God allowed Satan to test him, but not 'unto death'. Every evil trial and test could and would be explored. Job was rich in things of the earth; but much richer in things pertaining to God. Job lost every earthly possession, including his family. Accused of wrong and sin by his friends, he never gave in to Satan. He endured to the end of his trials in spite of the physical, emotional, mental, spiritual pain and sorrows he suffered. In his miserable state, he felt 'worthless before God'; and requested of Him only that he be allowed to 'go home and die'. Against all odds, he triumphed over Satan. Because he remained true and faithful, he was blessed with greater earthly possessions than he had before; and his family was restored to him. This Biblical example shows, and gives us hope, that anything is possible with God, through obedience to his laws.

We believe the 'glory of God is intelligence'. Learned and talented men of the world have created (often through the inspiration of the Spirit of God), many marvelous inventions that save time, toil, expense, and an improved life. This has given us more disposable time to improve the living conditions, and health around the world. Yet Satan has always found ways to corrupt good things, and turn their use to destroy the hearts and minds of men and women, in all generations of time. Today, his specialties include: media (in all its iterations), electronics, the arts, entertainment, medicine, sports, clothing, the internet; and this list is not all-inclusive. In fact, whatever our eyes can see, ears can hear, nose can smell; mouth can taste, or can be touched or felt; Satan (or those he influences) has used to change good to evil.

Media influences enter our minds through sight and sound; addictions arise from smell and taste; harmful substances enter through our noses and mouths (or are injected). The pathways into the body of the natural man are exploited by Satan, and are seemingly unlimited for use in the destruction of man.

The knowledge of who we are, should surely give us hope; we are the literal spirit children of Heavenly Father, and our spirits are perfect just like him. We have the capacity to become as he is. Immortal beings have a physical body permanently united with a spirit body, through the Power of the Holy Resurrection. Simply stated, when we overcome the natural man and we (our soul – the body and the spirit) become clean and pure through the Atonement of Jesus Christ. We must never allow Satan to take over our mortal body, which is literally a Temple that houses our Perfect Spirit.

We are placed on this earth, and asked by our Heavenly Father to call upon His Holy Name through his Son Jesus Christ. By living a Christ-centered life, worshiping our true Master the Savior Jesus Christ, and our Heavenly Father, we cannot fail. Once we have practiced and perfected this simple devotion, it becomes part of our nature, and we will have the strength necessary to resist the enemy.

I've heard some rationalize that they are strong enough to pick and choose a little sin in the smorgasbord of vice; here a little and there a little. It will be 'OK' in the end; I'll repent today and do it again tomorrow, believing God will show mercy for he is 'all-loving'. How many times have you made the following statements? 'It's just a game'; 'No one will know it's just you and me'; 'There's just one bad scene'; 'Everyone is doing it'; 'Just take one drink, there's no harm in that'; 'I'll only buy one $5.00 lottery ticket'; 'If I take this drug (just this once), I'll experience an out of body experience, with no side effects'; 'What's playing the slot machines going to hurt, it's only $20'. How easy it is for the natural man to devise an apparently endless list of excuses for our weakness to resist temptation.

By engaging in and supporting these 'vices', we're supporting Satan's work. As Christians we have a responsibility to insure that our actions match our beliefs; if they don't match, that's when the term 'hypocrite' becomes applicable. Participating in vices is no different than the man or woman who attends church on Sunday, then the other days of the week lies or steals. Satan is everywhere in the world except Holy places (where he is unworthy to dwell). We are commanded to stand in Holy places at all times. Once we break a commandment, law, or engage in an evil acts; we are on the slippery slope to bondage, and we'll repeat the behavior. Conceivably, the first few times a sin is committed, we are simply under the influence of the natural man. But then Satan sees the crack in our character, and enters in to take possession of the natural man and seeks to control your agency; the end result: freedom is lost. Skeptical this could happen to you? It happens to good people every day who've let their guard down. I can't stress this point too much: Satan's goal is to have a physical body even if just temporarily. Imagine having an evil spirit directing your every move; coming and going at its command. Your progression to eternal life is at a standstill as your heart becomes hard and cold, matching the darkness that constantly surrounds you. Your personality changes as the emotions of hate, anger, and misery are reflected in your treatment of friends, coworkers and loved ones.

As humans, it's impossible to live two lives for long. Satan tries to make us believe it's possible for as long as we need; then when it ends, he leaves us to suffer the consequences. The Savior taught us about serving two masters:

"No man can serve two masters: for either he will hate the one, and love the other; or else he will hold to the one, and despise the other. Ye cannot serve God and mammon." (Matthew 6:24)

In the world today, there are many who could be called mediums, Soothsayers, and fortune tellers. You no longer have to find a carnival, or go to the seedy side of town to find them; just log into your home computer or mobile device. These things known as 'priest crafts', describe those who use words of flattery, enchantment, or simply tell you the things you want to hear. Those practicing what could be called the 'dark arts', often claim to be of God. Their so-called revelations often come from Satan or are simply fabricated to get gain. People pay large sums of money to go to someone who may invoke God, but it is the god of this earth whom they channel. They build up their customers with a false sense of hope, telling them that no matter the sin, if you declare that you believe in Christ, you will be saved in the end.

There are many ways to worship Satan and his kingdom of darkness. Surprisingly (or not) there are actually many that openly and outwardly worship Satan himself, the father of all lies. There are the followers of the 'occult' who claim their allegiance to the Devil, and boldly say he is their 'Master'. There are the Voodooist's; a barbaric religion that originated in Africa, and is now in many parts of the world particularly the Caribbean, Central, and South America. There is the practice of witchcraft and sorcery whose power comes from Satan, and is a form of Devil worship.

Through the years, I've collected many stories involving board games; but today, the popularity of electronic games continues to rise. Some of these games don't contain parental advisory warnings of age; and even if they do, many parents don't pay attention to what their kids are asking for. Consequently, younger and younger children are being exposed to more racy and violent action games. Our greatest concern as consumers and parents should be the easy access to these tools of Satan. Allowing these influences into the home indirectly exposes all members of the family to evil. If a parents in engaged in this game play, it's only a matter of time before the children are exposed and asking to play. I've heard things like, 'Everyone at school is playing it'. Young teenagers and even pre-teens are asking for birthday and Christmas gifts of the genre of "Dungeons & Dragons" and violent 'first person shooter' video games. I went on line to read the instruction book for some of these games, and was shocked at the evil things that are suggested to be done to other players to obtain certain powers or a 'killing advantage'. I'm no expert in child psychology, or the effect of such things on the developing brain; but I do know the supernatural, the occult, death and destruction are of Satan.

What I'm suggesting is: if you buy one of these games, and bring it into your home, you are (by extension) supporting an evil industry; and inviting Satan's influence into your home. Sin can't be looked upon with the 'least bit of allowance'. Or in other words, the flames may be beautiful but if you touch them, you will be burned. Why would we willingly allow evil into our family room, our office, our children's room, or our bedroom? I can't imagine even being able to go to sleep at night when Satan's influence is in my game closet, my entertainment center shelf, in the hands of my children, or on my night stand

When I was a young Bishop I presented a fireside to a Young Adult group on the subject of Satan's influence in media and games. After the meeting, a young woman asked if she could speak to me in private; I could hear the trembling anger in her voice. For the next hour and a half, she tried to justify a particular game. I don't recall the title of the board game; but what I do remember was her total devotion to it. I asked her how much time she spent playing, and it was unbelievable! She had been role-playing a character in the game for nearly five years;

occupying multiple days and many hours every week. It wasn't just a one night party game; she was devoting every spare minute to being a fictitious character so she could improve her game play, and gain various powers over other players in the game. I compared it to being an impostor just like Satan. I told her that living in a fantasy world wasn't of God. The piece of plastic on the game board had taken on a life of its own, and dragged her into an addiction that had replaced normalcy in her life. Today on the internet there are 'gamers' who play in real-time competitions or war-games. In these games, people are totally immersed in the sights and sounds for hours and sometimes days at a time. They too often become addicted to the thrill of battle, and the carnage they inflict of the enemy or other players.

Cassie knew a woman from work with two young children. During one conversation, she mentioned that having two small kids had prevented her and her husband from gaming as much as in the past. She was resentful about how the children had changed their lifestyle. A few years later, Cassie discovered that this woman's attitude had completely changed. With her kids now older (6&7), she and her husband could game every day again. Certainly those children would be following the parent's example and become gamers also; and perpetuate poor-quality time between parents and children.

One of the worst of the satanic board games is the Ouija board. I'm told there are worse, but I have no desire to learn anything about them. I know without even examining their content, the goals are the same: to trap players into the satanic realm of fantasy; to gain trust in the supernatural; and experience a desensitized acceptance of mayhem and killing. I could write a book on the horrible events that have happened (to many of the special people I've known); when playing the Ouija board. Instead, I'll share just a few stories that testify to the evil caused by Ouija board play. The Ouija board is intended for use as a way to call upon Satan to get answers to questions; and in that way, invite him into your life.

When my older brother Sam was seventeen, one of his friends had gotten access to the game, and invited him and some other friends over to play with a Ouija board. In our religious community, every kid knows the reputation of the Ouija board. Of course being seniors in high school, they could handle anything. The owner of the game asked a couple general questions and then (as all teenagers do) asked life and death questions (which obviously to a rational adult seems very stupid). He asked, "When am I going to die?" It answered with, "Two weeks."

Then he followed with, "How am I going to die?" It answered with, "Car accident." My brother told us this story after the funeral of his friend; and 'Yes', both answers were correct.

As a LDS Bishop I was always trying to get my less active ward members to come out to church. There was a father in his late twenties who had 3 young children and new wife (he had just remarried for the third time). The first two wives passed away very mysteriously of rare sicknesses (or so I was told). After the deaths of his first two wives, he was excommunicated from the Church. I was interested if this family could consider coming back, and the husband re-baptized. I asked a good home teacher to visit with them, and report back. When he gave me his observations he said, "That is the strangest home I've ever been in. There's a feeling of darkness and evil." He said he saw an 'Ouija board displayed openly on the table in the middle of the living room'. I was in shock, and told the home teacher to continue fellowshipping. I called the father and asked him to come in for an interview. He agreed.

I'll never forget that interview. I asked him what I could do to help him get back to church and be re-baptized. His answer will ring in my ears forever. He said, "I'm afraid of the Holy Ghost, so I never want to be baptized again." I knew then, he was serving Satan and the interview was over. Once I realized he was serving the Devil, I was even more surprised that he would come to the church house. If I had raised my right arm to the square and cast out the evil ones, he would have called them back later. One final note; his third wife (along with her unborn child) were shortly after this interview killed in an automobile accident.

When I was still in High School, one of our coaches took five of us to see one of his previous school's ball games. As we drove, he told us a tragic story involving four of his high school friends when they were seniors. They like most teenage boys thought they could handle just about anything. One night they took a Ouija board to the town cemetery to try contacting another friend who had just died in an automobile accident. They received an apparition that they thought was their friend. The spirit told them his death wasn't an accident; instead he had purposely crashed the car to kill himself. As they listened to the demon disguised as their friend, they became convinced that their lives weren't worth living either. Each of these four boys cut their lives short by 'playing' a board game. One hung himself in his garage; another took his father's .357 caliber handgun and placed it to his head; the third was asphyxiation with car exhaust; and lastly the fourth by cutting his wrists.

These four suicides took place one after the other. After each funeral, the remaining boys returned to the cemetery, where again, they used the Ouija to call on the spirit of their recently dead friend. With each visit, a demon disguised as their dead friend, convinced another to take his own life. The evil spirits that appeared to those four boys were demons sent by Satan. Think of the pain, suffering, and grief of those four families left behind; as well as the community at large, grieving for these young men who had their futures hear of them. It just breaks my heart, and words cannot express the pain of losing a loved one to suicide. Once we've allowed the evil one inside our body, he will use 'familiar voices' and relentlessly tell us there is no Satan and there is no God. He will use any lie necessary to get you to do his bidding; even to the taking of your own life.

A family member told me the following story of what happened to her, her two sisters and their family, nearly forty-five years ago. Their parents were out, and one of her sister's friends came to visit and brought a Ouija Board. They were all curious about it and that evening, the parents and kids tried it out. Their dad thought the game was pointless and went up to bed. As the evening wound down, there was some talk about the mystique of the Ouija; then they all said their 'goodnights'. Their mother went upstairs and the girls to their room. The girl's room was in the lower part of the home adjacent to the family room where they had played the Ouija. Before going to bed they straightened their room and talked. Suddenly they could hear footsteps in the family room next door; "Nobody should be here", they whispered. They started to get scared, and began praying softly. They were huddled together praying, as the footsteps continued coming closer until the sound entered the room. They looked and could see no one where the sound of footsteps had been. Suddenly the footsteps began again, this time walking farther into the room, and in between the two beds. The sound stopped, turned around and walked to the foot of the bed. At this point it was more than these young pre-teen girls could handle; they started screaming and praying out loud. At that point everything that was on the dresser was thrown across the room. Their dad and mom now awoke to the screams, and came running. It took them quite a while to calm the girls. They decided to call the Stake Patriarch to come and bless their home the next morning.

That same night at the friends' home, they had gone to bed. They heard one of their teenage boys come home, and go to his room to get ready for bed. Then they heard someone else enter the house and they supposed it to be one of the other kids coming home. Suddenly, they heard fighting in their sons' room, and it soon got out of control; so they got up to break up the fight. To their surprise, their son was apparently alone, yet he was being violently tossed around the room. To their horror his face was contorted grotesquely. They called the Stake President and asked him come and cast out the evil from their son and home.

The next morning the family gathered around the breakfast table to discuss what had happened the night before. Specifically, they talked about not playing with the Ouija Board. A couple of the older children, who had missed the incident the night before, were very skeptical that such a thing could have happened. At that moment, the son who had been attacked by the evil spirit the night before arrived home and headed toward the bathroom. As the son passed, they noticed a breeze blow through the living room (later they discovered the windows were closed) and just thought it to be the morning wind. Suddenly, there were loud noises coming from bathroom; and they fearfully ran to see what was happening. Again their son's face was distorted, and he was being brutally thrown around the room. They called the Stake President again. This time he cast out the evil spirits, and promised them that if they wouldn't deal in evil things this would not happen again. They straightaway returned the game to its owner. They described what had happened and said that the church authorities advised them to 'destroy it'. They were mocked and laughed at by the owners of the game. These families never forgot the consequences of allowing a tool of the devil into their home.

These Ouija board stories happened many years ago. Does that mean that its influence for evil has become less 'popular' in today's world? All you have to do is ask anyone about the Ouija, and they will relate a story of evil and possession. The important point to understand is that Satan (or one of his 30 billion followers) will come at the drop of a hat. No matter your age or circumstances, you can invite them in your home through bad media of any type (books, magazines, movies, video games, board games, TV shows, music, etc.) and the devices that deliver that media (via satellite, cable, commercial TV and the internet). All these things can be used for good also; it's important to learn to monitor them; for protection, both personally and as a family. I can promise this, it doesn't take Satan long to destroy individuals, homes, families and communities; when he and his influences are invited into our lives.

In today's world, Hollywood makes Satan the hero. The most popular movies contain witches/warlocks, sorcery and wizards. These movies display and use supernatural and magical powers to get what they want. These things become sought after and idolized by our innocent children. These little ones don't have the maturity to comprehend the dealings of Satan and his underworld of evil disciples. The movies that portray the most violence, killing, adultery, sexual perversions, rape, secret combinations, and etc.; make billions of dollars in support of Satan and his cause. I've heard youth and adults alike make comments such as, "The thrilling movies are the most violent and scary." "That movie is way too religious and boring for me."

It seems that not a day goes by but that the NEWS outlets report stories about school teachers performing sex acts with students; young people as well as adults sending pictures of their private parts to others from their cell phones; spousal abuse, drug abuse, child abuse, mothers killing their children, 'mother against daughter', 'son against father', 'brother against brother', and the list goes on and on. Prophets have warned of our day: the 'Last Days'. It sounds all too familiar.

Satan's tools are many; he's so clever and creative. Just when we think we have 'seen it all', he unleashes old sins in new packaging that are unrecognizable to those who are not aware. Volumes could be written of his tactics, but remember this: Satan threatens not only our spiritual salvation; but also our physical lives.

I promise that if you study the Lords ways, and practice righteousness, you will be blessed. Satan knows his time is short; he will not hold back. I pray each of us can evaluate where our righteousness stands, and make the necessary changes to be on the Lords side.

(References: *King James Version of the Holy Bible*)

CHAPTER 11

Cain the First Son of Perdition in the Flesh

The world calls him 'Bigfoot' or 'Sasquatch'; I believe this being is none other than Cain the son of Adam and Eve, who killed his brother Abel over six-thousand years ago. The people, who have seen him, describe a being that is definitely of human, not animal form. Cain was the first man to commit murder on the planet Earth. In spite of all efforts, no one will ever be able to capture or kill this so-called 'Bigfoot'. In the modern era, there have been many written eye-witness accounts of this astonishing being; as well as oral traditions passed on by the Native Americans. There is also rock wall pictographs and cave wall renditions of this strange enormous being. He has been sighted by many throughout the ages, and all around the world; the majority of the credible accounts originate in North America. As I share scriptures and the personal accounts of many individuals who have had glimpses and even interactions with this big hairy person; I believe I can make the case that Cain and 'Bigfoot' is one in the same. You'll also see and come to realize that it is because of the cursing of God upon Cain, that it will continue to be virtually impossible to capture or video this mysterious, large, hairy being.

God cursed Cain and said he would 'roam the Earth for the entire temporal experience'; or for thousands of years. His wandering will end at the beginning of the Millennial Reign of Christ. At Christ's Second Coming, the Earth will be cleansed; Satan and his spirit followers (evil spirits/demons) will be bound or prevented from influencing man for a thousand years. Humans who are evil, and have been living wicked lives (essentially possessed by demons) will be burned. The spirits of those who are destroyed, along with Sons of Perdition (like Cain), will be sent to Spirit Prison for a thousand years.

In this chapter, I'll share my personal confrontation with this being that I accept to be the evil Cain. I'll also share an account written by David Patten. He documented in his journal, that he talked face-to-face with this giant who declared his name to be Cain. He told Mr. Patten, what his mission is on Earth, and how miserable he is. Some have said they've spotted multiple of these beings together; and even possibly a female. It's only speculation if other of Cain's family members were given the same 'cursing' and roam the Earth. We do know that Cain's third great grandson, was given an even greater curse. This history is recorded in scripture which I will site below.

Over the years, I have had several personal encounters with Cain. Needless to say, he is a striking figure: very tall, and completely covered with long, mangy, dirty, stringy hair from head to toe. Apparently because of his 'vagabond' status, personal hygiene is a problem thus accounting for his appearance and horrible odor.

Consider the age of Cain. As a child of Adam and Eve, he would have to be around five-thousand years old! Imagine, being the oldest living man, and being cursed to roaming the Earth for thousands of years. What a lonely, terrible existence! Cain holds the following ignoble distinctions of 'firsts' among men:

1. First to be possessed by Satan;
2. First murderer;
3. First Son of Perdition;
4. First to create a Secret Combination with Satan; and
5. First to worship Satan.

May I add: if God would have allowed him to suffer death (instead of the cursing), he would have likely been the first to commit suicide.

Turning to the Scriptures, we can learn firsthand about Cain and the Cursing that God placed upon him. Cain is mentioned in the Old Testament (Genesis 4: 1-25 & Hebrews 11:4); in the New Testament (1 John 3:12 & Jude 1:11), and in other apocryphal books of scripture. Modern revelation (Found in the *Pearl of Great Price*) gives the most detailed account of his life:

"And Adam and Eve, his wife, cease not to call upon God. And Adam knew Eve his wife, and she conceived and bare Cain, and said: I have gotten a man from the Lord; wherefore he may not reject his words. But behold, Cain hearkened not, saying: Who is the Lord that I should know him?

And she again conceived and bare his brother Abel. And Abel hearkened unto the voice of the Lord . . .." (Moses 5:16-17)

"For from this time forth thou shall be the father of his lies; thou shall be called Perdition; for thou wast also before the world." (Moses 5:24)

"And Satan said unto Cain: Swear unto me by thy throat, and if thou tell it thou shalt die; and swear thy brethren by their heads, and by the living God, that they tell it not; for if they tell it, they shall surely die; and this that thy father may not know it; and this day I will deliver thy brother Abel into thine hands.

And Satan sware unto Cain that he would do according to his commands. And all these things were done in secret.

And Cain said: Truly I am Mahan, the master of this great secret, that I may murder and get gain. Wherefore Cain was called Master Mahan, and he glorified in his wickedness.

And Cain went into the field, and Cain talked with Abel, his brother. And it came to pass that while they were in the field, Cain rose up against Abel, his brother, and slew him." (Moses 5:29-32)

"And the Lord said unto Cain: Where is Abel, thy brother? And he said: I know not. Am I my brother's keeper?" (Moses 5:34) "And now thou shall be cursed from the earth which hath opened her mouth to receive thy brother's blood from thy hand.

When thou tillest the ground it shall not henceforth yield unto thee her strength. A fugitive and a vagabond shalt thou be in the earth." (Moses 5:36-37)

"Behold thou hast driven me out this day from the face of the Lord, and from thy face shall I be hid; and I shall be a fugitive and a vagabond in the earth; and it shall come to pass, that he that findeth me will slay me, because of mine iniquities, for these things are not hid from the Lord." (Moses 5:39)

I personally believe there is significant symbolism in this account. Through modern prophesy, we know that the Earth is alive and has a spirit just like all things that were created. The Earth is often called 'Mother Earth' because of the life she gives to God's creations here. Even though Cain was born before Abel, because of Abel's righteousness he was chosen to carry on the patriarchal order from his father Adam. When Cain killed Abel, his blood was spilled on the earth and penetrated to its very soul. As the scripture states, "The earth which hath opened her mouth to receive thy brother's blood..." indicates the severity of Cain's actions by the indicated punishment Cain would be, "... cursed from the earth...". I believe that Mother Earth was so repulsed by Cain's deed of death, that she did not want Cain's body buried in the Earth. Then the cursing continues with, "When thou tillest the ground it shall not henceforth yield unto thee her strength." Cain would never be able to grow fruit or vegetables to eat.

Cain had a perfect knowledge of God; as part of the family of Adam, he talked personally with Him. With that perfect understanding, he then came out in open rebellion, fought against God and his ways, worshiped Satan, and killed his brother Abel. Cain became the first man on Earth to murder. The first secret combination was established between Satan and Cain. Cain's sacrifice was rejected because it was offered at Satan's command, not in the Lord's prescribed manner. Cain was cursed and told that the Earth would not yield to him its abundance. In addition he became the first man to be cursed as a Son of Perdition.

Cain's punishment was not only because of murder. After having accepted Heavenly Father's plan in the First Estate (Preexistence); and having received the Holy Ghost in this Second Estate (earth life); and having received a greater light and sure knowledge of Jesus Christ; he still denied the Holy Ghost. This qualified him as a Son of Perdition.

Even Cain has a distinct advantage and power that Satan doesn't. As a result of his earthly birth, he is assured a tangible body of flesh and bone in eternity. This enables him (and other mortals who become Sons of Perdition) to rule over Satan because he will never have a body. The Lord placed a unique 'mark' on Cain; a mark of 'dark skin'. This was not a race or genetic mark; but a mark that would identify him to all mankind so they would know not to kill him; thus preserving his cursing to roam the Earth as a fugitive and a vagabond until the millennial reign of Jesus Christ. He along with Satan (and other mortal Sons of Perdition) will then be bound for a thousand years until the end of the Millennium. Because of the Lord's cursing on Cain, he could be easily identified. Cain could come and go, and no man could kill him. This cursing in found in the *Pearl of Great Price*:

"And I the Lord said unto him: Whosoever slayeth thee, vengeance shall be taken on him sevenfold. And I the Lord set a mark upon Cain, lest any finding him should kill him." (Moses 5:40)

As I stated at the beginning of the chapter, Cain continues to roam the earth today. He has been seen and described by many people throughout the ages in North America, and been given the name of 'Bigfoot' or 'Sasquatch'.

In the book *The Miracle of Forgiveness* by Spencer W. Kimball, is repeated the account of an early Apostle of the Church of Jesus Christ of Latter-day Saints (LDS), who saw and described, a very remarkable individual who had represented himself as being 'Cain'. The Apostle's name was David Patten, here is his account written in his personal journal of that meeting:

"As I was riding along the road on my mule I suddenly noticed a very strange personage walking beside me; his head was about even with my shoulders as I sat in my saddle. He wore no clothing, but was covered with hair. His skin was very dark. I asked him where he dwelt and he replied that he had no home, that he was a wanderer in the earth and traveled to and fro. He said he was a very miserable creature and that he had earnestly sought death during his sojourn upon the earth, but that he could not die; and his mission was to destroy the souls of men. About the time he expressed himself thus, I rebuked him in the name of the Lord Jesus Christ and by virtue of the holy priesthood, and commanded him to go hence, and he immediately departed out of my sight."

In my lifetime I've never heard of anyone having a conversation with Cain such as David Patten's. Typically when someone has seen him, it's just for a moment, and then he disappears. He always appears to be walking away from the people that have spotted him. I, like David Patten, had a very unique experience with Cain. There were no words exchanged between us; but his presence was real and witnessed by another.

I was seventeen years old and a senior in high school. My good friend Blake and I were in the mountains in the Monte Cristo area of Utah, hunting deer during the annual Bow Hunt. The area we were hunting is called Dry Bread Hollow.

We were driving my Dodge Opal down into the canyon on a primitive jeep trail. We shouldn't have taken such a small/low, two-wheel drive car down such a rocky, rugged road. But we were kids, willing to try anything, and deal with the consequences later. After traveling a couple miles we came into an open meadow where the road broke off in several directions.

We encountered a few nice bucks but couldn't get close enough to shoot at them. As we continued on the main branch of the road, suddenly there was a loud sound, and smoke started streaming from under the hood of my car; we realized we were in big trouble. We were in the middle of nowhere with a broken radiator hose. Of course this being 1974, we had no way to contact the outside world, and we were stranded. Darkness was about an hour away; and with no desire to stay the night, we decided to start walking down toward the main highway which was (we estimated) at least three miles away.

Making the best of it, we continued to hunt as we walked out of the area. My friend had a bad leg; and at 260 pounds he was a big boy. We knew it wouldn't be a fun walk (especially if it ended up being ten miles), but we really didn't have a choice. As we walked down the winding road, we could see that the road ahead straightened out and had hills on both sides. To pass the time, I took a few shots at a porcupine. The wooden arrows I carried were destroyed, leaving me only two for that 'big buck', if we saw it.

As the sun was just about to set, we noticed something very large and dark, standing on the ridgeline about a half mile from us. We both thought it was probably a moose; it was definitely larger than a deer or elk. We stopped and watched as it began gradually making its way down the ridge. We continued walking down the canyon, and soon noticed that the 'animal' had started to parallel our position; and was making progress towards us. This struck us as very strange and unusual behavior for wild game. It didn't take long before we realized that whatever it was, walked on two legs! Even at a distance we could see that it was much taller than a man, with walking strides much longer than anyone we had ever seen. By now we knew it wasn't a moose, and we didn't think it was a bear. I've hunted since I was a boy and have seen every kind of animal we have in the Utah Mountains; this was like nothing I had ever seen before. Naturally, our eyes became glued on his every move.

I knew I had a weapon, but the thought had never crossed my mind that I might have to use it for protection from a giant human-looking creature! Closer and closer it came off the hill. My mind was racing as I thought out loud, "How are we going to get out of this?" In a few moments we were going to be face to face with whatever it was. It was seven or eight feet tall and could move twice as fast as us. I knew my little re-curve bow and two arrows would be hopeless in our defense.

When the creature was less than a hundred yards away, it was crossing through a small grove of trees, and it dawned on me what this thing was. I had read newspaper articles about it and even seen a movie; it had to be the creature known as 'Bigfoot'. I had done a lot of research on this creature and came to understand that it was actually Cain. From my study I knew that Cain couldn't be killed; so my arrows would have been useless. Blake and I froze in our tracks. He continued towards us and was now only fifty yards away. The breeze blowing in our direction caught the stench of his body. It was horrible and reminded us of something dead. I also knew that he wasn't capable of harming us. At fifteen yards I could make out his bloodshot eyes behind a face and head covered with matted hair.

We almost said in unison, "We've got to do something, and do it now! The Spirit whispered to me, 'Raise your right arm to the square', and I knew immediately what I should do. I raised my arm and said, "I command you to leave in the name of Jesus Christ, my master!" He immediately stopped in his tracks, turned in the opposite direction, walked back over the ridge, and out of our sight. He went over that ridge at a speed and pace like it was flat ground. Words cannot describe the feeling of danger we both had in those minutes; nor the feeling of calmness and peace that came over us when it was over. I can testify that Cain is alive, and he does come and go on the Earth.

I know with all my heart and soul that the name of the Lord Jesus Christ has power over Cain, Satan or demons. We dropped to our knees and prayed to our Heavenly Father with hearts full of gratitude for sparing our lives. As you can imagine, the memory of this experience has been embedded in our memories forever. Almost twenty years after this experience, I ran into Blake for the first time. The first thing out of his mouth was, "Joe, do you remember that experience up in the mountains of Monte Cristo, and what you did to get rid of that hairy giant?"

The second encounter I had with Cain was about fifteen years later in a dream. Using the words I recorded in my journal, I'll recount this awful experience. It was Monday February 27, 1989, and I had just started a period of fasting and praying, in preparation for a talk I would give to a youth group (LDS Stake Young Women) the following night. As I tried to go to sleep, it just seemed impossible, with all I had on my mind.

After about two hours of tossing and turning, I finally fell fast asleep. As the dream opened, I could see Cain about fifteen feet in front of me. He was staring at me with those flaming red eyes from across what appeared to be a very small empty room with only a chair at his end. I'll never forget the furious big bloodshot eyes piercing me to the core. No words were exchanged, but I could feel his immense hatred and anger toward me. His facial expressions intensified, and his whole being emanated pure evil. Then he began moving toward me as he picked up the chair. I thought I could hear the sound of grinding and gnashing teeth as he approached me in pure rage! My subconscious mind (or spirit) prompted me, in that split second, to raise my right arm to the square and I said, "I command you to leave in the name of Jesus Christ, my master." It was at that very moment that he was going to smash the chair over my head. I sat up in bed wide awake, dripping wet with sweat; I looked at the alarm clock, it was 3:05 in the morning. Cassie at my side awoke, and asked me 'what [was] wrong'? I told her my dream, and she could feel an evil presence and was scared. We fell to our knees and prayed, thanking our Heavenly Father for his protection and deliverance once again. I arose and using the Holy Priesthood rededicated and blessed our home.

In July of 1996, my father, brother, and my boys Joseph, Grant and Rick, were on a trip in the Four Corners area of South Eastern Utah. We were scouting for deer in preparation for the upcoming Bow Hunt the next month. In the mountains around Monticello, we saw several deer but not very many big bucks.

We decided to go into a very remote area towards the Colorado border, which was approximately fifteen miles from our location. In that area we knew there were many grain fields with deep dark canyons breaking off from them. The deer had a history of feeding there at night, and then, in the early morning hours, making their way back through the canyons. As we were driving, we came to a fork in the road, and my brother spotted three nice four point bucks feeding along a ridgeline.

They quickly ran down into the canyon. We took the road in that direction and went a couple miles down to the bottom of the canyon; where we discovered a lot of deer tracks along the road. The majority of the tracks were on the West side of the road, where the hill was fairly steep and thick with trees. I asked my three sons to make a 'brush' up through the trees; then circle back towards the road where we would slowly move up in the truck, and meet them at the top. Every hunter knows this is a good strategy to get the boys to do the work and the adults to take it easy in the truck. Anyway, the boys liked to hike, and hopped out of the truck thinking it was a great idea. They spread out about fifty to a hundred yards apart and started heading up through the trees. This made it possible to cover a lot of area looking, not only for tracks but hopefully flushing out some deer as well. The boys disappeared up the hillside, and we slowly moved up the road. What the boys encountered in their 1.5 mile hike was astonishing! They were so affected by what they saw that two of them (the oldest and the youngest) were already waiting on the road by the time we got to the designated stop.

They were hot, sweaty, and out of breath from running up the mountain; and had a look of terror in their eyes. I looked at them and asked, "Did you run the whole way so you could beat us here?" "Where's Grant? Before they could answer, Grant came running as if he was being chased! The three in unison emotionally shouted, "You won't believe what we saw! We've never seen or smelled anything like that before!" Joseph and Rick said the smell was 'horrible and nasty' and like someone who had 'never taken a bath'. Grant agreed and said "Oh yeah, it smelled like somebody had died down there!"

All three boys described the tracks they had seen. They said the tracks were 'about eighteen inches long and about twelve inches wide'; they were very 'deep in the hard ground' as if the person was 'big and heavy'. They could see the clear impression of 'five toes of a very big man'. The boys never saw who made the footprints, but they could smell him, and felt his presence. And 'no way' were they going to go 'back to show' the rest of us! Not even to take pictures or impressions of the footprints.

I wouldn't wish this on my worst enemy. Cain is evil, and I don't want to be around evil. In the years since, just mentioning this experience to my sons, sends chills down their spines. To this day, I wish we'd have gone back there and taken pictures of those big foot prints to show the world. Without weapons, my boys would never have returned to that area. These are the hair-raising encounters with Cain that my family and I have witnessed through the years.

Many of my friends are LDS return missionaries and over the last thirty-five years we've had many talks involving some of their most personal confrontations with the adversary. I don't think there's been a single one, that didn't have an encounter with evil during their time of service to the Lord. In each case, it has involved a situation where someone was in the process of accepting the Gospel of Jesus Christ in their lives. And as my own, these were experiences that are indelible memories of the circumstances and events involved. Each and every one of them has testified to the fact that Satan tried to stop the Lord's work. The Gospel of Jesus Christ is the 'good news' that brings men and women to the true happiness and joy of life; Satan doesn't want that for anyone; in fact his goal is to destroy it all. In an upcoming chapter, I'll relate some of those missionary experiences that involved evil spirits and Satan's followers.

As I had mentioned at the start of this chapter, after Cain had murdered his brother, he was given the title of 'Master Mahan'; and the first secret combination was formed with Satan the 'father of all lies'. In a subsequent chapter, I'll reveal more from the scriptures about this subject and show how throughout history, these 'secret societies' have come to destroy many nations, the complete destruction of generations of people, and countless murders. These groups and people do it to get gain, and out of hate, jealousy, and the lust for power.

Consider some of the recent events in just the United States; could they be tied to 'secret combinations'? I know this is 'way out there' but; could it be possible that one of the anti-gun activists groups could have hired the mass murderer that carried out the shootings in the theater at Aurora Colorado? When a secret combination is formed, money talks and evil power is formed. After the mass murder in Newtown, Connecticut; many 'special interest groups' (think: secret combinations) began vehemently lobbying the government to pass legislation and laws that could take away the Constitutional Rights of the Second Amendment. Considering this, sheds quite a different light on the efforts of Cain (since the beginning of time) to control the world through secret combinations.

Reading from Moses we learn more about the title of 'Master Mahan' given to Cain, and another person who received an even greater cursing: Cain's third great grandson, Lamech:

"If Cain shall be avenged sevenfold, truly Lamech shall be seventy and seven fold;

For Lamech having entered into a covenant with Satan, after the manner of Cain, wherein he became Master Mahan, master of that great secret which was administered unto Cain by Satan; and Irad, the son of Enoch, having known their secret, began to reveal unto the sons of Adam;

Wherefore Lamech, being angry, slew him, not like unto Cain, his brother Abel, for the sake of getting gain, but slew him for the oath's sake.

For, from the days of Cain, there was a secret combination, and their works were in the dark, and they knew every man his brother.

Wherefore the Lord cursed Lamech, and his house, and all them that had covenanted with Satan; for they kept not the commandments of God, and it displeased God, and he ministered not unto them, and their works were abominations, and began to spread among all the sons of men. And it was among the sons of men." (Moses 5:48-52)

It's very important to know that (by association) Cain and his family (wife and children), were 'cast out' from the rest of his family. This would have included his parents Adam and Eve, brothers, sisters, and all other descendants of Adam. Cain was worshipping Satan and had no more contact with or even a desire to talk with God. Before his revolt and unthinkable murder of his brother Abel, Cain had talked with God face to face on several occasions. The greater sin (even above murder) is after having a perfect knowledge of God, and then denying that knowledge and the Holy Ghost. This sin has no forgiveness in this life or the life after and results in the Son of Perdition designation.

The title of 'Son of Perdition' is given to all those guilty of this 'unpardonable sin'. For that reason, I suggest that Lamech (Cain's third great grandson) had no contact with religion, and was never taught the Gospel of Jesus Christ. This made it impossible for him to commit the 'unpardonable sin'. Lamech was definitely guilty of creating a secret combination and murder. The subject of his worship was Satan.

I would like to relate another experience that I had as an LDS Bishop. It involves someone that had the same title as Cain, 'Master Mahan'. What's most disturbing to me is Cain received this title because of murder. There were many people who had problems that would come to counsel with the Bishop. One such person was a young woman who was very sexually active. Because of her transgressions, she spent a lot of time working through her issues with me, her Bishop. I tried everything possible, giving her priesthood blessings, fasting, and praying for her. She put her membership in jeopardy and eventually was excommunicated from the Church. She had religious upbringing in a very supportive family; they were solid, faithful, and true stalwarts in the Gospel of Jesus Christ. She had just allowed Satan to enter her life through her errant lifestyle, and take control. She did have faith she could change, and she knew she could trust me to do everything I could, as her Bishop, to help.

During one of our counseling meetings, she divulged some information about a satanic group of fifteen teenagers and their adult leader who had the title "Master Mahan." She indicated that she wasn't member of the group; but that she had watched as three of the young men demonstrated their 'powers'. She described how they had taken what they called 'voodoo dolls', and used them to inflict pain on others. By labeling the dolls with the names of individuals that they didn't like, and placing 'cursing' on that person; they would cause those persons to become ill, She told me that she had actually witnessed these people become sick with the stomach flu, chest pains and other minor discomforts and illnesses.

At this point in the conversation, I expressed a great concern not only for her, but also for the others who were part of this evil group. I told her, "People who enjoy inflicting hurt or pain on others are calling upon Satan as their master." I knew that those involved with this had stopped their eternal progression, and were on a downward spiral that would be very difficult to overcome. The powers they were demonstrating were from Satan, and he would never support them in the end.

As the meeting progressed, she told me that there were three members of the group that wanted to get out of the 'Satanic Cult', and meet with me for help. I knew that the leader was the one I needed to target to destroy this satanic assembly. I thought that perhaps I could get to the leader by first trying to help the three young men. I asked her to get word to them that I would meet with them at a designated date and time in my office at the church building. As she left, I immediately got on my knees, prayed, and started to fast for the young woman, the three teens and the rest of those involved in the group.

A couple of days before the meeting, the Spirit told me that the boys didn't really want help. Their goal was to try their powers on me, an LDS Bishop. I wasn't surprised that nobody arrived at the appointed time for our meeting; and I never saw anyone from the satanic group. The next time the woman and I had a meeting, I told her what the Spirit whispered to me about the boys. She said, "The spirit was right." I told her how I prepared for the encounter and what would have happened as I met them just inside the doors of the church. Once in the building, and looking directly at them, I would have raised my right arm to the square, and say the words, "I command Satan and his evil followers to depart in the name of Jesus Christ my master."

I know by the witness of the Spirit, that those boys had demons in them, and after my pronouncement, they would have collapsed to the floor as the evil ones left their bodies. It was also made known to me the reason they hadn't come to the building. They certainly had gone to their adult leader, who knowing of powers of God and the sanctity of a dedicated church building, didn't want them in a situation that was dangerous to the demons.

If they had come, after casting the demons out, and the boys regained their strength, I would have given each one an individual Priesthood blessing making them whole again. This would have given them the ability to eschew the evil and begin afresh with their lives. Satan and his evil followers know who Jesus Christ is; they also know that if they can bring down one of the followers of Christ, others will fall too. We should do everything in our power to never have even a single link of Satan's chain wrapped around us; not even for a moment. Darkness will overpower us if we allow even the slightest degree of opening to Satan.

The young woman continued to go through many difficult and challenging tests; but eventually she was able to see the light, and overcame the powers of darkness; allowing Christ and His atonement in her life. Five years later, she met a fine young Priesthood holder, and they were married in the Holy Temple.

Any son or daughter of God, after having received the 'Second Comforter' (the personal witness of Jesus Christ), who then goes out in open rebellion by denying the Holy Ghost, becomes a Son of Perdition just like Cain. Like Cain, they have a body that will rise with them on resurrection day. Because they have a resurrected body, they will reign over Satan and his followers (the one-third of the hosts of heaven that will never receive a mortal body). Final Judgment happens at the end of the thousand years 'Millennium' and the 'little season' when Satan will wage one final war with the children of God. Eventually, after the Final Judgment is complete, they will be cast into Outer Darkness for all Eternity. This will be the end of their 'progression' for all Eternity. Here is a perfect description of Cain:

1. Hair that goes from the top of his head to the bottom of his feet. I think a big reason for this is he knows that he is naked, and wants to hide his nakedness, and also his shame.
2. He can't wear clothes because of the cursing. God told him he could not disguise himself, when someone looked upon him they would know exactly who he was instantly.
3. He has a horrible odor. He can't even bathe (if he was a spirit there would be no odor) another reason that he can't hide the smell. It's like a dead human which definitely identifies him having been in the area.
4. His eyes are red blood shot, and dark for lack of sleep. Always wandering as a fugitive and a vagabond, homeless with no family.
5. Seven to eight feet tall, but without question a human man.
6. Void of the "Light of Christ" he has no light within him just darkness.

As I close this chapter I would like to testify that Cain is real and he is alive. He wanders the Earth a very miserable and lonely being. He has a body of flesh and bone just like all of us born to the Earth. With God's cursing, Cain's physical body was changed or transformed so he could come and go without suffering death. This is how he was able to survive the flood of Noah, and has never been killed or captured.

(References: *King James Version of the Holy Bible, Pearl of great Price, Doctrine and Covenants, and "The Miracle of Forgiveness* by Spencer W. Kimball)

CHAPTER 12

Control of Self
Spirit / Natural Man / Possession

Every child born to the Earth has a perfect spirit body and a physical body (aka natural man / woman - appetites of the flesh). At this point in the reading, the definition of 'possession' should be well-understood. However, just to be clear; when a person has another spirit (or numerous spirits) dwelling inside their body (such as the person described in the New Testament who had 2000 demons inside him – one calling itself 'Legion'), they are 'possessed'. In a possession, the person essentially loses their original identity and becomes 'someone else'. They have little to no control of their physical body because the demons have taken over.

The most priceless gift from God to His spirit children is agency; in other words, the ability to choose 'good from evil'. Agency was given by God and He cannot rescind that gift, or He would cease to be God. That's why it's such a serious matter when one becomes possessed by an evil spirit whose master is Lucifer or Satan; Satan has taken control of a gift God has given (even though initially we allowed the evil through disobedience to one (or many) of God's laws.

This is how serious it is: the very Light of Christ is darkened, and the person falls under the influence of Satan. The full attributes of the natural man are exposed, love diminishes, feelings of hate enter in, actions become 'carnal and devilish' to the point that agency is totally removed, and Satan is in charge. Now the demon is in control and evil of any kind is possible. These evils include (but are not limited to) rape, incest, same-sex attraction, murder, secret combinations, and suicide; the list could go on and on. Now, realistically, not *every* rape, murder, suicide or evil action is the result of a possession. I am saying that either a person has allowed the natural man (the appetites of the flesh) to become evil enough to do such deeds; or the person has become possessed (through their disobedience) with an evil spirit (or spirits); and committed these acts or crimes against humanity.

Let's look at some examples. King David, the leader of all Israel, committed two very serious sins. The first was adultery with Bathsheba. As a result, Bathsheba became pregnant with his child. He tried to cover up the scandal by bringing Bathsheba's husband home from battle; then sending him to the front lines of battle to certainly ensure his death. The more grievous of the two sins was murder, of which there can be 'no forgiveness in this life'. The point I want to make is this, David knew what he was doing in both instances. He was not possessed, but he allowed the natural man to rule. He lusted after Bathsheba, and acted upon those lusts. Then he tried to cover-up the sin by committing murder, and creating a secret combination.

When someone takes another person's life (if not in justifiable self-defense; or during an act of war wherein the soldier is under direct orders by a superior officer), it is murder. Only God holds the power to give and take life. It is God's decision alone to determine when one of his children's mortal probation experiences has to come to an end. By committing murder, the murderer has taken the role of God by eliminating someone's agency.

Consider the young man in Connecticut who without provocation entered an elementary school and gunned down twenty innocent kindergarteners along with six adults. He had killed his mother earlier in the day, and after the terror he inflicted, he also killed himself. A feeling, loving and compassionate person could never have perpetrated such a horrible crime. This causes me to believe he was not himself; he had become a sociopath. I believe this young man was possessed with one or many evil spirits which caused him to lose normal human feelings for mankind. He was definitely not in control of himself.

Then there was the young man in Colorado, who killed a number of people in a movie theater. He prepared for and planned his attack, including booby-trapping his apartment. This wasn't the act of an insane or mentally ill person. He came prepared with firearms, ammunition and a bulletproof vest. He chose the location because he knew it was a gun-free establishment where it was unlikely that anyone would fight back. This person, like King David, knew what he was doing before he did it. He may have been acting under the direction of some evil person or a demon, but he had full knowledge that people would be harmed and killed; and the consequences for his actions.

These kinds of events are used by conspiring men to justify their attempts at limiting the constitutional rights of the free people of the United States. In secret, they make pacts or secret combinations with groups who want to curtail legal access to firearms. Their reasons are ultimately to control the populace. Legal firearms owners are sportsmen, hunters, and those who desire to protect their rights of 'life, liberty and the pursuit of happiness'.

As previously been mentioned, evil spirits are always at the wait for an inroad to the natural man. The paths are many, but generally disobedience to God's commandments, in one form or another, is how it starts. The next few paragraphs describe another more and more common foothold Satan and his hosts are exploiting; that of same sex attraction. First some basic understanding; God created all of us in his image male and female as spirit bodies. Then our earthly parents provided a 'tabernacle' of flesh and bones to house this special perfect spirit. God is perfect; he could never accidentally place a female spirit in a male body or vice versa. God sent us to earth to gain a physical body that matched our spirit and gave us agency to be tried and tested. His primary command from Adam's time (that has never been rescinded) is to 'multiply and replenish the earth'. Having families provides us with the opportunity to teach them the difference between right and wrong. The basic format is found in the Ten Commandments (whether you believe in God or not), and the doctrines of Christ. These guide our actions on not a restrictive, but a responsible path to happiness. The only God-designed family unit comes through and by marriage between a man and woman.

When a person indulges in things that are inappropriate, it soon becomes a habit. Habits must be fed, and sooner or later the individual needs more and more to experience the same or greater thrill or high from the activity. Before long, actions they once thought of as 'wrong' become 'justifiably right'; this assuages the feelings of guilt, the 'conscience', 'Light of Christ', and the 'Spirit' provides to help us avoid or turn from sin. Eventually as the feelings of guilt are suppressed, they deny God and continue down the forbidden paths they've chosen to follow.

One inroad to the natural man is same gender attraction. I believe that when a man is attracted to another man, and then acts on that attraction; the appetites of the flesh or the 'natural man' is controlling that man's perfect spirit within him. In the case of the other male (or two females) it's the same. This opens the door for Satan and his evil followers to take possession of them. This is something that will be covered to a larger extent in an upcoming chapter. It's interesting to note the change in demeanor and even voice that takes place as a man 'becomes' more feminine; or a woman 'becomes' more masculine. In these cases, I believe that an opposite gender evil or demon spirit has taken over that person.

Another example of these inroads is through some medications. When a person is ill, they seek out a Doctor or Psychologist who often will prescribe medicine. Do we question the physician about the side effects of these medications? It can be very disconcerting to know of all the possible problems a drug can cause; especially if the medication is for a physical medical condition that must be addressed. But what if the medication is prescribed for a psychological condition such as depression? If the medication has potential negative psychological effects, the value must be weighed. Do the benefits outweigh the possible harmful effects? I feel we often become test subjects when a physician suggests we 'try' a medication to 'see if it helps'. Medication isn't always the answer, as studies have shown the mind has powerful curative powers. Having a positive and cheery attitude, getting physical activity, engaging in service, showing increased love, and sincere prayer, actually helps the body and mind overcome illness. Often, we overlook God in the equation. Those who serve in their church, pray, help their friends and neighbor generally have better health. We can turn to God and trusted church advisors who can assist in the process. Family members, friends, associates at work; rallying around us, can strengthen us and give us courage to overcome. We are what we think about.

When one of these (or other) inroads is taken by Satan's hosts, we notice the change in people. Their 'personality shifts', and they're 'different' than the way we've known them all their lives. We may start to avoid them because we don't want to 'step on their toes' or invade their privacy. We may think, 'They're just going through a phase or a hard time', and we excuse their behavior. They may express hate toward us, or perhaps jealousy; anger seems to become their common emotion. They experience feelings of isolation, and loneliness; they become convinced that no one cares or loves them. Depression sets in; love for self disappears. At this point they can start to have thoughts of hurting themselves, and even suicide; thinking that 'Everyone will be better off without me'. Satan loves this.

We all must *recognize* and *help* those who become possessed, *because the person in this situation cannot see it.* The evil within has convinced them they don't need help; they are truly living in denial. This is a critical time for them; we need to run to them, embrace them with our love and attention; and help them. You see, when they reach this 'all-time low' in their lives, is when the evil spirit uses 'familiar voices' to convince them: 'You're not worth anything, you're going to hell anyway, just kill yourself and end this pain'. It becomes easier and easier to make an impulsive decision; get that knife, find those pills or pull that trigger and end their suffering. This happens in seconds, and the deed is done immediately or in minutes. Please look for the warning signs of mood changes, or the person you know becoming unrecognizable as your friend or loved one. Don't allow them to have idle time; love and embrace them no matter what they've done; there is always hope! They are a son or daughter of a loving Father in Heaven. Look into their face, what kind of image do they reflect? Has some of their light gone? Are they as you have known them; or do they appear as someone very dark, evil and hateful? Don't allow them to give up.

Casting out Unclean Spirits, Demons or Evil Spirits

"And it came to pass afterward, that he went throughout every city and village, preaching and shewing the glad tidings of the kingdom of God: and the twelve were with him,

And certain women, which had been healed of evil spirits and infirmities, Mary called Magdalene, out of whom went seven devils,

And Joanna the wife of Chuza Herod's steward, and Susanna, and *many* others, which ministered unto him of their substance." (Luke 8:1-3 – *emphasis* added)

Here Luke talks about a very important doctrine that needs to be addressed: The casting out of evil spirits by Jesus Christ *which happened in every city to which he traveled.*

Hopefully I'm making a convincing case for how important it is to cast Satan and his followers' out of our lives before we can have full faith and a strong testimony of Jesus Christ. Concerning those who are being held hostage by Satan, their perfect spirits can never appeal for help; it takes the power of the Priesthood to free them. In other words, a righteous Priesthood holder must call upon the Powers of Heaven in the name of Jesus Christ to cast out the unclean spirit that has taken hold of one of God's children. This Priesthood is described in Hebrews chapter 7 in the *New Testament* of the *Bible*.

Were these women evil described in Luke above? No, but they had been possessed and were healed. Mary Magdalene is said to have been the Lord Jesus Christ's companion; and she was a disciple of Christ. She witnessed his trial, his crucifixion, and his resurrection. She knew nothing of Lucifer and his demon spirits until the Savior made her whole. Satan in his evil designs knew that if he took her, that was so close to the Savior down, he could then get many others as well. Satan lacks wisdom, but has knowledge; he looks for those little cracks in our natural man so he can enter and take possession of the body. This only happens when we allow the natural man to take control over our perfect spirit. Then it's only a matter of time!

The Veil and Satan's followers

When Satan was cast down, he and the one third of the host of heaven were not given a 'veil of forgetfulness' to 'cover' their memory of their pre-earth experience. Being spirits, they can never experience what a body is like, but they know each of us; we were their family and friends. The ultimate goal for Satan and his followers is to have temporary possession of a body. They know that God's Plan included saving the most valiant spirits for this the 'latter days' of the Earth. Many of God's spirit children come to earth and don't realize their full potential. They allow the natural man to rule their lives as they make choices or experience trials. They don't fully understand or comprehend the Love of God. Satan doesn't have to put too much work into them; they fall without much effort on his part. He goes after the very best; the most righteous, those who are disciples of the Lord Jesus Christ. Those who promised they would fulfill their mission, and never let the Lord down.

I have a Time magazine from the summer of 2012. On the front cover, is a silhouette of a US soldier and a caption that reads: 'ONE A DAY'. I opened up the story to this description: "The greatest military in the world, the US is losing one soldier a day to suicide." Then a little over a year later, I was watching a TV show about disabled veterans. It talked of the emotional problems these former soldiers were suffering caused by war. The leader of this group was pleading for help from all Americans because the suicide rate at that point in the military was twenty-two a day!

Who is the real enemy? The Lord God says that he has two enemies: 1. the natural man; and, 2. Lucifer or Satan and his 30 billion followers

In an upcoming chapter, I relate the story of a seventeen year old young man who was possessed. I had cast the demons from him and his apartment, and then gave him a blessing, and dedicated his apartment to be free of evil spirits. It was a new day for him, and my hope was that he would realize that Satan would still be relentless in trying to possess his body. Previously, I talked about Mary Magdalene and how she had seven evil spirits within her. The scriptures also say, when one is cast out, Satan will send seven more wicked than the first evil spirit to try to possess the body of one of God's children.

Can you see how we are outnumbered, and can be overwhelmed by Satan and his one-third of the hosts of heaven? He has a military-like organization of generals, lieutenants, and frontline soldiers. Once a person has a demon spirit removed, Satan will regroup and send his best to renew the battle for the soul. These evil spirits work tirelessly, twenty-four hours a day and seven days a week to intimidate, convince, and prod mankind. They are relentlessly on the prowl for the next opportunity to possess what they can never have: a body of flesh and bones. Once they've taken over, agency is gone, and they start to make the decisions of that person.

Satan loves a challenge. He has vast knowledge; he knows who the great and noble ones are from his time in the preexistence. He knows those who will have great influence over many, and he pursues them relentlessly. It's a simple matter: get one of those to fall, and many others will be brought down just from their bad example; little or no effort is required of Satan. He uses all the greatest inventions of mankind to promote and pervert the truths of God and entice the natural man. Satan's followers have largely eliminated God from the schools, government, and even the language of the people; except to profane it. He convinces community and government institutions that, to be 'politically correct' and 'sensitive to all people', overrides the will of the majority to have prayer or religious conversations in their communities, agencies, or organizations.

Many, who have died and returned, have witnessed scenes of Satan's tactics. Because their work wasn't done here on earth, they were able to relate to us warnings that should be a wake-up-call to all. In the book *Return from Tomorrow*, by George G. Ritchie; he tells of what he saw on the other side of the veil while he was dead for nine minutes; and then was revived. Mr. Ritchie was in the spirit without his physical body, which still lay in the hospital room. What he witnessed he saw with his spirit eyes, not the natural eyes. From the book, I begin quoting from the third paragraph, page 59:

"Gradually I began to notice something else. All of the living people we were watching were surrounded by a faint luminous glow, almost like an electrical field over the surface of their bodies. This luminosity moved as they moved, like a second skin made out of pale, scarcely visible light.

At first I thought it must be reflected brightness from the person at my side. The buildings we entered gave off no reflection, neither did inanimate objects. Then I realized that the non-physical beings didn't either. My own un-solid body, I now saw, was without this glowing sheath.

At this point the Light drew me inside a dingy bar and grill near what looked like a large naval base. A crowd of people, many of them sailors, lined the bar three deep, while others jammed wooden booths along the wall. Though a few were drinking beer, most of them seemed to be belting whiskies as fast as the two perspiring bartenders could pour them.

Then I noticed a striking thing. A number of the men standing at the bar seemed unable to lift their drinks to their lips. Over and over I watched them clutch at their shot glasses, hands passing through the solid tumblers, through the heavy wooden counter top, through the very arms and bodies of the drinkers around them.

And these men, every one of them, lacked the aureole of light that surrounded the others.

Then, the cocoon of light must be a property of physical bodies only. The dead, we who had lost our solidness, had lost this 'second skin' as well."

If we could see with our spirit eyes, we could look at other living people and see this same luminous glow. I believe this to be the Light of Christ, combined with the perfect spirit that God created for each of us, glowing through the physical body of every son and daughter of God.

When individuals do evil things or place evil things in their bodies, the Light of Christ leaves; they become unworthy of Christ's presence. People possessed with evil spirits won't have this radiance because their spirits have become suppressed and contain no light, only darkness. In this condition, they can't comprehend 'light'. Immortal, resurrected beings, whose physical bodies and spirit bodies have been reunited, have the brightness of the sun (as many Prophets have testified). Continuing from the book, first paragraph at the top of page 60:

"And it was obvious that these living people, the light-surrounded ones, the ones actually drinking, talking, jostling each other, could neither see the desperately thirsty disembodied beings among them, nor feel their frantic pushing to get at those glasses. It was also clear to me, watching, that the non-solid people could both see and hear each other. Furious quarrels were constantly breaking out among them over glasses that none could actually get to his lips.

I thought I had seen heavy drinking at fraternity parties in Richmond, but the way civilians and servicemen at this bar were going at it, beat everything. I watched one young sailor rise unsteadily from a stool, take two or three steps, and sag heavily to the floor. Two of his buddies stooped down and started dragging him away from the crush.

But that was not what I was looking at. I was staring in amazement as the bright cocoon around the unconscious sailor simply opened up. It parted at the very crown of his head and began peeling away from his head and his shoulders. (Mr. Ritchie witnessed the "Spirit of Christ" leaving his body giving entrance for Satan and his followers) Instantly, quicker than I'd ever seen anyone move, one of the insubstantial beings who had been standing near him at the bar was on top of him. He had been *hovering like a thirsty shadow* at the sailor's side, greedily following every swallow the young man made. *Now he seemed to spring at him like a beast of prey.*

In the next instant, to my utter mystification, the springing figure had vanished. It all happened even before the two men had dragged their unconscious load from under the feet of those at the bar. One minute I'd distinctly seen two individuals; by the time they propped the sailor against the wall, there was only one.

Twice more, as I stared, stupefied, the identical scene was repeated. A man passed out, a crack swiftly opened in the aureole round him, one of the non-solid people vanished as he hurled himself at the opening, almost as if he had scrambled inside the other man.

Was that covering of light some kind of shield, then? Was it a protection against disembodied beings like myself? Presumably this substance-less creature had once had solid bodies, as I myself had. Suppose that when they had been in these bodies they had developed a dependence on alcohol that went beyond the physical; that became mental, spiritual, even. Then when they lost that body, except when they could briefly take possession of another one, they would be cut off for all eternity from the thing they could never stop craving." (*Emphasis* added)

I should clarify some of the concepts of this last paragraph. When one dies, the attitudes, appetites, and desires that an individual has acquired during life (whether good or evil), will remain with them in the afterlife. If they use the powers of the Atonement while alive on the Earth, they can have all their sins removed through the simple process of repentance. This repentance can also take place in the spirit world up until final judgment at the end of the millennium. However, it's a hundred times more difficult when the body and the spirit are separated to repent and use the power of the Atonement. Thus the counsel: 'don't procrastinate the day of repentance'.

Those who've lived and died on this Earth, will never enter into another body other than their own; and that will happen at the time of Resurrection. The spirits that Mr. Ritchie witnessed diving into the live people were demons under the direction of Satan. They are as a *shadow* always here, hovering around every living being. Just the thought of a demon diving into me and controlling my every move, sends chills down my spine. In my life, I have been very blessed; I have never tasted any alcoholic beverage, or taken illegal drugs of any kind; only those prescribed by my doctors for various physical ailments. I was blessed to never desire to take substances into my body that could play a role in allowing me to be controlled.

In January 2014, an incident happened that made the national news. The news media report of the story, gave the impression that this type of thing is rare. The report was of a mother who killed her two children declaring that she was, 'performing an exorcism'. The photo that flashed across the screen showed the mother of the children who appeared to be wide-eyed and deranged; implying that she had killed her children in a crazed state of mental instability.

Another story aired as an investigative news program. The journalist seemed to make light of the circumstances of the story with almost a 'joking' attitude. The lead-in announced that a family was being possessed by demons; and it had been witnessed by the police officers in the home and later in the hospital. The story unfolded with the account of the officer in charge describing how he had watched as the nine-year-old son climbed up the wall backwards and did a somersault. The story revealed that the mother of the boy had four previous exorcisms performed on her before this incident. And an expert on the subject declared that the house was infested with about two hundred demons.

The way this story was handled by the media, exposes just how strongly Satan influences the media to downplay the reality of evil in the world; these types of possessions are real. It's not a joking matter; it isn't Hollywood; and most definitely isn't rare. With millions of suicides and millions of murders, there must be millions of possessed human beings roaming the Earth under the influence and power of the Devil. The questions that should have been asked by the investigative reporter are: 'What is happening in that home'? 'Was devil worshipping going on'? 'Was there an Ouija board present'?

Those who will be highly critical of my theories may ask, 'If there are millions possessed with devils or demons, why aren't there millions of horror stories like these happening every day'? The answer to this is clearly: Satan doesn't want to be on the front cover of every newspaper, or radio, and TV news cast. If he were, it would be counterproductive to his efforts to control mankind. If his true involvement were revealed to the public, people everywhere would begin to accept him as the instigator of all the evil in the world. As a result more and more of God's children would come to believe in Jesus Christ and his saving powers. By promoting these stories as 'rare', Satan and his true motives are kept in the shadows, where he can continue to slowly and quietly deceive the hearts of men, and lead them down forbidden paths to temporal and spiritual death.

Satan's greatest prize is the body of man; the very thing he can't ever have, because he never earned it. You and I accepted the Father's Plan and earned this Mortal Experience because of our desires to become like God, and receive the special gift of agency. Remember, Satan and his followers had the same agency to choose, but by choosing to follow Lucifer, gave up their opportunity.

As has been mentioned, the hosts of heaven who followed Satan are spirits. Spirit matter is very 'fine' or 'thin'. That means that numerous spirits can infest a living body; recall the two thousand (one of whom called himself Legion) that were inside the poor man of the country of the Gadarenes? If he had two thousand inside him, then anyone can have just as many. This book has been almost impossible to write because of the opposition of Satan. Whenever I've mentioned it vocally outside of my dedicated home, Satan has done everything possible to disrupt my life and the lives of my family. It's an indescribable blessing to know that Satan can't read our minds; but be cautioned: when we vocally expose him in any way, his hate will be kindled upon us and emulated by his followers' seemingly right before our eyes.

I received a phone call a couple of years ago from a person who asked me to give a fireside talk on the subject of 'Satan's Tools', to the youth in a small community. The date was in about two months, and I told him I would be happy to come and present the topic. The next day, I went out to feed my goats and noticed something very strange and impossible: my heavy, 300-foot irrigation system pipes were lifted out of the metal stakes that held them in place; and were twisted and moved into a snake-like shape. I knew immediately that Satan was not happy that I would be exposing his nature and lies to a youth group. As the date of the fireside quickly approached, I hadn't heard from the fireside organizer on any updates about the event.

As many times in the past, Satan intercepted and many of those firesides never happened. I found the organizer's number and called and confirmed the date and time. Within thirty seconds of hanging up the phone, there was noise like someone trying to break in my front door, and the whole house began to shake. I knew instantly that Satan wasn't happy with me again. I went to the earthquake site on the internet, and confirmed there hadn't been any earthquakes in my area. What a great blessing it is to hold the Holy Priesthood of God; enabling me to bless and dedicate my home to make it possible (through righteous living), for my home to be hallowed ground where Satan cannot enter.

About six months ago I had another experience while fasting and praying about the writing and contents of this book. I had made the mistake of leaving a window open in my home, where I'd knelt in prayer, pleading my case before my Heavenly Father. With the window open, Satan could listen in. As I arose from my prayer and looked out the window, I couldn't believe my eyes; my back yard was in total disarray. Starting from that window, the destruction spread outward through my yard. Two heavy swing sets were wrapped around the tree, metal lawn chairs and a heavy decorative wooden 'well' were thrown several feet from where they had been, children's playground equipment thrown completely over the raspberry patch, and lastly a large hole had been broken through the vinyl fence that separates our home from our neighbor's. There were no footprints, no fingerprints, and no wind. It just happened.

Satan can and will take possession and conceal his identity. A close friend told me this story about an ex-wife. She had been seeing a psychiatrist for counseling. After several visits, my friend received a phone call from the doctor expressing his concerns; he said, "While asking your wife several personal questions, her answers came from thirteen different voices; including some that were male voices." Stunned, my friend thanked him for the phone call as the thought entered his mind: 'I'm sleeping with the enemy'. That night he waited for his wife to go to sleep and as a Priesthood holder, laid his hands on her head and cast out the demons. He then gave her a priesthood blessing. When she awoke the next morning, he witnessed a miraculous change in her personality and demeanor; she acted like the girl he first fell in love with; she was herself again. It was short lived, lasting only two or three weeks. She quickly called the evil spirits back because her desire to live righteously, no longer existed. She only desired to turn to alcohol which allowed Satan back into her body.

This next story illustrates that Satan doesn't have any limit or bias toward those he will hold hostage. It's all up to the individual; Satan has no power, only the power which we grant him through our actions.

A co-worker named Phil, told me of a horrifyingly evil story that happened to a LDS missionary, serving in his mission. This account happened many years ago, but it still happens today. A missionary in my faith is a disciple of Jesus Christ who sacrifices two years of his personal life to testify of Jesus Christ and His Gospel anywhere in the world he is sent.

Phil's missionary companion had received a phone call from another missionary in distress. He had been violently thrown against a window by his companion; was injured and bleeding, and needed help. "He's gone crazy, please come right now before something worse happens!" The phone went dead. They ran to their car and drove in 'panic mode' to the other apartment. As they drove, they discussed what they were going to be dealing with. What's happened to this young man? Can we really help? En route Phil made a call to their Mission President (who was about 30-minutes away) and briefly explained the situation; and asked him to come as quickly as possible.

While Phil was relating the story to me, I could feel the stress and tension in his voice. When they arrived at the apartment they found the injured missionary outside holding his bleeding arm. He was totally beside himself with fear. They asked, "Where is your companion?" He responded, "Upstairs in the apartment but he's crazy, be careful." With trepidation, they approached the door and found it open. They could see the disturbed missionary standing across the room glairing directly at them as they entered. As they entered the apartment, the door slammed shut behind them. They immediately realized that evil spirits were in the apartment. The missionary had an evil appearance, his face was contorted and he looked as if he had been in a horrible fight. In a deep voice as if from the underworld, he said (pointing at a picture of Christ), "This is not my master!" Then he snatched the picture off the wall, and pointing to the wall underneath said, "This is my master!" Immediately Phil's companion raised his right arm to the square and commanded the demons to leave 'in the name of Jesus Christ our master'. The affected missionary immediately collapsed and fell to the floor as if he were dead. The Mission President arrived shortly thereafter and gave the young man a priesthood blessing and rededicated the apartment. Phil never saw the possessed missionary again. Even though traumatized, the companion missionary was sent to a new area and was able to remain in the mission field.

What was that young missionary doing to become possessed by evil spirits? He had to invite them into his life at some point, which could have been long before the mission. Had he lied to both his Bishop and Stake President? Hopefully, he repented and was able to live a righteous life from then on; making it totally impossible for Satan to enter into his body again.

I end this chapter with these chilling thoughts: If you were asked, 'who is the 'most wicked', or 'evil person' to have ever walked the Earth?" Perhaps names like Adolf Hitler, Mussolini, Stalin, Mao, or maybe even the first murderer Cain might come to mind. Would it be Judas Iscariot, who betrayed Christ? Perhaps it was one of the Caesars who had Christians killed in the Coliseum, Henry VIII, or Marie Antoinette. Could it be a leader of the Babylonian empire, who ransacked Jerusalem and took the Israelites captive? Or, it might even be the future antichrist with his 200 million-man army going against Israel at Armageddon?

You can only pick one, even though there have been many worthy of the title 'most wicked'; you be the judge of who fits the criteria. Now, imagine you are in the presence of this person, and under their command. You can feel the very darkness that surrounds him, the evil and wickedness he exudes. Could you stand up to him and challenge him on the decisions of horror, oppression, torture, and murder he commands? Or, would you wish to be far from this person, so you could be outside his influence?

Now with these feelings, and thoughts racing through your mind, ask yourself two questions, 'could this really happen'; and 'could you have a confrontation with someone or something more wicked than the most wicked person to walk this earth'? The sobering answer to both questions is 'YES'!

To address the first question, it is only a matter of time. When you die, if that evil person lived long ago, you will see him or her up close in the Spirit Prison if your works have been evil as well. If your works have been righteous, then you will look upon him from a distance because you will be in Paradise.

Now for the second and most important question; this happens every day of your mortal life. Every son and daughter of God including the most wicked, evil person at the top of your list, were born and came here with the Light of Christ; and most importantly chose Heavenly Father's plan of happiness. All others chose Satan's plan and were cast out from the presence of God down to the earth. *Satan's least wicked spirit, most timid private spirit, is more wicked and evil than any human that has or will come to this earth.* Doesn't that statement send chills down your spine and open your eyes to the reality of Satan.

Evil spirits are hovering around you and me every day of our lives. Every time we step out into this wicked world, the battle rages nonstop; twenty-four hours a day, seven days a week, and three hundred sixty-five days a year. Each demon or evil spirit only needs a few seconds to dive in; and then, direct and destroy our agency to choose correctly, 'good over evil'. This thought should scare anyone to the point of never placing themselves in the position to be possessed by Satan and his hordes!

I don't know about you, but I would rather face an enemy that I can see with my natural eyes, than the unseen enemy. It's good to know that one enemy is seen every day in the mirror. And it's even better to know the unseen enemy can only work on the natural man to accomplish his evil agenda. If we can control the natural man, then we can defeat Satan! If Satan has no weapons, giving him power or influence, we can literally crush his head. His power comes from our evil actions.

'It's okay, just take a little drink'. That comes from the voice from the unseen world. 'This life is nothing but pain; the gun will quickly take away the pain'. What? That sounds like my voice, or a familiar voice. 'You can have this out of body experience, just inject the drugs and feel the sensation'.

These evil shadows will diminish and disappear just like a shadow disappears in the noon-day sun; when we live a Christ-centered life, Satan becomes powerless. He is a mastermind at trying to ruin our progression, but he can't be in our presence when we become Christ-like in every way, because he is unworthy. Jesus Christ is the Savior of the world; He is the Master Healer, Master Teacher, and Master *Physician.*

(References: *King James Version of the Holy Bible* - 27 Chapters of the 68 total chapters of Matthew, Mark, and Luke address the casting out of evil spirits. True stories about real individuals, some stories are repeated because this doctrine is so important to know and understand. Many other stories and experiences are contained in other books of the *New Testament* by apostles like Peter, James, John, and especially the Apostle Paul in the book of Acts, Romans, Ephesians, 1 Timothy; and let's not forget the revelations of John in the book of Revelations; and the prophets and apostles in *The Book of Mormon, Doctrine Covenants*, and *Pearl of Great Price.*)

CHAPTER 13

Suicide

Once a son or daughter of God has fallen motionless to suicide, Satan, his lieutenants, and soldiers celebrate and praise each other for their success. Satan looks up to heaven and shouts:

'You see father, I won! They were miserable and had no love for thee. I took control of them, and destroyed their agency. They became mine, and they followed me. I had possession of their body at the time of their death. Revenge is so sweet. Look at this motionless body, they bowed down to me and worshiped me. Look at the chaos I have created; now, I will work on their family and friends. I am the master of this world. Father, this adds to the millions of other mortals that have fallen to me; not accepting Jesus Christ as their Savior.'

This book has been an ten-year process in writing. There were periods of pain, sorrow and striving to endure this effort. Writing this chapter was the most difficult of all, because of my own son Joseph's death to suicide. That is the reason I choose to speak so boldly; that hopefully, you'll come to know and understand how devastating, cold and heartless this action called suicide is to anyone touched by it, and to mankind as a whole. Suicide is not of our Heavenly Father or his Son Jesus Christ; but was solely instituted by the Evil One, the Father of Lies.

Suicide is a very serious sin. The Lord tells us in scripture that murder, or the 'shedding of innocent blood', isn't forgivable by God in this life. I'll add that the taking of one's free agency also rises to that same level, and that is Satan's specialty. Several years ago I knew of a person who had committed suicide, and prior to their death, hadn't been to the LDS Temple to receive what is known as their 'temple blessings'. Under 'normal' circumstances when a person dies without having received their temple blessings, their family is allowed to do their temple work by proxy in one year. At that time, and in that particular case of suicide, it wasn't allowed. The Church policy has since changed, and now the work can be done one year after their suicide. This allows the earthly work of Temple ordinances to be conducted; and leaves the judgment of the correctness of the process to the 'True Judge in Israel', the Lord Jesus Christ. Only He knows the status of an individual's progression while on Earth; and when they are in the Spirit World. Obviously as mortals, we don't have all the answers, and must exercise faith until we meet the Savior face-to-face. That being said, suicide remains a sin that cannot be dismissed and remains very close to the sin of murder.

From the Ten Commandments given to Moses in the Old Testament, we learn how God feels about the sin of killing (taking one's own life or that of another):

Thou shalt have no other gods before me. (Exodus 20:3)

Thou shalt not make unto thee any graven image, or any likeness of anything that is in heaven, or that is in the earth beneath, or that is in the water under the earth:

Thou shalt not bow down thyself to them, nor serve them: for I the Lord thy God am a jealous God, visiting the iniquity of the fathers upon the children unto the third and fourth generation of them that hate me; (Exodus 20: 4-5)

Thou shalt not take the name of the Lord thy God in vain; for the Lord will not hold him guiltless that taketh his name in vain. (Exodus 20:7)

Thou shalt not kill. (Exodus 20:13)

The first three Commandments clearly define the role of God, and what our relationship with Him should be. It's stated very clearly that no person or thing should be placed above God. Why was it important for God to set this standard at the outset? Whenever man thinks, acts, or tries to replace God with themselves or another being or object, they are in jeopardy of the wrath of God. Breaking one of the first three Commandments is a serious, salvation threatening, action that God commanded us against. Let's consider five examples of human actions where man attempts to usurp God and chooses to control aspects of life which only belong to God:

1.   Murder. We were put on the Earth to gain a body, gain experience and knowledge. This is a probationary state to prove ourselves worthy to return to God, our father in heaven. It's for God alone to know and choose the day appointed for the death of every living soul. The only exceptions to this rule are in cases of self-defense, defense of others, and in times of war (in defense of the God-given right of freedom from tyranny).

2.   Abortion. At conception life is created. The developing fetus is the sacred vessel of the spirit that enters into that body. As in the case of Murder, it's for God alone to give life and take life (to determine when mortal life comes to an end). The exceptions to this are rare, and can be affected by the health of the mother or circumstances surrounding conception that resulted from rape or incest. In any case, application of an exception requires fervent prayer to Heavenly Father in making these difficult decisions.

3.   Suicide. The shedding of innocent blood (even if it's self-inflicted), is again to God alone to judge. There may be a fine line of distinction drawn between suicide and murder; the common thought is that we 'belong to ourselves' and have the right to make such a decision. The truth is, we belong to God, and only He has the right to make life and death decisions; and determines the resulting judgment. Only God knows the content and state of our hearts and minds in the extremity of our earthly existence. In the early chapters of this book, I talked of two suicides in my family (Uncle Dean and my son Joseph). I am confident that Heavenly Father will take the circumstances of their deaths into consideration in His infinite wisdom and perfect judgment.

4. Transsexual operations. The willing alteration of the physical body we were given at birth is a mutilation of one of God's creations. The correct gender spirit (that was created by God) is always placed in the correct gender fetus. God is perfect and would never send a female spirit to be housed in a male body or vice versa. To change the form or function of this perfect union of spirit and body could be considered a blasphemy before God. There are rare occasions, where the child is born with both male and female sex organs. This 'birth defect' as with other physical abnormalities will usually need to be repaired surgically. Parents in this situation should prayerfully approach Heavenly Father in

mighty prayer and fasting to decide which spirit (male or female) is housed in this infant body. DNA must be considered as the ultimate evidence of correct gender assignment.

5. Judging others unto salvation. We are saved by grace only after all that we can do in this life and by and through the name of Jesus Christ. The Lord Jesus Christ will be our final judge for all eternity. Each of us only has the right to judge or choose for ourselves; right from wrong, and judge good from evil; that's called agency. No human has the right to take away another's agency.

These five examples are very serious sins in the eyes of God. Each of us must work out our own salvation. Accordingly, each situation we face, presents unique conditions and challenges. Above all we must, think, ponder, and pray to our Heavenly Father for guidance in every significant life decision; to make the correct choice. Answers will come from our loving Heavenly Father; these will be tailored specifically for us. Asking, 'what would the Savior do' is a good thought process; but never assume you know the Mind of God. Always go to Him in prayer, and receive His guidance that is confirmed by the Spirit of the Holy Ghost.

There is a false concept in the world today known as 'pre-planned repentance'. It's basically a revival of 'eat, drink, and be merry for tomorrow we die'; the thinking is the same: I can do these things and repent tomorrow; and everything will be square between me and God. There is a law of physics that illustrates reality: 'for every action, there is an equal but opposite reaction'. The same concept can be said in a more common way, 'if you pick up one end of a stick, you automatically pick up the other end'. You cannot plan your suicide and have it justified in the eyes of God because you were 'not yourself' or 'out of your mind' with alcohol and/or drugs, and think now I'm justified in pulling the trigger. Don't walk the tight rope between murder and suicide, it's not worth it. Suicide has never been the solution to the problems or challenges of life. The Lord promises no matter what our circumstance, or trial, or test, he will never allow anything to come before us that we are not capable of overcoming *while here on Earth*. What a great blessing and promise this is. The conditions that exist now were the same at the time when Adam and Eve were cast out of the Garden of the Eden. We are all mortal and must contend and battle with Satan and the one-third of the hosts of heaven. Yet we have the power to conquer Satan.

When Satan and his followers left the pre-existence there was no veil placed over their eyes like it was for us. He wants possession of all mortals, and he knows who the valiant and faithful spirits are; they are those upon whom he works overtime to destroy. Once he possesses one of God's children, he will do everything in his power to destroy the very soul of that person. I believe he evilly wrings his hands in gleeful anticipation when we speak of suicidal thoughts; and he rejoices in every suicide that is carried out.

When someone becomes possessed with an evil spirit, it's only a matter of time before others will try to enter them also. Once evil has taken possession of a person's body, there are only two methods by which they can be expelled:

1. A righteous Priesthood holder (after much fasting, prayer and faith) raises their right arm to the square, and uses these words: "Satan I command you to come out of this person in the name of Jesus Christ my Master"; then, by the laying on of hands, gives that person a Priesthood Blessing.

2. Death of the person. Either way, once the evil spirits are removed, they will seek to enter into someone else.

I have a dear friend who witnessed the releasing of demon spirits from a person who committed suicide. Susan is originally from Sweden, where she spent her youth. Her father was an angry, mean, and very abusive man when she was young. He was especially abusive to her mother who was kind and loving; totally the opposite of her father. Susan and her brother were abused both verbally, and physically. As a child, she didn't understand why he was abusive, and couldn't accept that someone could be that hateful and mean; always shouting bad language and cursing God.

Then the unthinkable happened, Susan's father was standing at the top of the stairs holding a shotgun. She and her little brother were at the bottom of the stairs looking up. Before the children could understand what was happening, he pointed the shotgun to his face and pulled the trigger. Susan recounts what she experienced:

"Brother and I stood in shock at the sight of our dad's face being destroyed, as he instantly fell dead before our eyes. It was a terrible scene that forever haunts our minds. Suddenly, there was total chaos, as if a tornado wind went through the house. Books were thrown from the bookcase, light fixtures were shaking, things were flying off the shelves and chairs were overturned. We couldn't see the evil spirits leave him, but we witnessed instantly what they did to the house the moment the trigger was pulled. Even though our dad never showed love to us, we still loved him."

When demons are inside a person, there are changes that should be very noticeable by the loved ones and friends around them. Please recognize, and don't ignore, the warning signs. Ask questions, get out of your comfort zone, and help their perfect spirit that's crying out for help. They may do crazy things, insane acts, or verbal assault, violence, or hate. They may eventually get to the point that they stop loving themselves and their own life. The demon(s) never stop telling them they are worthless, that their body is nothing but pain and suffering. 'Get rid of it! 'Why don't you just give up and kill yourself'? This will go on and on, until the person is without feeling. To them, the Light of Christ seems to fade to darkness; and the love of God becomes faint, and thoughts of death turn into the reality of suicide. Sometimes the person 'tests the waters' with suicide attempts, but once that knife is in their grip, the rope is around their neck, the pills in their hand, or their finger on the trigger; the possibility of death is real. Always remember, whether you are a victim of these thoughts, or a family member or friend: YOU have the power to crush Satan's head, he only has the power to bruise your heel. The power he has is only what you allow him to have; period.

Throughout these chapters, you've read instruction and examples of how evil can be eliminated. This is such important material, that I feel compelled to repeat it at other points in the discussion. Please understand that this information can save you, or your loved ones, from being possessed by Satan and his evil spirits.

Again, if you're a woman, an innocent child, or man who doesn't hold the Priesthood of God, you CAN act. Using the power of the name of Jesus Christ, endowed to every man, woman, and child through the Light of Christ, you can stop evil and prevent evil actions of those possessed. This is how to proceed: Having faith in the Lord Jesus Christ, raise your right arm to the square, and say "I command you to leave in the name of Jesus Christ my Master." By the power of Jesus' name, those persons have to leave. Please note that you can't cast the demons out of their bodies because you don't have the Authority from God (through Priesthood) to do such; but when the Son of God's name is announced, they have to obey.

Satan simply waits patiently for the window of opportunity to 'leap' into a body. All it takes is one too many alcoholic drinks, or one too many pills. It doesn't matter if the substance is legal or illegal; anything which can cause you to lose control, or relinquish your agency, can be just what Satan needs. Seeking that high or endorphin rush, whether it is from a substance like drugs; or visual stimulation such as with pornography; if it causes you to lose control and become addicted; it can take over your life. Building the courage and strength of character to say no, ultimately is easier than trying to be cured of an addiction. 'Avoid the very appearance of evil' is good advice when it comes to the strength to be in control of the natural man at all times.

I've spent twenty-five summers coaching Little League baseball in the various communities in which I've lived. I've become very attached to every one of the young boys and young girls who've played for me. It's as if (for me and the assistant coaches) they become one of our kids; and their families become part of our family. One day I received a phone call from one of my former assistant coaches. As we began to speak, I could tell he was emotional and sobbing softly. He told me that one of his best players had just committed suicide, and how devastating it was on the boy's family, to him as his former coach, and to the whole community. I could literally feel through the phone lines the great depths of grief he felt for his best friend's boy. This is a story I must tell; but please understand that it's very personal to me. Suicide affects so many; not just dad and mom, brother and sister; it affects the extended family, friends, classmates, and whole communities.

Ryan was at the top of his junior high school class; he was the student body president, and loved by his peers. He was on the school baseball team, had a beautiful girlfriend, and it seemed everything was going his way; except he was struggling with one of his classes. On this particular day as he arrives home from school, his mother (in an effort to help) asked him about his homework, and whether he had completed the assignments and the necessary makeup work, to be able to pass the challenging class. His response was, "Mother, leave me alone!"

His mom told Ryan that she had to leave to do some grocery shopping, and would be back soon; his father was still at work, and his sisters were gone to their friends for the evening. Ryan was home all alone. When his mother returned, Ryan's room was tossed all around, clothing and things in his closet, and mattresses off the bed; everything was thrown all over the room, as if somebody was looking for something. There was no sign of Ryan, and no messages or note indicating that he had gone out. As his dad arrived from work, he called our mutual friend (the one who had called me) to come over and help find his son. A search by the local community began. It was soon dusk, and still no sign of Ryan. As light began to fade to darkness, Ryan's father found his body in a ditch about two hundred yards behind their home. He had shot himself in the chest with a 12 gauge shot gun.

His dad collapsed to the ground with grief, and when he gained his composure and strength, picked up Ryan's body and carried him back home. His mother was beside herself with grief, and blamed herself for pressuring Ryan earlier that afternoon. A few days later, Cassie and I attended the viewing and could see the pain of their loss, in the eyes of each family member. When I embraced Ryan's dad he didn't want to let go of me. The Spirit told me at that moment, 'this father won't recover easily from his heartache and anguish'. His emotions had overcome him, and in the months ahead, it would become more than he could bear. During our time there, I tried to talk to everyone in the immediate family, and group of friends. I asked them to keep me informed, and pleaded with them to 'stay close' and 'support' the family; and to please 'sacrifice their time' to be with Ryan's dad and mom.

With a suicide, emotions and feelings are never resolved with the end of the funeral, and the burial; the family that's left behind, continues to grieve and suffer with unanswered questions. About a year later, I learned that Ryan's dad was in a coma, and by all accounts, it was felt that it was from a 'broken heart'. He couldn't get over losing his son, in that way. Ryan had been the only son, his dad's best friend, and hunting partner. His body was run down from his emotional stress, and he contracted a brain infection. The doctors said he was going to die if he didn't respond soon. They called me to request a Priesthood blessing. He needed it that night, but I had just started a new job, and couldn't make it to Salt Lake in time. Consequently, his younger brother gave him the blessing. Because of the faith of those around him, a miracle happened, and the healing Power of God was manifest.

He awoke from the coma, almost before his brother had said, 'Amen'. As was later related to me, some of the words of the blessing were, "You will recover; you will realize in your mind and your heart that Ryan is in a better place and he's progressing." But the most revealing words in that Priesthood Blessing were, "Ryan wants you to know that his mom and his sisters need you more staying with them, than coming to me." Ryan's dad had an amazing experience while comatose that took him to the other side of the veil. He said he was walking down a beautiful pathway towards an extremely bright light. There, in the distance stood his son, Ryan. Ryan was whole and he had a beautiful glow around him. He beckoned to his dad, saying almost the same words that were in the Priesthood blessing, "Mom and my sisters need you more than I do." Both pronouncements were spoken at nearly the same time, on both sides of the veil.

A few years ago my neighbor Bill stood at the podium in a Sacrament Meeting and spoke of an incredible experience he had with his friend Jake when they were seniors in high school. Jake called and asked if Bill would come get him so they could go for a ride. He could tell something was wrong, because of the tone of Jake's voice. Jake had been going through the stages of loss and depression in recent months following a breakup with his girlfriend. As Bill arrived to pick up Jake, little did he know how in the next hour, his life would be changed forever. As they started to drive, Jake expressed the desire to get on the freeway. Bill entered the interstate highway and brought his car up to speed. At this point, Jake looked directly at Bill and said, "I'm going to open my door and jump out, if you try to stop me or stop the car, I'll get out and walk in front of the next car coming down the road."

Jake was dead serious, and Bill knew it. He was going to commit suicide with the help of his best friend. Just imagine yourself in Bill's situation; if Jake carried out his threat, he could be accused of murder! What would he tell Jake's parents, let alone the police? How could he ever erase this horrible scene from his mind? Bill knew that Jake's words would haunt his mind forever; and he would spend many sleepless nights repeating the scene over and over, and asking himself, 'what should I have done to stop my best friend from doing the unthinkable'?

As Bill pondered these thoughts, his level of stress multiplied; but then an overwhelming feeling of peace came over him. He felt the love of God, for him and for Jake. He came to know through the Spirit of the Holy Ghost that it wasn't Jake's appointed day to die. Bill started to sing Church hymns and Primary children's songs; and expressing his love for Jake, and Heavenly Father's love for him. Jake started to cry, and kept repeating, "I'm worthless, I'm no good to anyone." Bill continued to sing of the Savior Jesus Christ; song after song. He told Jake, 'You have a great mission to do in this life. What will your family do without you? Think of your mother who brought you into this world, risking her own life to give you yours; she loved you more than she loved herself. Your brothers and sister would be so heartbroken. Stay with me Jake the only one who wants you to jump from this vehicle is Satan. Don't let him win, he's the loser'. Bill basically commanded through song and unconditional love for his Savior, the evil to leave that car. In that hour, he saved Jake's life.

How many Jakes are out there? How many sons and daughters of God have given up hope? As the scriptures predict, 'men's hearts shall fail them in the last days'; and 'the love of God will wax cold'. Satan through his deceptive voices are continually telling the natural man within each of us that this body is nothing but pain, sorrow, and something to discard. One of his deceitful tactics is to disguise himself with your voice, or another familiar voice.

Once I was having a serious conversation with a coworker. He told me about an experience that his mother had. This was at a time when she had four children under the age of nine, and with the pressures of caring for the children, taking care of the home, with meals, and laundry, and cleaning; she was becoming discouraged and frustrated with life. It was about nine o'clock in the evening and his father was out working in the barn. His mother was standing at the kitchen sink tidying up from supper. As she looked out the kitchen window, she could see herself reflected in the glass as if looking into a mirror. Then, a voice out of nowhere said, "It isn't worth it, there's too much work and pain. Just end your life now." What bothered her most was it was the sound of the familiar voice, as if she was talking to herself. She simply left it at that; and being a righteous woman, never gave up hope and carried on in faith. She knew full well that she had a Savior who went through every pain and sorrow that any of us would ever go through in the garden of Gethsemane, and on the cross at Calvary. She felt she had no right to complain; her responsibility was to be faithful and endure to the end.

Over the past several years I've collected statistics on suicide from newspapers, magazines, television news, and investigative reporting programs on TV. From Time magazine dated July 23, 2012, the cover reads: 'ONE A DAY', then in lower case "Every day, one U.S. soldier commits suicide. Why the military can't defeat its most insidious enemy." In the background is a soldier standing at attention and blowing a bugle. I turned to the cover story that started on page 22. There was a young military wife carrying some of her late husband's belongings. On her face was an expression of defeat; hope for the future was dashed, life had lost its meaning, as the love of her life had taken his own life. There was story after story of military officers, husbands and fathers; individuals who had bright futures; all gone. The stories broke my heart. That tragic Sunday morning March 5, 2006 when I lost my son to suicide, forever haunts my memory. Oh how much I would give to hug and embrace my son again.

Life is so valuable and priceless, yet so fragile and irreplaceable. As I wrote this book, I prayed that somehow, some way, I could provide words of counsel and instruction on how suicide can be prevented by knowing the true enemy, and understanding his weapons of war. In the above-referenced article, the Secretary of Defense, Leon Panetta is quoted concerning this major problem of suicide:

"The U.S. military seldom meets an enemy it can't target, can't crush, can't put a fence around or drive a tank across. It has not been able to defeat or contain the epidemic of suicides among its troops, even as the wars wind down, the evidence mounts that the problem has become dire."

The true instigator of this epidemic is the unseen enemy; Satan and his 30 billion followers. Satan knows he's going to lose the war in the end, but he is winning the battles against the natural man. His convincing powers are taking over people by the millions. Suicide never only affects the 'one'; the article goes on to say that 95 % of the cases are men, and the most are married. Satan applauds every suicide because he knows it has a devastating effect on the family unit; and sometimes the family never recovers. Another quote from the Pentagon:

"No program, outreach, or initiative has worked against the surge in Army suicides. No one knows why nothing works. The Pentagon allocates about $2 billion, nearly 4% of its $53 billion annual medical bill – to mental health."

I can't say it enough, 'IT'S NOT ALWAYS A MENTAL ILLNESS'. If the military were doing the right things to combat this unseen enemy, then this epidemic *would* turn around. The numbers would be going down instead of skyrocketing. I just read the other day the number of suicides in the military has multiplied from one, to twenty-two a day. We are talking about the greatest military in the world, where more are dying from self-inflicted wounds, than are from the bullets and bombs of the enemy forces. I believe with the power of the Priesthood of God, all things in righteousness can come to pass. If they could only realize there is HOPE in every situation that we will ever encounter in this life. God himself said, 'I will never let you go through anything that you personally can't handle'. With his help, humbly ask in prayer, acknowledge his hand in all things, and give thanks to him for our blessings.

On average, there are over a million suicides per year. Sons and daughters of God simply are not enduring to the end; they're giving up hope. Our Heavenly Father just wants us to call upon his help through his only begotten son Jesus Christ. When his name is pronounced the evil spirits have to leave. They are not worthy to be present even when Jesus Christ's name is mentioned.

Kim Ruocco the director of TAPS (Tragedy Assistance Program for Survivors), and whose husband committed suicide, said this:

"These were highly valued, well-educated officers with families, with futures, with few visible wounds or scars. Whatever one imagines might be driving the military suicide rate, it defies easy explanation."

Please listen: Satan can be stopped; he is only a spirit who wants to possess your sacred and unique mortal body; that you alone have earned. It's up to each one of us to help and love each other enough to keep our agency intact and suppress the evil one.

The obituaries describe too many suicides, and the numbers are increasing at an alarming rate, that has become almost daily. We see headlines such as, 'too many Utahns are killing themselves', 'What can you do?' 'Suicides slam our Community', 'Suicides skyrocket' and 'Suicide: A Local Concern'. One of the biggest problems we humans have is we are proud. In fact we are so proud that we hate to burden someone else with our problems. When we're asked, 'do you need any help'; we say, "I'm great; I can handle anything"; in reality this is far from the truth.

Satan will never stop prodding, and tormenting mankind to hurt themselves or others around them physically, mentally, and morally in any way possible; to destroy the sons and daughters of God. I'm so grateful for the Light of Christ that is given to every child born to this Earth. It is through this Spirit that all may know 'good from evil'. I testify that the gift of the Holy Ghost can be our constant companion at all times and in all places; otherwise, I could not have survived the tests of my life.

If we could only see with our spiritual eyes and hear with our spiritual ears, we could all recognize these truths. We could look upon others and know instantly if the adversary has taken control of them. Their countenance would not glow, and darkness would surround them. There have been many people that have died for just a few minutes and then came back to life. They describe things on the other side of the veil that is beyond our knowledge and understanding. They are allowed for a few moments to see with their spiritual eyes. As I've mentioned, the spirit world is all around us. We can't see those spirits, but if we could, we would see how their actions while here on Earth, have dictated the consequences of their actions, when now in their post-mortal state. For example, when someone who has smoked cigarettes for 20 years dies; they take with them the urges and desires they had during their life; the urges and desires don't die. In the spirit world, cigarettes do not exist, so those who have smoked will constantly be seeking relief from those desires. They'll keep putting their hand to their mouth to take a puff. They'll wander around with mortals constantly grasping at their cigarettes, tormented because they can't touch them.

Below I include another excerpt from the book *Return from Tomorrow.* Here I quote from Pages 58 and 59:

"In one house a younger man followed an older one from room to room. "I'm sorry, PA!" he kept saying. "I didn't know what it would do Mama!" I didn't understand.

But though I could hear him clearly, it was obvious that the man he was speaking to could not. The old man was carrying a tray into a room where an elderly woman sat in bed. "I'm sorry Pa," the younger man said again. "I'm sorry, Mama." Endlessly, over and over, to ears that could not hear.

In bafflement I turned to the Brightness beside me. But though I felt his compassion flow like a torrent into the room before us, no understanding lighted my mind. Several times we paused before similar scenes: A boy trailing a teenage girl through the corridors of a school. "I'm sorry Nancy!" and, a middle- age woman begging a grey-haired man to forgive her.

"What are they so sorry for, Jesus?" I pleaded. "Why do they keep talking to people who can't hear them?" Then from the Light beside me came the thought: *They are suicides, chained to every consequence of their act.* The idea stunned me, yet I knew it came from Him, not me, for I saw no more scenes like these, as though the truth He was teaching had been learned." (*Emphasis* added)

I think of my own son Joseph; I believe he's around every member of our family trying to tell each one of us: "I'm so sorry", "Please forgive me." I believe he'll be required to do this until we have passed this life, and are on that side of the veil to frankly forgive him; Or, until our Heavenly Father witnesses that we have developed Godly forgiveness for Joseph, I believe at that point, he will stop coming to us and asking for forgiveness. If we allow such a tragedy to overcome us to the point of failing health or developing the desire for death, we stop our progression, and we stop their progression as well. We need to go on with life, and so does our loved one. Just like Ryan's father in the story above, he became despondent to the point of ill health, which nearly killed him. When he had the experience in the spirit with his son, he realized it was time to let go of Ryan and concentrate on life and living. We'll never forget them, but we must let them go, for their good and ours.

My son's death has made me work harder in faith and righteousness, so I can be with him again and embrace him in love for all eternity. A few months ago I witnessed a miracle with my son Joseph. I came home from church one Sunday afternoon and went to my room to change clothes. I looked at his picture on my dresser, and without glasses I could look right into his beautiful blue eyes and I could see the Savior's image in his countenance. The spirit bore witness to me that Joseph's progression is amazing after these eight years in the spirit world.

With over one million suicides each year in our world today; think of all those spirits trying to do the same things in the spirit world, which Mr. Ritchie witnessed during his near death experience. Forced to come back to their loved ones, and endlessly beg their forgiveness; can you feel their pain? Suicide is never the answer to any of life's challenges; it doesn't solve anything. Life is so precious, and such a priceless gift from the loving God who created us. He is the Father of our spirits; we are created in his image, and have the ability to become as He is for all eternity. His power is pure love. He gives us a lifetime to repent. He has appointed the time and date of our death; He is the judge of when life should come to an end. Don't try to take the place of God in that decision. Suicide is Satan's way to destroy agency, the sacred gift given each of us.

If the thought ever enters your mind of destroying your life by committing suicide, please consider my words, the words of a father with a broken heart that can never be repaired, because Satan convinced my son to end his life. Picture the scene before your eyes; Joseph with the barrel of a rifle in his mouth. The trigger is pulled, and the barrel now lies on his lifeless chest; the empty silence. I could not bear the pain as I saw my boy on the floor before me. I passed out trying to go up the stairs. My denial, "That's not my son, it's someone else." How I made the '911' call, heaven only knows? I made my way to the bedroom, and fell face down on my bed; I felt so hopeless, and my strength was gone. Lee's father (Lilly's father-in-law) gave me a Priesthood blessing, and Rick and Grant still had to literally carry me from our home, to the neighbors across the street. My lack of strength persisted, I didn't have enough strength to lift my face from my lap; I was completely defeated. I only wanted to be with my son; life was no longer important. For hours and days I wanted to go 'home' and be with my dead son. Suicide never entered my mind, but thoughts of being a worthless father did. What could I have done to save him? Did I help him enough? Is this my fault? I pray for the day when I may hug and embrace my Joseph again. He knows of my love for him.

At the gravesite, my four year old granddaughter saw Joseph and Uncle Dean standing at my side. Joseph was begging to stay, and Uncle Dean was motioning to Joseph that it was time to go. Joseph had already realized the pain he had caused. He was asking for forgiveness from his broken hearted father. I did feel his presence but wasn't worthy to see him. We were all touched when she told of this experience.

If I could prevent or stop any suicide I would. I would go to the ends of the Earth to talk, give blessings, and bear testimony that God lives and knows each one of us personally. No matter what, he loves us unconditionally. Keep hope alive, believe in Jesus Christ, and have faith in his Eternal Atonement which heals all wounds.

(References: *King James Version of the Holy Bible, Book of Mormon, Time Magazine* July 2011, and *Return from Tomorrow*)

CHAPTER 14

Homosexuality

What a controversial subject to address in today's world! This subject *seems* divisive only because those individuals involved in this behavior, immediately go on the *defensive* when the subject is broached. It seems that if you don't automatically support their point of view, you are immediately labeled an enemy. Since the point of view I present here is from God's word and perspective (as contained in the sacred scriptures), I pray that this chapter will be read with an open mind; before I am regarded as hateful, condemning, or judgmental. I understand that those who identify themselves as homosexual may also be 'believers'; my hope is that these persons might be able to recognize God's truth, and not dismiss this information at first glance as prejudicial.

I have unconditional love for every son and daughter of God; just as I know Heavenly Father has love for each of His children. We are all created with the ability to be attracted to many different people. Some may find that they experience a stronger attraction to those of the same gender. That *attraction of itself* is not a problem in God's plan. Where it becomes wrong in the eyes of God, is when that attraction is *acted upon* and crosses a line into physical contact. Once a person takes the step to homosexual *activity*, is when Satan has the opportunity to enter into a person; and begin to influence them into further involvement in a homosexual lifestyle. This aberration of God's perfect Plan, doesn't come from the individual's perfect spirit, or because society has come to accept it as 'normal'. It is clear that the influence for this 'natural man' behavior comes from 'the imposter', 'the great liar' and his hosts; who constantly work to make that which is *natural between a man and a woman*, SEEM natural between two of the same gender. The person entrenched in this behavior is not the guilty party in this activity; it is the spirits of Satan who have entered within them. I believe that no matter the sin, inside each of God's children is the desire to return to a state of purity before God. Our innate Light of Christ (or conscience) deep inside our souls, desires to escape from the state of sin into which we have fallen. I believe we never forget the desire, borne deep in our spiritual roots, to become like God.

I am witness to the truth that when homosexuals have the evil spirits cast out of them, they change back to their true identity almost instantly. To me, this proves the 'True Innocence' of those involved.

The first story I'll relate, involves Tracy, Joseph's fiancée. Early in the book I described how she had a challenge with same gender attraction. Joseph became aware of her interest in women at the drinking party they attended the night before his suicide. I believe that at this stage in their relationship, they each had become possessed with many evil spirits. These were able to enter into their bodies from alcohol use, and other violations of God's guidelines for happiness such as premarital sex. Satan was working overtime to destroy their relationship, eventually tempting her with same sex-attraction.

At the party, Tracy and Joseph had a fight where she yelled, 'I would rather have sex with any woman than with you'! Then she called off their engagement. This downward spiral of emotion ultimately culminated in Joseph's suicide the next morning as I described in Chapter Three.

Of all the circumstances surrounding Joseph's suicide, I believe the greatest contributor was Tracy's inclination toward homosexual behavior. That being said, I can also bear testimony of Tracy's *true innocence*; it was evil spirits that convinced her to engage in homosexual behavior. It simply wasn't her natural woman or her spirit body; it was the impostors that had taken control of her mortal body.

Shortly after the funeral, we learned that Tracy had become pregnant four days before Joseph's death. Eventually, I met with her step-father and asked him to cast the evil spirits from her; he agreed, and the miracle happened instantly. Tracy's original identity and spiritual beauty was restored; she was once again 'herself'. Her family and ours witnessed the inner beauty return; she had a glow in her countenance. We were able to see with the same eyes that Joseph had when they first met. He had seen her individual worth and divine potential. My family embraced her as one of our own. She was her normal self through the entire pregnancy and birth of our grandson (who, by-the-way looks just like his father). Eventually, feeling defeated from the pressures of single parenthood, and many people not accepting the changes she was trying to make in her life; Tracy started doing things that allowed Satan to reenter into her life. She started to drink again and associate with others who did not care about the standards of true happiness. She's now a professed lesbian and her life isn't what it could have been.

Please accept my special witness that when someone engages in homosexual behavior, they do it under the direction of Satan; because he has taken possession of their body. The cure is casting out the evil ones, and then giving the person a Priesthood Blessing. This story, and others that I'll share later in this chapter, will further show that I love those who have the affliction of evil spirits that have driven them to sin.

I know the family unit is the greatest organization in the world. If anyone had a right to hate, seek revenge, demand justice and want nothing to do with a person such as Tracy, it would be me and my family. Yet only one week after Joseph's death, we embraced her and showed unconditional love for her. This should be proof that I don't have hate for anyone; whatever a person's worldly challenge. I know that Satan is the culprit, not the perfect spirit within each of us.

Satan doesn't have a body; he wants us to hate ours. He doesn't want us to have the joy of a spouse of the opposite sex – nor a family. His plan is a plan of *imitation*. Perverse sexual sins such as (homosexual behavior) are grievous, and a great abomination in the eyes of God. Every child born to the Earth is perfect; each created in the image of a loving Heavenly Father. Each child can become like Him through the gift of agency. Agency is God's gift that makes it possible to choose the good from evil; there is only one or the other; either we serve God, or the Devil. Under the influence of Satan our actions can definitely be evil, if we choose to follow him. It's wonderful to know that every child is born with the Light of Christ (the Spirit of Christ), giving them the power to discern right from wrong.

(Note: All scriptural references and scriptural footnotes in this and other Chapters, are sited from the LDS Edition of the *King James Version of the Holy Bible*)

In the New Testament book of Romans, the Apostle Paul describes the feelings of God on the subject of homosexuality:

"Wherefore God also *gave*[a] them up to *uncleanness*[b] through the lusts of their own hearts, to dishonor their own bodies between themselves:

For this cause God *gave*[c] them up unto *vile*[d] *affection*[e]: for even their *women* did change the natural use into that which is against nature:

And likewise also the men, leaving the natural use of the woman, burned in their *lust*[f] one toward another; men with men *(woman with woman*[g]*)* working that which is unseemly, and receiving in themselves that recompense of their error which was meet." (Romans 1:24, 26-27 – *emphasis and explanation added*)

a. Acts 7:42
b. See Topical Guide (TG): Uncleanness
c. Greek (GR) Translation: abandoned, delivered
d. GR: sufferings, passions of dishonor. See also 2 Tim. 3:3
e. Affections see also Judges 19:22
f. TG: woman
g. Added by author

According to Paul, it's very clear how God feels about homosexuality. There are also many scriptures going back to the beginning of time where God speaks of his divine counsel on homosexuality. Homosexual behavior is not natural, and therefore a great abomination and grievous sin in the sight of God. There are scriptures that use the word abomination in place of homosexuality.

In Chapter Eighteen of the Old Testament book of Leviticus, God speaks about the multitude of sex perversions that Satan has instilled in the hearts of men. Here's a partial list: incest, homosexuality, sodomy, infidelity, fornication, adultery, and every other sexual perversion. By Satan's deception, he convinces the people of the Earth to partake of these things to specifically destroy their souls.

Of course nobody instantly becomes someone who is involved or commits these acts. Satan works on the natural man continuously to get us to gradually give in to unnatural acts for pleasure and carnal gratification. Little by little, the natural man takes over and controls our every move. It doesn't take a lot of disobedience to God's laws to provide that window of opportunity for Satan to enter in and take possession, leading to permanent darkness and devastating consequences.

For to be *carnally*[a] minded is *death*[b]; but to be *spiritually*[c] minded is life and peace. *(The word death in this verse refers to spiritual death or the second death*[d]*)*

Because the *carnal*[e] mind is *enmity*[f] against God: for it is not subject to the law of God, neither indeed can be. (Romans 8:6-7 – *emphasis and explanation added*)

a. TG: Carnal Mind; Chastity; Man, Natural, Not Spiritually Reborn
b. TG: Death; Death, Spiritual, First
c. TG: Spiritually
d. Added by author
e. TG: Fall of Man
f. TG: Opposition

The word *enmity* (opposition or opposite) describes Satan or the devil. He is an enemy to God, and if an enemy to God, an enemy to man. By giving in to carnal desires, or perverting the procreative powers in unnatural sexual acts, we mock God and His laws. Freely succumbing to the appetites of the flesh (or natural man) will cause the Spirit of the Lord to withdraw from us. Always remember: no unclean person can dwell in the presence of God; and Satan is literally our common enemy in all things pertaining to the salvation of our souls.

When people read or hear talked about weakness or sin in which they are involved, the first reaction is defensive. The second reaction is to justify the false bill of goods Satan has sold them that says: 'it's ok to sin, it doesn't matter, I'm still a good person; if I want to change, and I can always repent later. I only do it once in a while, it's not hurting anyone'; or any of the other lies they've come to believe as truth.

Homosexual behavior is not a solo activity. It affects immediate and extended families; it affects the workplace, the church, the neighborhood, and even communities; it's most insidious trait is that it takes God out of the life of the follower. It's literally possible to see its effects on the appearance of the person involved; whether men or women, their very image changes. Their mannerisms, voice and body movements change. The Light of Christ becomes diminished, and darkness overshadows them as their true identity becomes disguised and distorted. The reason for this is: they now serve a new master, Satan.

What I've observed of same gender 'couples' reinforces Satan's involvement in these two specific ways:

1. There is always one that takes the masculine role; and the other the feminine role. This is because God's plan (which is natural law) intends mates to be male and female. In these relationships Satan attempts to provide a counterfeit to the man-woman relationship, to make it an artificial-couple. You'll note that this goes so far as

for the voice and mannerisms to change to the opposite gender. This happens out of a conscious willingness to play the proper role; as much as it is the evil spirits that have taken up residency in their body. This is evidence the evil one, now has control of this person's voice. For those who have known them, it's as if someone else speaking through that person.

2. Satan's involvement causes their demeanor to change. Friends and family might notice extreme mood changes; expressions of love for family diminish; anger becomes more prevalent as a dominant character trait; or they appear to be someone else and don't act like themselves. Friends and loved ones soon begin to wonder: 'what happened to my brother (sister, father, or mother)'?

As family and friends, when you see these kinds of changes that may even include pushing loved ones away, and avoiding family and friends; pay attention, these are warning signs. These are red flags of concern that they are in a dangerous place. With the help of Satan, they are sliding into a deep, dark pit of bondage from which they won't possibly be able to escape, without your loving intervention.

The spirit of God, the light of Christ which is housed in their perfect and immortal spirit, is being controlled or pushed aside by Satan, and often, they can't plead for help. Please, we all must recognize these signs, and help them before it's too late. Don't fall into the *politically correct* or *societal norm* trap and say, 'it's okay, everyone's doing it' and support them in their homosexual behavior. It's not helping them to enable them. Jesus loved the sinner; but not the sin. Real love is trying to stop or prevent a tragedy. Taking time to be there for them and listening; leaving the ninety-nine to seek out the one is sometimes necessary. Forgetting ourselves in service to others is the Lords way. When we focus on others' needs, we forget our own pain and challenges. We can become 'angels on Mount Zion' by helping others return to God, clean and pure. We need to help each other stay on the straight and narrow path of righteous living. Enduring our trials well and emulating God's love through our actions.

In the beginning, God created man and woman and gave them the command to 'multiply and replenish the Earth'; and He gave them *agency*. A modern day Prophet Harold B. Lee said, "Next to life itself, *agency* was the greatest gift from God." The procreative powers endowed us from God Himself, are only realized between man and woman. Marriage between a man and a woman is the only way man and woman can fulfill the 'full measure of their creation'; it is ordained of God and is verified by His words as contained in the Holy Scriptures.

The Story of Sodom and Gomorrah

Most people are aware of the names of these cities and the story as described in the Old Testament; in fact these names are still used today to describe debauchery. These cities are the greatest examples of sexual perversions and wickedness that have ever been on the face of the earth. In these cities, the people were involved in every form of sexual aberration imaginable; which would have included pedophilia, bestiality and homosexuality. The people had totally and completely abandoned God, and instead, worshiped the carnal desires of the flesh, stoked by Satan's influence. It would be safe to say that they had abandoned any desire for righteousness.

In Sodom and Gomorrah, homosexuality, sodomy, and other sexual perversions were so widespread that Satan had taken hold of the hearts of every man, woman, child and family. Can you imagine Satan's delight in his control over their bodies? They had gone to the point of no return, ripened in iniquity and wickedness; and were ready for destruction. God knew they would never repent and return to him, because Satan had become their master. God was not ever mentioned in their conversations and the people worshipped only the flesh, and how it could be used for personal gratification. The Holy Ghost could not dwell there; and had totally withdrawn from their society.

Genesis 18 and 19 is where you can read the full account of Abraham and his nephew Lot. In brief summary, there was strife between the herdsman of Abraham (Abram at the time) and Lot over grazing rights. To keep the peace, they mutually agreed to go to different parts of the land; Abraham went to dwell in the land of Hebron, and Lot took his family to what was known to be the most fertile part of the land, the Plains of Jordan. Lot and his family settled in Sodom.

Abraham was visited by angels and told that Sodom and Gomorrah had become so wicked, that God was going to destroy the cities and everyone in them. Abraham was going warn his nephew Lot, but also being a loving and merciful man, he asked the Lord if he would spare the cities if he could find 50 righteous persons. As the story goes, he made several attempts at finding good people, but not having any luck, continued to implore the Lord to spare the cities with less and less numbers of righteous people. Eventually, he couldn't find any righteous besides Lot and his family; and the cities were slated for destruction.

The night before the annihilation of Sodom and Gomorrah, the same two angels that had visited Abraham, came to Lot's home. Men in the surrounding area heard of the visitors, and quickly wanted to 'be with' these strangers. They tried to force themselves into Lot's home. Demanding to be with these 'holy men' so they could perform homosexual acts with them. In an effort to bargain, Lot was even willing to give these evil men his two daughters as alternates, telling the people to, "Do with them as you please". But the men of the city rejected the women; they wanted to be with men. The men of the city had no idea that these were angels sent from God to destroy them. The evil men threatened Lot and tried to break down the door of his home to take the holy men. The angels took command of the situation, and smote the men at the door with blindness so they wandered away. Once they were safe, the angels left with the command to, 'Prepare your family to leave early in the morning'; they were to go into the mountains to escape the destruction of the cities. Lot tried to convince his two sons-in-law to leave with him, his wife, and two daughters, but they mocked him.

When the morning came, the four family members departed toward the mountain with the command given in chapter 19, verse 17, 'Don't look back'! I think the Lord did this to test their obedience one last time, and to see if they regretted leaving their earthly possessions. As you recall, Lot's wife looked back and lost her life. In the end, God rained brimstone and fire upon the cities to their complete destruction. The destruction was so thorough, that little evidence has ever been found of these ancient cities.

Sodom and Gomorrah is only one example of people becoming so wicked and iniquitous with sexual perversions, that they were ripened for destruction and had to be wiped from the face of the earth. Through the ages, as mankind becomes wicked and perverse to a point that there is no hope for their salvation, God has stepped in and cleansed the Earth of their presence.

Sodom and Gomorrah's 'bad' example illustrates how a people make a complete mockery of God. They had no light; only darkness was reflected in their total allegiance to Satan. They, as the people in the days of Noah, were at the point of no return, where there was no desire to repent and return to God. A friend once said, "To choose a life without

God and the family are unfathomable." That is the 'life' that the author of all evil promotes as he counterfeits all that is holy in this world of sin.

The people of Sodom and Gomorrah, exceeded the boundaries of nature, acted upon, and embraced abominations that are beyond the nature of reasonable, thinking, men. All other creatures of the Earth obey their creator and mate with 'their own kind', never 'recreationally using' the bodies of others for indulging in ungodly acts, or perverting the procreative powers ordained by God.

When men and women entertain perverse thoughts and act upon them, they become possessed by the spirits that follow Satan. The pure and perfect spirit created by God for each of his children, must be in charge; must be in our image, and in our countenance. If we fall, there is a way prepared by which we can use our God-given agency and choose righteousness; we can cast the demons aside, and return to our Heavenly Father; the Father of our spirits. Later in this chapter, I'll share a few more personal experiences showing how those afflicted with homosexual behavior can become whole again.

Sexual sin in all forms has been an abomination among mankind since the beginning. Largely it has been practiced in the shadows until our time. Today, with advances in communication and entertainment, these perversions are in full display; and the impact on the world is worsening at alarming rates. The moral state of the world today is a fulfillment of prophecy, that 'in the last days, men will declare, evil good, and good evil'.

For a moment, let's review some of God's words on the subject, as recorded in the Old and New Testaments:

"*Thou_*shalt not lie with mankind, as with womankind: it is *abomination.*" (Leviticus 18:22 – *emphasis* added)

    a.   OR With the male you shall not lie as one lies with the woman
    b.   TG Homosexual Behavior

To be clear, the law applies to women having sexual relations with other women also; it too is a great abomination in God's eyes.

"If a man *also lie with mankind*[a], as he lieth with a *woman*[b], both of them have committed an *abomination*[c]: they shall surely be put to death; their blood shall be upon them." (Leviticus 20:13 – *emphasis* added)

a. HEB lies with a male
b. TG Woman
c. TG Homosexual Behavior

In the early days, this sin was considered a capital offence and the judgment was death. In today's world that penalty (although still practiced in some religions), is looked upon as barbaric. Yet is the sin any less impactful on the spiritual lives of men and women?

"The shew of their countenance doth witness against them; and they declare their *sin*[a] as *Sodom*[b], they hide it not. Woe unto their soul! for they have rewarded evil unto themselves." (Isaiah 3:9 – *emphasis* added)

a. Gen. 19:5   TG   Apostasy of Israel   *(Gen. 19:5 refers to men of Sodom)*
b. Gen. 13:10 (10-13); Deut. 32:32 *(Homosexuality)*

In this scripture Isaiah talks of their evil acts that were obvious by their 'look' and the 'evil' or 'darkness' that emanated from their person for all to see. They had personally invited Satan to possess their mortal body.

"And they were haughty, and committed *abomination*[a] before: therefore I took them *away*[b] *as*[c] I saw good." (Ezekiel 16:50 - *emphasis* added)

a. Jer. 23:14   TG   Homosexual Behavior
b. Gen. 19:24 (24-29) *(destroying the people of Sodom & Gomorrah)*
c. HEB   when I saw it

God is speaking here, declaring he will remove those from the earth who do not turn from the commission of these horrible sexual perversions. People who do these things are worshiping the appetites of the flesh, or the natural man; to a point, where Satan becomes that person's master. The love of God has grown cold as they defiled their earthly body that houses their perfect heavenly spirits.

"Know ye not that the *unrighteouss*[a] shall not *inherit*[b] the kingdom of God? Be not deceived: neither *fornicators*[c], nor idolaters, nor *adulterers*[d], nor *effeminate*[e], nor *abusers*[f] of themselves with mankind," (1 Corinthians 6:9 – *emphasis* added)

a. See 1 Ne 10:21;Alma 11:37; 40:26; Moses 6:57 TG Worthiness
b. See John 3:5; 1 Cor. 15:50

c. GR sexually immoral persons, male (or female) prostitutes, TG Fornication
d. TG Adulterer; Sexual Immorality
e. GR catamites (a boy or youth who is in a sexual relationship with a man)
f. GR male homosexuals TG Homosexual Behavior

Don't be deceived by Satan; no unclean thing can enter into the kingdom of God. In this scripture the word *abuser* is used synonymously with the term 'homosexual'. To me homosexuality is a mockery of the procreative powers given to man from God to create a family. Some homosexuals and especially pedophiles are predatory in that are always looking for their next victim to use or abuse; and then leave damages and abandoned for their next prey. I've seen many converted to these sins and 'way of life', only to be left behind for new flesh. These people become Satan's missionaries for his doctrine of 'anything goes'; which is open rebellion against God.

"For *whoremongers*[a], for *them*[b] that *defile*[c] themselves with mankind, for *menstealers*[d], for liars, for perjured persons, and if there be any other thing that is contrary to sound *doctrine*[e];" (1 Timothy 1:10 – *emphasis* added)

a. TG Whore
b. GR homosexuals
c. TG Homosexual Behavior
d. GR kidnappers
e. 2 Tim. 4:3

Here the word *defile* is used for homosexual behavior. The last words of the scripture, *contrary to sound doctrine,* reminds me of the words in 2 Tim. 4:3 which states, "They will *not endure sound doctrine*; but after their own *lusts* shall they heap to themselves *teachers*, having itching ears;" (*emphasis* added)

This says: I won't follow the living prophets (who's words call me to repentance); I'll listen to the pleasing words of the secular prophets of the day, or the philosophies of men which declare: 'these things are OK', 'God's word isn't relevant', 'if it feels good, do it', 'if it's fun and pleases the lusts of your eyes (and your friends are doing it), it won't hurt you', and 'this is the modern age, change from the old ways are good'. The natural man seeks the crooked and wide path of Satan's doctrine. The man of God seeks the straight and narrow way of God's unchanging path to happiness. God is the same yesterday, today, and tomorrow; the

God of the Old and New Testament, and our time.

By now, the doctrine of God has been explained very clearly. If you struggle with same-gender attraction, or if such feelings have only been a fleeting thought, there is help available. If you haven't acted on those feelings, or are not fully engaged in homosexual behavior, go to a trusted member of your family, or a friend; hopefully you'll come to an understanding that you are in danger and need help right away!

If Satan takes possession of your body, his goal is to destroy your agency (ability to choose), and then life itself. But he doesn't takeover quickly; he's very subtle and patiently takes control a little at a time. He'll cleverly give you ninety-nine truths, to get you to accept one lie that will engage you in sin. He works slowly, until he has full control, knowing that once he has you, he can use you to influence others. When darkness has overshadowed you to the point that the Light of Christ is only a glimmer, Satan will put his chains of hell around you, and looking upward, declare, 'God, I have taken another one of your children to myself!'

If we involve Jesus Christ and his infinite Atonement in our lives, *all* sins can be overcome and forgiven. If we have a sincere desire, having hope in Christ, believing in him, with love for God, and especially a love for ourselves; we may repent and God will remove our sins. You have the power to make this change in your life's journey. Through God's love, and the love of your family and friends, you can do it! I testify that there is hope for each of us, God's children; no matter the situation or circumstance, or how far we think we may have fallen, God will not forsake us, because of His unconditional love for each of us.

One Sunday afternoon Cassie received a phone call from a friend who lived in a nearby town. She was crying, but her tears were tears of joy. Her son, who had struggled with same gender attraction for many years, had finally announced that he was ready to make a change in his life. As a teenager, he had been unhappy, but until now he hadn't made the connection; his homosexual behavior was the source of his sorrow and deep depression. His personal revelation had come after several evenings of scripture reading with his mother. The Holy Spirit had touched his spirit, and he had been humble enough to receive spirit-to-spirit instruction in that moment. A loving Father in Heaven heard his pleading, and the prayers of his family; God's Spirit literally witnessed to him that he was going in the wrong direction, and needed to change.

Of course the story of the miracle hadn't started only a few days ago. The boy's mother had been praying and pleading for months that Heavenly Father would intercede; that he might change and come unto Christ. As a desperate single parent, she had her own struggles; but her focus had been primarily on those of her family and most particularly her son. As a family they had been working to make scripture reading a daily part of their routine. Her hope had been that they would receive personal revelation, to help them better align their lives to Christ, and become a Gospel-centered home.

This was the situation; her son wasn't coping well with his job, either physically or mentally; he believed that was his biggest challenge. Then here was his mother, living in a small home with very little income, and trying to be mother and father to her little family. There was love in the home, and this mother had a testimony of Jesus Christ, believed in the power of the Atonement, and had faith and understanding that families can be together forever.

I had been introduced to Cassie's friend only once, and had never met her son, nor was I aware of his situation. Through Cassie, she asked me if I would sit down with her son, give him some counsel, and a priesthood blessing. I agreed, and Cassie shared with me a brief summary of the challenges this young man was going through. I had fifteen minutes to prepare to lovingly counsel a complete stranger.

Knowing this young man was a son of God, my spirit brother, made it easy to relate. And I knew that, 'when you are in the service of your fellow beings, your only in the service of your God'. I immediately went to my knees in private prayer, asking Heavenly Father to send the Holy Ghost; so that through me, the proper words of inspiration would be conveyed to him. I prayed that he would feel the power of the Priesthood of God; and God's love as his Heavenly Father. My hope was to inspire him to 'come unto Christ', and receive the power of the Atonement and the ministering Angels in his life. I prayed that he would be blessed with hope, and faith to move in the right direction (I knew this course change – if embraced) would eliminate the anxiety, depression, and suicidal tendencies that tortured him. I prayed that he might be made clean and whole from his affliction, and become again like a little child. I knew that all of this could be realized through his faith in Jesus Christ, and the administration of a Priesthood Blessing. Many thoughts flashed through my mind after my prayer. I knew God knows this young man personally, and all would be well if he had the faith and desire to change.

As they arrived at our home, Cassie greeted them and took them outside to see our large garden. Through the open window I could hear the young man's voice; and at that moment, the Spirit whispered to me that he was in a dangerous situation. Immediately the words of Isaiah came to my mind, 'their very countenance changes when they engage in homosexuality' (see Isaiah 3:9). This young man had a feminine or girlish voice; and the Spirit bore witness to me that his homosexual behavior would be the main focus in the counsel and Priesthood Blessing I would be giving. As I walked down the stairs, I uttered a silent prayer in my heart. I asked that the Holy Ghost be present, and touch his spirit.

The mother introduced her son John; we shook hands, and the four of us retired to the family room. I began our conversation with some basic questions to get to know him. "What is your relationship with Heavenly Father?" He replied, "Lately mother and I have been reading the scriptures, and I've felt His love at those times." Then I asked, "When was the last time you went to church?" He said, "It's been a few years." I replied, "I want you to know no matter where you've been or what you've done, God loves you unconditionally! He may not like your actions, but He will always love you as an individual, and as His spirit son. God is the definition of love; He allowed his Only Begotten Son to be sacrificed and crucified for us his spirit children. The Atonement is that one, great gift, which makes it possible for us to return home, to God's presence.

Before I ask the next couple of questions, I want you to know I love you even though we have just met. You're my brother and a son of God, so you too can become just like him. Feeling the inspiration of the Holy Ghost to speak boldly about his sexual preferences, I asked, "Do you have a girlfriend or boyfriend?" He answered, "At this time I have neither. But same sex attraction has been a problem for a few years." Let me ask another question before we talk about the last one. "Have you ever thought about suicide?" "Yes" John replied, "I've tried to do it a couple times but failed." His answer caused me to pause and reflect on my own son's suicide. We'll return to John's story later in the chapter.

My son was 23 years old when he committed suicide; and there was a string of events that led up to his death. These included, his fiancée Tracy, turning to lesbianism; and her telling him (on several occasions) to 'go shoot yourself'. On the last night of Joseph's life, she told him that she was 'done with him', and would rather 'be with any other woman' instead. I can imagine the thoughts that must have been running through his mind. He had many setbacks in the time leading up to his death. He had been in jail for 30 days for a DUI five months before his death; he lost his car to the bank, unable to make the payments because of court imposed fines. Then, two months before his suicide, Tracy told him, "If you get me pregnant, I will have an abortion." The influence of alcohol in his system, when he pulled the trigger, was also a factor. Joseph simply wasn't himself; He had allowed Satan and his followers into his body through the cracks he had created by his actions. These demons were controlling his every move for months before he took his life. Three months before his suicide, I tried to give him a Priesthood Blessing; they had convinced him to not allow me to lay my hands on his head. If I had that opportunity, I would have been able to cast the evil spirits out of his body.

In Tracy's relationship with other women, she took the role of the masculine partner; and began taking on a mannerism of toughness. She started to wear male clothing, walking like a man, and talking with a deeper voice. She lost pride in her God-given beauty and now has a body full of tattoos and piercings. These kinds of physical changes are typical of those involved in homosexual behavior; as they become occupied by evil spirits that take control of their actions, and even their physical appearance.

When I see same sex 'couples' on the news lining up to get married, I can't help but think of the traditional families that are being destroyed. This activity leaves families in turmoil and confusion; and I wonder what the children think when they ask their parent, "What has changed? "Why can't we be a normal family?" I picture Father in Heaven with tears in his eyes as his 'little ones' are offended, and the structure of the family is destroyed. When Tracy indulged in lesbian behaviors, she became possessed with evil spirits; this prompted her to deny the God-given love between a man and a woman. When I see two men or two women kissing it brings on a sick feeling as the Holy Spirit whispers to me, 'This is wrong and offensive before God'.

A few weeks after Joseph's death, Tracy was picked up by the police. She had missed her scheduled court appearance months earlier, and a warrant had been issued for her arrest. She was taken to jail, and during routine jail intake blood tests, it was discovered that she was pregnant; it was Joseph's child. What a blessing to know Joseph had given us another grandson! But the question lingered, 'Would our future grandchild be killed in an abortion'?

During the few weeks that Tracy was in jail, I was talking to her step-father who was also a worthy holder of the Holy Melchizedek Priesthood. As we talked of her situation, I asked him to cast the demons out of her body to protect our grandson; and to help her resolve the homosexual behavior issues. He told me he would.

After her release from jail, she was willing to receive the blessing. Her step-father cast the evil from her, and gave her a Priesthood Blessing; as the blessing was pronounced, Tracy became a changed woman! She was civil to those around her; she wasn't as quick to anger; and she wasn't hateful in her speech. She had a renewed love of herself and others, as was evident in her words and actions. The most significant miracle is she showed no further inclination toward homosexual behavior. We all looked forward to the birth of her (and Joseph's) son. When he was born, he was perfect and beautiful; and we were grateful for the Priesthood that made it possible.

After the baby was born, Tracy faced struggles as a single mother trying to support her little family. She tried time and time again to get work, but no one would hire her. It wasn't long before she gave up on life's challenges and returned to the enticing of evil. The saddest part of the story is that about a year after the birth, she returned to the homosexual lifestyle; and she remains in that wicked state today. Our family and hers still love her unconditionally, just as the Savior would. But we will never accept that homosexual behavior is anything but Satan's way to subvert the family, and take control of those who allow themselves to be involved in this insidious lifestyle choice.

While in California visiting my daughter Emily and her family, we went to Disneyland. While there we saw many same-sex couples; they were easy to spot, not only because they're 'different'; but their countenances are not normal because the Light of Christ has been overshadowed by darkness and evil. In every case haircuts, voices, body movements, demeanor, they basically become impostors betraying the gender with which their body and spirit were created. Their master has become Satan, the great deceiver; he has marked them through his deception, and they have lost their true identity as sons and daughters of God.

The incidences of sexually transmitted diseases such as AIDS are high among the population of men (and women) involved in homosexual behavior. These diseases are then often spread to innocent victims. More than half a million people in the USA have died from AIDS and AIDS-related illnesses. An estimated 1.2 million people in the

United States carry HIV; over 150 thousand of whom don't know they are carriers. There are over 50 thousand new cases of HIV every year in patients over the age of thirteen. As the world seeks to find a cure for this scourge, suicide continues to grow among this group. This is particularly true of those who have lost their support group due to the dramatic changes they've made in their lives. Satan seizes upon those in this situation and whispers untruths such as 'how can you stand yourself', 'you aren't worth anything', 'you are a sinner, why even try to be something you're not; you're going to Hell anyway, kill yourself'. First they feel depressed, then unwanted and alone; and soon they lose all hope. Satan blinds them to the reality that there is a God who loves them; and whose son Jesus Christ made it possible to repent and receive forgiveness through His atoning blood; and be clean again. Instead, many turn to suicide, which only brings more sorrow and broken hearts. Suicide allows Satan to affect whole families as recrimination, blame and contention takes over the whole family; dragging them down for years as they try to deal with their loved ones untimely death. Let us show renewed love for the homosexual; pray for them, and help them find the way back home.

Now, returning to my interview with John. I had discovered in my brief conversation that he was struggling with same-gender attraction and has considered suicide; I continued with this instruction: 'John, I'm going to be very bold and direct with you, so please resist the urge to go on the defensive; that is what Satan would want you to do. The Spirit of the Holy Ghost tells me there's an unclean or evil spirit inside you. This same thing happens frequently throughout the world as Satan takes control of the lives of sinners every day. But John, you are one of the lucky ones, because you have expressed a desire for stronger faith in Jesus Christ and his Holy Priesthood. I can help you through the power of the Priesthood of God which I hold, by casting away the evil spirit or spirits that are inside you; and give you a Priesthood Blessing to heal you from your affliction; and make you whole again. You can be freed from the chains of Satan, and be yourself again; a clean, loving son of God, on the pathway back to Jesus Christ. Right now, you are in a very serious situation and risk losing your salvation.'

Let's take a few moments here, and review some of the doctrine surrounding this topic. In the New Testament Book of Luke, we read of those who have demons cast out of them, and how their situation could become even worse. (I told John he needed to understand this before I could cast out his demons):

"When the *unclean spirit*[a] is gone out of a man, *he*[b] walketh through dry places, seeking rest; and finding none, *he*[c] saith, I will return unto my house whence I came out.

And[d] when he cometh, he findeth it swept and *garnished*[e].

Then goeth he, and taketh to him seven other spirits more wicked than himself; and they enter in, and dwell there: and the last state of that man is worse than the first." (Luke 11:24-26 – emphasis added)

a. See D&C 50:31 (31-33)
b. See JST Luke 11:25 ... it ...
c. Ibid
d. JST Luke 11:26-27) And when *it* cometh, *it* findeth the house swept and garnished. Then goeth *the evil spirit*, and taketh seven other spirits...
e. GR put in order

These verses describe when a person has evil cast out of them, there is a risk (as Satan and his followers try to find new people to inhabit) that the demon spirit will return with reinforcements to retake possession of that body. Satan does not give up easily. As was described in this scripture, he doesn't just double or triple his efforts; he actually increases it by seven hundred per cent!

As I read this, the Holy Ghost bears witness to me that this tactic *is* reality; he will return with a vengeance. Satan is certainly organized in his attack strategy and methods. With his anger kindled at the loss of a mortal body, he will personally choose even stronger and more effective 'soldiers' from among his male and female, captains and generals. It is possible that in this way, female demons would be in charge of a male physical body, or vice versa, a male demon in a female physical body. I believe this is why we see, such dramatic changes in appearance and mannerisms, by those involved in Homosexual behavior.

I believe this is exactly what has happened in the world since the beginning of time. This doctrine is very clear to me, and I testify that it is true. The only way back to our Heavenly Father or the Kingdom of God, is in and through the name of Jesus Christ.

Another scriptural account where a person had seven evil spirits in possession of their body is found in Luke:

"And certain women, which had been healed of evil spirits and infirmities, *Mary*[a] called Magdalene, out of whom went seven devils," (Luke 8:2 – *emphasis* added)

    a.   See NT Mark 16:9 (1, 9)

These are the main ideas I'm inspired to point out:

1. This can happen to anyone;
2. There is a way out of the chains of Satan;
3. Mary became a disciple of Christ;
4. It's possible that Mary was the savior's companion or wife;
5. Anyone who sincerely seeks to have evil cast from their lives, will desire to dedicate their lives to the cause of Christ.

(Continuing my conversation with John) 'Do you understand the seriousness of your situation? I can cast out the evil that's within you, but it's up to you to start living a righteous life, and always keep the Commandments of God. And in all places avoiding the temptations of Satan and enduring to the end. Satan and his demons will never give up. You're a special child of God, and Satan wants you. You just can't allow him to enter in your life in any way. He can bruise your heel but you have the power to crush his head. His power is only what you allow him to have through wickedness and iniquity.'

Raising my right arm to the square, I commanded the evil spirits out of John by the Power of the Priesthood of God; and in the name of Jesus Christ. Laying my hands on his head, I called upon the powers of Heaven, and bestowing a Priesthood Blessing making him whole again. I, Cassie and John's mother all witnessed a 'mighty change' come over this young man. It happened, almost instantly as the power of the Priesthood literally restored him to his true identity. His countenance glowed, and the most noticeable change was his voice. His normal male voice returned, and his mother saw her son; and no longer an imposter. The very next Sunday, John went to church to prove his commitment to follow Jesus Christ. He was holding his mother's hand as they entered the chapel. He's now praying daily and reading the scriptures in his efforts to thwart the evil one and his minions.

In the 1980's a co-worker made this statement to me about Homosexuality. He said his male friend who turned gay, was born with (in his opinion) a female spirit. I asked, "So he acted like a female from birth?" He answered, "Well no, just when he became an adult." I told him that the scriptures were very clear; God created us first with spirit bodies, then physical bodies secondly to house our immortal perfect spirits. In his opinion was couched the erroneous concept that God made a mistake by placing a female spirit in a male body.

Let me make a point here: having thoughts or feelings of attraction to a person of the same gender, but never engaging or acting upon them, is not a sin. But it's important to understand that if Satan becomes aware of the inclination, he will become relentless in bringing you down to his level and attempt to destroy your agency.

It's important for us to avoid the very appearance of evil. If we always pray for help, and live a Christ-like life; we will know who our master is. Please don't risk t testing the boundaries. Stay focused on the Light, and listen to the Holy Spirit. With Christ, we are never alone; for when we are with God, there are more for us (loved ones on both sides of the veil praying for us every day) than against us (Satan's evil forces).

If you, or someone you know, have fallen into homosexual behaviors, there will always be a way back through the power of the Infinite Atonement of Jesus Christ. He has already paid the price for sin; He is the only one that can overcome the demands of justice. This is accomplished through his loving mercy, as we follow the established process of repentance. With the help of a worthy Priesthood holder, the demons can be cast out by the authority and power of the name of Jesus Christ. Through the Power of the Priesthood, this Priesthood holder can place his hands on your head, and bestow a Priesthood blessing upon you, making you clean and whole again.

From the beginning of time, the primary organized group in the world has been the family unit. This consists of a Father (male) and Mother (female) who are legally married. They (through use of their God-given procreative powers), create physical life [bodies] for the spirit children of God. By doing so, they invite children into their home to complete their family unit. This is the plan of happiness and there are NO substitutes, only imitations. Neither two men nor two women can physically create offspring. If the whole world embraced homosexuality, the human race would be doomed to extinction. Of course this would thwart the Plan of God to share all He has with his children. Homosexuality is one way Satan tries to frustrate that Plan.

It always astounds me how men and women want to take upon them the mantel of God, and try to take control of nature. Transsexual operations, for example, can only alter the physical body; the spirit remains the same. Man and woman are God's greatest creations, to alter that creation is solemn mockery of our Heavenly Father. Satan applauds these actions and any other that attempts to modify or deface the human form. This also includes sexual perversions that put to unnatural use the sacred creative power. When we engage in open rebellion to God's laws, we become subject to the devil, and worship him.

The 'homosexual community' and 'liberal thinkers' agenda is to change public education curriculum to introduce these perversions to children at ages as young as kindergarten. Exposing our children to such thought, images and actions (that are clearly against God's law), must not be allowed to happen. Only a vocal ground-swell of indignation from good families will keep the perversion of sacred matters out of the schools. These things used to be hidden away from public view. Today it is everywhere in the public forum, LGBT (Lesbian, Gay, and Bi-sexual & Transgender) groups band together; and cry out, 'we deserve to be happy too', and 'we should be treated like any other *family*'. 'What we do is just a natural thing'; all the while undermining God and the Heaven-ordained unit of the family. The reality: only living God's commandments bring true happiness; Satan's counterfeit only brings brief euphoria and then destruction. I personally believe (and heard many such stories) that in the psyche and reasoning mind of every homosexual, they believe that the behavior is wrong, and would admit it on their death-bed if they still have a belief in God.

History DOES repeat itself; from Cain, to Noah's time, to Sodom and Gomorrah, to the Savior's time, to our day; evil is constantly in play for the souls of man. From the time Cain was cast out of the land of his inheritance (because he hated God and worshipped Satan); wickedness spread throughout the whole Earth. By the time of Noah, Satan's influence was rampant to the point that everything had to be destroyed by flood. Homosexuality was reintroduced to Noah's descendents by Ham and Egyptus and again became an acceptable practice among the followers of Satan. God destroyed the people of Sodom and Gomorrah, and Jesus and living prophets spoke against these things in the times of the early Church of Jesus Christ. Today this insidious plague continues to infest the world because the natural man loves Satan more than God.

Evidence of this is found in the scriptures. God's first commandment to Adam and Eve (multiply and replenish the Earth) was given so that all His spirit children would have the opportunity to gain a body, and experience life on earth. Only through this opportunity, could our first parents' 'glory in [their] posterity'; but it also brought glory to God. This was the same commandment given to all flesh, animals, fishes, and fowls of the air; and NEVER was it to be accomplished without males and females performing their individual roles in perpetuating the species.

At the Flood 'all living' was destroyed except for the eight humans and animals on the ark (one pair [male and female] of all other living things [7 pairs male and female of the clean animals and fowls of the air]. When they were released from the ark, their first commandment was to 'multiply'. The earth was as if it had a new birth just as in the days of Adam and Eve.

> "Bring forth with thee every living thing that is with thee, of all flesh, both of fowl, and of cattle, and of every creeping thing that creepeth upon the earth; that they may breed abundantly in the earth, and be fruitful, and multiply upon the earth."(Genesis 8:17)

> "And God blessed Noah and his sons, and said unto them, Be fruitful, and multiply, and replenish the earth." (Genesis 9:1)

> "And you, be ye fruitful, and multiply; bring forth abundantly in the earth, and multiply therein." (Genesis 9:7)

These scriptures are very clear: the great gift of procreation cannot be carried out without the male, and the female each in their role. Marriage between one man and one woman is ordained of God; and all others are impostors created by Satan!

Homosexuality started in the time of Cain and with his posterity because they were worshipping Satan. Satan's doctrine is primarily anything that is evil or the complete opposite of God's doctrine. The Flood destroyed the wicked from the earth. The question becomes: When did it come back to the children of man? The answer is found in Genesis 9. Not too long after the Flood, and a few hundred years before Sodom and Gomorrah was destroyed, homosexuality made reappearance. The person who reintroduced it was one of the eight people who were saved from the cleansing waters of the flood. He at one time, had to have been a righteous, God fearing, man or he wouldn't have been able to board the ark.

"And the sons of Noah, that went forth of the ark, were Shem, and Ham, and Japheth: and Ham is the father of Canaan.

These are the three sons of Noah: and of them was the whole earth overspread.

And Noah began to be an husbandman, and he planted a vineyard:

And he drank of the wine, and was drunken; and he was uncovered within his tent.

And Ham, the father of Canaan, saw the nakedness of his father, and told his two brethren without.

And Shem and Japheth took a garment, and laid it upon both their shoulders, and went backward, and covered the nakedness of their father; and their faces were backward, and they saw not their father's nakedness.

And Noah awoke from his wine, and knew what his younger son had done unto him.

And he said, Cursed be Canaan; a servant of servants shall he be unto his brethren.

And he said, Blessed be the Lord God of Shem; and Canaan shall be his servant.

God shall enlarge Japheth, and he shall dwell in the tents of Shem; and Canaan shall be his servant." (Genesis 9:18-27)

It is sad to me that these eight people had the potential of the whole earth, and all the blessings of God, given to them. In this 'new beginning' for mankind, evil was completely washed away from the earth; yet they again allowed wickedness and the influence of Satan to creep into their lives.

Sometime before the flood, Ham (Noah's youngest son) married Egyptus a descendant of Cain (this was forbidden and against the wishes of his father Noah). Noah was not only their father but also the Prophet who was trying to teach the doctrine of God to his family. I think Egyptus must have been a righteous woman or God wouldn't have allowed her to board the ark. But perhaps Ham's righteousness was only superficial and he deceived his father? Or, possibly, Noah (a loving father) couldn't bear to lose him and was protecting him from the flood. Whatever the case, Ham was preserved.

In the verses above, it is declared that, 'Ham is the father of Canaan'. That (Canaan) is eventually (along with Egypt), where Ham and his family settles. One of Ham's sons is named Canaan; and the land of Canaan is where Sodom and Gomorrah were located.

The analogy is drawn that (just as Adam and Eve), Noah's family would populate the earth once again; and Noah began to be a husbandman (farmer) and planted a vineyard.

The story starts to take a turn when the scripture records that Noah, 'drank of the wine, and was drunken; and he was uncovered within his tent'. The scripture leaves a lot unsaid in this matter. Perhaps Ham had placed something in his drink which made him drunk or put him to sleep. Could Ham have taken him to the tent; or was Ham the one that removed his clothes while asleep in the tent?

As the scripture relates, Ham 'saw the nakedness of his father and told his two brethren without', we begin to wonder, 'What's going on here'? It seems that Ham didn't just open the tent door and 'happen' to look in; he entered the tent and DID something to his father. Afterward, he went and (possibly) told his brothers what he had done to his now naked father.

In Shem and Japheth's response we see their love, respect, and especially their righteousness; for the way they handled the situation. They took a garment or large sheet (animal skin) between their two shoulders and walked into the tent backwards to cover the nakedness of their father; never seeing his nakedness.

Make NO mistake; this story reveals the homosexual acts of Ham on his own father. The scripture says Noah awoke from the wine and *he knew what his younger son had done unto him*. It doesn't take much imagination to picture what happened in that tent that day. Was Ham so desperate for sexual gratification that he had to rape his father? This is beyond my understanding or comprehension that something this horrible could even be conjured up in the mind of any human being. Ham had to be possessed with many evil spirits.

Ham's actions were so serious that Noah cursed not only Ham, but all of his posterity. A 'servant of servants' he would be to his two brother's families; a similar cursing that was given to Cain from God. Noah disavowed his own son, and sent him away to the land of Canaan. We each are punished for our own sins, but when a father, mother, brother, or sister engages in wickedness; it can affect the whole family. It also results in the sinful behavior being passed on to succeeding generations; making it difficult to break the cycle of sin.

Noah declares that Shem and Japheth's God is not the same God that Ham worships. Ham's descendants were Sodom and Gomorrah and the African nations. Shem's descendants inhabited the Middle East and Abraham (father of the faithful) who had Isaac who had Jacob (Israel) who had the 12 sons (12 tribes of Israel) or the Patriarchs of old came through his family lines. Japheth's descendants inhabited the eastern European and Asian nations of the world. I want to testify that as I read these scriptures, I can feel Noah's Godly sorrow, anger, disappointment, but also the love he felt as a father of a wayward son who fell from the teachings of God.

In time, if you are practicing homosexual behavior, you will fall under the control of Satan. Repentance and freedom from his chains will never come to pass UNLESS your thoughts and desires return to God. God loves you, and I love you! You can find the person God so lovingly created you to be. Forgiveness will come from a loving Savior, your brother Jesus Christ. Through the redeeming power of the Atonement, you can become clean and pure again. I call this, "True Innocence." Understanding who you are; having real remorse for your sins; seeking for a remission of your sins (by confessing to God and your Church Leader), and then seeking to make restitution (to those who have been hurt or harmed by your actions); when this has been accomplished, you will be truly forgiven by God and become clean and innocent again.

Please, please know that my words here are not homophobic in any way. The challenges of the flesh (the natural man) are not who you are. They are simply a part of this world that must be overcome as part of our Earthly test or probation. I know good people who have 'given in' to same-gender attraction and expressed that attraction through their sexual behaviors. I love them, and pray that they can be healed. In the meantime, they as all people should have civil rights and privileges; but the sin cannot be condoned. If you would like to read more on this subject, here are more scriptures that reference and boldly speak of homosexuality and other sex perversions:

Gen. 13:13, Gen. 18:20, Gen.19:5, Lev. 18:22, Lev. 20:13, Deut. 23:17, Isa. 3:9, Ezek. 16:50, Roman 1:27, 1 Cor. 6:9, 1 Tim. 1:10, 2 Tim. 3:3, 2 Peter 2:10, and Jude 1:7 *The Book of Mormon*: 2 Nephi 9:40, and 2 Nephi13:9 (Reference: *King James Version of the Holy Bible*)

CHAPTER 15

Secret Combinations or Secret Societies

'Secret combinations' can be defined as two or more individuals who meet together to establish oaths and covenants (one could be a human and the other, one of Satan's followers or an evil spirit) that will: harm, do evil, steal, plunder, destroy, impair, downgrade, segregate, create lies, impose wrongful judgments, imprison, create conspiracies, threaten bribery, establish sinister plots, and commit murder. This list isn't all-inclusive, and could go on and on; listing every way humans conspire against other humans for self-aggrandizement, and to obtain power. These groups will stop at nothing, and will go to any expense to accomplish their designs; even if it requires murder to maintain the secrecy of the group.

The mastermind of these ungodly alliances is none other than the great deceiver, Satan himself. He is the author and creator of these devastating things called secret combinations. These 'secret societies' have only one leader, and only one goal: the complete destruction of the individual, the family, and the nations of the world.

There are those who would discredit the notion that such secret societies exist. Certainly the idea makes for good book or movie material; but these types of organizations couldn't exist without being discovered; or could they? They do exist, and they are well-hidden behind blood oaths, threats of death and the actual murders. Conspiracy theories abound; but if you know what to look for, you can read the clues in any deal, agreement, or program; in government, business, or organizations that secretly take advantage of someone else. Just refer to the list of the traits of these groups as outlined in the first paragraph of this chapter. Any effort to hide truth, to hurt others, or enslave people would fit the definition. Sound familiar; it's Satan's plan in full bloom.

The contrast between the Lord's way, and the way of Satan is clear by the Savior's statement, 'When two or more *meet in my name even Jesus Christ*, I will be in the midst of them and the truth will be established'. If decision-making in organizations is based on the love of mankind, the building of hope in individuals, always seeking ways to do good, and being totally honest in everything they do; these organizations become established as Christ-centered institutions where God is placed above all else, and the good for the people involved is a close second. When a righteous plan is discussed, designed, and implemented, by leaders who are an example of the best intentions for all involved; then that plan is the antithesis of a secret combination; and the love of God is present.

There are many scriptural records of individuals, groups, cities and even nations whose destruction became assured, when sin and evil became established through secret oaths and covenants. When governments are infiltrated by secret combinations, then Satan and his demons step in; inevitable annihilation is the end result. God forewarns mankind through his servants the prophets; but only until their hearts become hardened and cold to the Spirit; then when it is obvious that there is no hope, and they've become totally allegiant to Satan, they are ripe for destruction.

I love how the Apostle Paul describes (in a very concise way) who the real enemy is:

"For we *wrestle*[a] not *against*[b] *flesh and blood*[c], but against principalities, against powers, against the *rulers*[d] of the *darkness*[e] of this world, against spiritual *wickedness*[f] in high places." (Ephesians 6:12 – *emphasis* added)

   a.   Joseph Smith-History 1:15 (15-17) Real enemy to righteousness & spiritual death - the Devil himself and his followers one-third of the hosts of heaven wrestling them every day of each of our lives.
   b.   TG: Opposition (Satan)
   c.   TG: Flesh and Blood (mortals)
   d.   2 Cor. 4:4) God of this world (or worldly people) the Devil
   e.   TG: Darkness, Spiritual, Secret Combinations (Devil)
   f.   TG: Governments, Wickedness (lead by Satan)

The Apostle Paul outlines the way we may escape the enemy of God and man:

"Wherefore take unto you the whole armour of God, that ye may able to with*stand* in the evil day, and having done all, to *stand*.

Stand therefore, having your loins girt about with truth, and having on the breastplate of righteousness;

And your feet shod with the preparation of the gospel of peace;

Above all, taking the shield of faith, wherewith ye shall be able to quench all the fiery darts of the wicked.

And take the helmet of salvation, and the sword of the Spirit, which is the word of God:

Praying always with all prayer and supplication in the Spirit, and watching thereunto with all perseverance and supplication for all saints;

And for me, that utterance may be given unto me, that I may open my mouth boldly, to make known the mystery of the gospel,

For which I am an ambassador in bonds: that therein I may speak boldly, as I ought to speak." (Ephesians 6:13-20 – *emphasis* added)

In *The Pearl of Great Price*, Moses recounts the story of Cain (and his third great grand-son Lamech). Cain was the first in the BAD and EVIL things introduced to the Earth. He was the first Son of Perdition (having denied the Holy Ghost) and partaker of the 'second' or 'spiritual death'; where there may be no forgiveness given. He was the first to set up a secret combination or oath with Satan. This not only affected Cain himself, but also his entire family for 'all time', as they also received a curse from the Lord. Then, we read of Lamech who received an even greater cursing:

"And Cain *loved* Satan more than God. And Satan commanded him saying: *Make* an offering unto the Lord.

But unto Cain, and to his *offering*, he had not respect. Now Satan knew this, and it *pleased* him. And Cain was very wroth, and his countenance fell.

If thou doest well, thou shalt be *accepted*. And if thou doest not well, sin lieth at the door, and Satan *desireth* to have thee; and except thou shalt hearken unto my commandments, I will *deliver* thee up, and it shall be unto thee according to his desire. And thou shalt *rule* over him;" . . .

"And it came to pass that Cain took one of his brothers' daughters to *wife*, and they *loved* Satan more than God.

And Satan said unto Cain: *Swear* unto me by thy throat, and if thou tell it thou shalt die; and swear thy brethren by their heads, and by the living God, that they tell it not; for if they tell it, they shall surely die; and this that thy father may not know it; and this day I will deliver thy brother Abel into thine hands.

And Satan sware unto Cain that he would do according to his *commands*. And all these things were done in secret.

And Cain said: Truly I am Mahan, the master of this *great* secret that I may *murder* and get *gain*. Wherefore Cain was called *Master Mahan*, and gloried in his wickedness." (*The Pearl of Great Price*, Moses 5: 18, 21, 23, 28-31 – *emphasis* added)

"And Lamech said unto his wives, Adah and Zillah: Hear my voice, ye wives of Lamech, hearken unto my speech; for I have slain a man to my wounding, and a young man to my hurt.

If Cain shall be avenged sevenfold, truly Lamech shall be *seventy* and seven fold;

For *Lamech* having entered into a covenant with Satan, after the manner of Cain, wherein he became Master Mahan, master of that great secret which was administered unto Cain by Satan; and Irad, the son of Enoch, having known their secret, began to reveal it unto the sons of Adam;

Wherefore Lamech, being angry, slew him, not like unto Cain, his brother Abel, for the sake of getting gain, but he slew him for the *oath's* sake.

For, from the days of Cain, there was secret *combination*, and their works were in the dark, and they knew every man his brother.

Wherefore the Lord *cursed* Lamech, and his house, and all them that had covenanted with Satan; for they kept not the commandments of God, and it displeased God, and he ministered not unto them, and their works were abominations, and began to spread among all the *sons* of men. And it was among the sons of men." (*The Pearl of Great Price*, Moses 5: 47-52 – *emphasis* added)

There are many scriptural accounts of secret combinations. There is only room here to describe a few; but these will show sufficient evidence that secret combinations have been a 'true evil' everywhere in the world, and among all nations, since the beginning of time; and continue today.

I love the first three Gospels: Matthew, Mark, and Luke for their descriptions of Christ's life and teachings. The Gospel of John takes a different perspective and focuses on the conspiracies of the Jews. Even though his intended audience is members of Christ's Church, he elaborates on the actions of the Jews against Christ. In nearly every chapter of John we find the Jewish religious leaders plotting to kill the Savior of the world.

They conspired in secret, and openly, to kill the Son of God. And what were His 'crimes'; healing the sick on the Sabbath; teaching the doctrines of God, casting out devils, and raising the dead. He fulfilled the 'old law' and taught prayer, faith, repentance, baptism, and love for everyone, including our enemies.

Yet even His inner circle, were not immune from the conspiracies. Judas Iscariot one of His 12 Apostles (of whom Jesus had once said he had a 'devil'), met secretly with the Jewish leaders and conspired to entrap and betray the Redeemer for 30 pieces of silver.

The Sanhedrin wanted to avoid the scandal of an illegal 'religious' trial and arranged a trial before Pilate. From the crowd, the Chief High Priest and other religious leaders called for His crucifixion; the perfect and innocent Son of the Father. These Jewish leaders were consumed with jealousy, planted in their hearts by Satan. They perpetuated the lies that His miracles were performed by the power of the devil; when the opposite was true. Their secret combination was to have Jesus destroyed; this simple carpenter's son, who was the greatest of all.

It's very clear to me that the hand of God was in the discovery and colonization of what is now the United States of America. The Founding Fathers were inspired of God, to create and establish a first-of-its-kind Republic, founded on a Constitution 'of the people, by the people and for the people'. These men were not perfect, yet they were good and noble men, willing to fight to the death to be free from tyranny; and to keep that freedom intact. These were honest men doing everything in their power to establish a form of governance that would assure freedom of religion/speech, and other freedoms as outlined in the Bill of Rights (First Ten amendments to the Constitution).

I have faith that the government of the United States was established by God through men that were influenced by the Holy Spirit, to righteously form the manner in which it would be governed. The three branches of government (Legislative, Executive and Judicial) were established to be equal, yet separate. I think it's reasonable to trust that those elected to office by the voice of the people, are representative of the majority, and are the most honest and forthright people for the job. However, if evidence surfaces that any elected or appointed officer of government (at any level) has been influenced by a secret society of any kind, they should be prosecuted. If after proper investigation and trial they are found guilty of deceit, lies, or any collusion with secret combinations, they should be removed from office immediately.

Looking back at the 2012 Presidential Elections, it was discovered that election fraud was rampant. Members of the Black Panthers organization were discovered outside polling locations where they were seen pressuring and threatening people to vote a certain way. There were voting districts that were reporting an unprecedented number of 'zero votes' for one of the presidential candidates. One media story attributed as many as 5 million votes that were cast in behalf of deceased persons. There were observations of voting machine 'hacking' where the vote registered was for a different candidate than cast. Still others were seen voting as many as five times. Requiring photo identification at the polls would surely curtail voter fraud. Satan himself is the author and creator of secret combinations, and anyone involved with these secret societies represents evil and a satanic influence. Satan, and those he influences, want these processes altered, because he knows by controlling governments, he can have power over hundreds of millions of people through the repressive and enslaving policies of corrupt government.

When impropriety is exposed, and the truth established, involving anyone in an office of public trust, they should be removed from office. The Scriptures teach that the 'love of money is the root of all evil'. When special interest groups and lobbyists persuade elected officials to vote in favor of a bill favorable to their cause, through favors, influence, money or gifts; (and it isn't in the open for all to see); this rises to the level of a secret combination. Satan enters into these 'backroom deals' and takes charge; he controls (even to the point of possession) that person or persons in the position of influence.

Let's consider some of the scandals that have been in the news in the last few years, and let's see if there 'appears' to be secret combinations involved: Starting with Benghazi, Libya. In this incident, four Americans including the U.S. Ambassador were killed. The circumstances surrounding this incident were lied about and misrepresented to the American people by our leaders at the highest levels. In spite of this, those involved have not been prosecuted nor have they acknowledged their cover-up. The fact remains, innocent people died.

The IRS scandal has targeted conservative groups and sanctioned discrimination for political gain. Untold millions (possibly billions) of dollars were spent by the IRS, possibly at the behest of those in high positions of power. Many regular Americans were the target of IRS audits that destroyed or damaged their financial futures. Many small businesses failed because of this secret abuse of power for political gain.

The Affordable Health Care Act (aka Obama Care). False promises and outright lies were made to the American people. Instead of making health care insurance more affordable, just the opposite resulted. Sky rocketing costs have made health insurance unaffordable to millions of people. This flawed law was rushed through Congress without most of those agreeing to it, ever having even read it. Many who voted for it ignored the wishes of their constituents to stop the bill's passage.

I believe that if this law is not repealed in the near future; it could be the fulfillment of one of the prophecies of John. In the book of Revelations, John the Revelator (an Apostle of Jesus Christ) declares that in the last days (before the second coming of Jesus Christ), the 'mark of the beast 'will be forced upon people. Without 'the mark' people won't be able to conduct the business of buying or selling. It is said that this will take some form of three sixes (666), and will be established by Satan as a way to enslave the children of men. There has been speculation that in this electronic age, it could take the form of an implanted chip that would contain all personal information such as: financial accounts, political affiliation, medical history, family history, and the list could go on. Something of this nature is already being implemented (as mandated by law) in the credit card industry.

A few years ago one of the most popular members of Congress made a statement to the American people. He exposed information about one of the most influential terrorist groups in the world. This is the statement he made: "We in the Congress have evidence that the Muslim brotherhood have infiltrated all levels of government in United States of America." The news media immediately squelched the story, and nothing was heard about it again. It's possible this Congressman was threatened (even with his life) for broadcasting true information of which he had personal knowledge; and now it has ended his political career. I suggest that if we only knew the extent to which our government has become influenced by secret societies and combinations, we would be more fearful of the future of America; and continuously pray for our leaders to make righteous decisions based on God-inspired precepts, rather than kowtow to the brokers of evil.

Satan has had a hand in the destruction of many civilizations and governments during the thousands of years of his reign on Earth. All the (so-called) great empires of the Earth have fallen under his greed and influence: From the Greeks and Romans, to the Jews and the Ottomans, the Chinese and Mongols, to Great Britain, Japan and Germany; and more recently Uganda and Cambodia. These countries were all (at one time or another) lead by evil men such as Adolph Hitler who killed millions of innocents. As I've proposed before; in the end, when Satan is through with these men, he convinces them (like Hitler) to commit suicide; or someone else to kill them. Today, the atrocities continue and are escalating as the 'wrapping up scenes' of the Earth are seen before our eyes. Every country or group that is an enemy to freedom will continue to wreak havoc in this world. At some point in time, Satan's proxy will appear who will be the 'anti-Christ'; then we can expect the Second Coming of the Savior, who will rescue the world from Satan's grasp.

Consider this: could it be possible to set up secret combinations to conduct mass murder; with the goal of putting more focus on 'gun violence'; with the end to attempt to destroy Constitutionally guaranteed rights? Because the Second Amendment (the right to bear arms) has been called into question with these events; it's difficult not to consider the possibility. With the rapid dissemination of news through internet media outlets, 'smaller scale violence' has escalated; and the blame never seems to fall on the source: Satan and his influence for evil in the world.

Every act of violence is inspired by Satan; and perhaps in many, secret combinations are involved. This could be particularly true if the violence serves a political or simply a satanic purpose. Look at the Trolley Square shooter in Salt Lake City; the movie theater shooter in Colorado; or the Sandy Hook Elementary shooter in Connecticut. All these events and many more, have been used to promote an anti-Second Amendment agenda; and raised questions of how we handle individuals who are considered mentally ill.

In each of these cases, the individuals were thought to be completely rational weeks or months prior to the killings. The clear explanation is that at some point, Satan and his demons took possession of these men. In most cases, these heinous acts are pre-planned, prepared, practiced and carried out in an intelligent, conscious and methodical manner; leaving no room for doubt that the persons involved were completely sane during the course of the crime. The evil spirits that were allowed to enter into their bodies caused them to do acts that the normal person would never do. Still, public defenders and criminal defense lawyers, attempt to paint a picture of insane behavior to rationalize their client's actions. One thing is for certain, none of these men were 'themselves' at the time of their crimes. In every case, family and friends describe them as normal in every regard yet they killed with impunity. If they had been 'themselves', they couldn't have taken the lives other sons and daughters of God.

Situations such as these leave many unanswered questions; but it seems clear that those drawn into acts of mayhem and murder are mentally disturbed; and suffer this affliction from the possession of Satan or one (or more) of his followers. Satan causes those who are affected to no longer value their own lives, let alone the lives of others; their love of life had disappeared.

Through the media, many today have become more desensitized to death and killing; and the horrible scenes of carnage that are created during these crimes. Movies and video games have become more graphic in the past two or three decades as standards and rating systems have 'evolved' to accept and allow more realistic scenes of death and destruction. I read a statement several years ago, "By the time an average boy reaches the age of 18, he has committed 20,000 'virtual' murders." It doesn't matter if these fictional killings are of animals, robots, cartoon characters, machines, or people; over long-term exposure, *actual* life can become less valued. I'm convinced that this helped my son make the decision to pull the trigger ending his life. He had also frequently listened to music that influenced his depression and hopelessness. Let's consider outlawing violent video games rather than guns.

Satan being a spirit cannot directly take a life; if he could, we would all be dead. His power and influence is only what we allow him to have. He does this through the natural man because in our weakness we can't rule ourselves righteously.

Satan and his demons are constantly working on us; digging, prodding, inching closer, exposing our wickedness, and exploiting our imperfections and failings; making evil seem good and good evil; and whispering to us with a familiar voice (that may even sound like your own), convincing us to commit just the slightest indiscretion; and that's how he gets us.

There once was a television show that starred the comedian Flip Wilson. The line he made famous was, "The devil made me do it!" It became a catch phrase that we kids used all the time. We didn't know just how close to the truth those words were. With the change of only one word, the tables turn from the devil's responsibility for our actions to our own: "The devil *convinced* me to do it!" As he exploits our weaknesses through our five senses, he explores all our flaws until he finds that weak spot and enters in and destroys our agency.

We are truly innocent when we come into this world, and no matter what sin we later commit, we can find true innocence again. The Savior Jesus Christ paid the price for us; any pain, sin, sorrow, disease, and imperfection of man, can be healed through our faith and His redeeming power. By completing the prescribed steps of repentance, we can return into his loving arms of mercy; and be forgiven of any sin including the most grievous that can be imagined; except denial of the Holy Ghost.

Because secret combinations have been so damaging to every level of society throughout history, we have an obligation to take a stand for truth and righteousness; and speak out when we see the signs and symptoms of secret combinations. Certainly we should expect those running for public office to be examples beyond reproach of integrity, honesty, and a willingness to give their lives in service to this uniquely free nation. We expect them to equally and fairly represent all people, at all times, and in all situations, without favoritism. If they fail in fulfilling those expectations, then they should be removed from office by the vote of the people.

It seems that expectation may be 'pie-in-the-sky' thinking based on the wickedness we see in our government today. Nevertheless, it is our right as citizens to hold our public officials to a 'zero tolerance' standard of integrity. If they are found guilty of creating or engaging in any secret combinations, then we, through our representatives need to request that the impeachment process begin.

The scriptures are replete with accounts of peoples and nations that were overthrown, enslaved, and destroyed by secret combinations. These often take root after years of prosperity where men have forgotten God. I believe this beautiful country of America is in a head-on collision course with just such an ending; and we risk the loss of freedom which has been so dearly fought for and earned. For over two hundred and forty years we have enjoyed this freedom, and perhaps we are reaching a tipping point of sorts. These secret combinations created by Satan and orchestrated by the powers of darkness that he controls, are becoming stronger every day. Untold millions have died at their hands, and they will continue to grow *if we allow it.*

When I make the statement, "There are no evil sons and daughters of God born to this Earth," you might counter with the question, "What about someone like Adolf Hitler? He had a hand in killing over six million Jews, isn't that the definition of evil?" Even so, he was only being *used* as a pawn, and a puppet of Satan.

I think it's highly probable that Hitler was so evil that Satan himself had possession of his body (and no other demons). Satan is so selfish about taking credit, that he doesn't want anyone else to be recognized, even his evil followers. It's no coincidence that Satan convinced Hitler to annihilate the Jews; they are scripturally God's chosen people. Satan was able to distort Hitler's thinking to justify naming the German people the 'master race'. In Satan's reasoning, if the chosen people of God were eliminated from the earth, he could become the 'antichrist', and rule the world! Satan is the self-avowed 'god of this world'. As such, he will employ any means, and use any person to accomplish his designs. Then, when Satan has no further need for those persons; he moves on to fresh innocents to corrupt. When Hitler's Satan-inspired designs began to fail, and the war had become lost, Satan's support withdrew as well, and Hitler was left to fail on his own.

So in the end, after Satan had abused Hitler, made him a sexual deviant, a paranoid schizophrenic, and driven him to madness; Hitler killed his girlfriend Eva Braun, and killed himself. Hitler was an instrument set up by Satan; to accomplish the extinction of six million Jews and countless thousands of other children of God who were caught up in his 'unholy' war of 'ethnic cleansing'. The human suffering perpetuated by World War II, has affected the world for generations. I realize it's difficult to consider, but even Hitler was truly innocent when he came into this world; until through his natural man, Satan began to take over.

Evil perpetuates evil. Consider this: secret combinations or secret societies often thrive quite well on their own, even without the help or influence of Satan and his devilish hordes. Suppose a person becomes so prideful and caught up in the euphoria of power, they start to worship themselves as 'all powerful'; as god of their 'world' just as Satan does. Soon, like Satan, they become sociopathic where they are beyond feelings of regard of love for their fellow man. They're so 'into themselves' that the natural man takes total control; darkness enters their life and the lives of everyone who surrounds them. The light of Christ becomes just a flicker, and eventually is totally extinguished.

The same thing happens in families, cultures, religions, business organizations, thrones and principalities. Humans who are so evil that they no longer need Satan to inspire their actions are the most frightening of all. Oppression of others becomes second nature; they never have feelings of compassion for those they injure, or guilt for their actions. They've become so blinded to the worth of humanity, that they can hurt, maim, or kill with impunity; to them, the wellbeing or life of another human means nothing.

With these people (businesses, organizations, cultures, religions, etc.), Satan only needs to occasionally 'check on his investments', just to see how things are going. Humanity is dead; all that matters is perpetuation and aggrandizement of themselves and their interests. Like Adolf Hitler, they become so wicked that the 'darkness' actually begins to show in their countenance. They no longer have that aureole of light that surrounds the God fearing and righteous individual. At this point, they are in open rebellion against God and begin to believe they are above the *fictitious* 'God of the masses'.

Sadly, possibly you (as I, in reading this chapter) have caught yourself thinking, 'this sounds like our government and many of the elected officials who we trust to run the [city, state and] country'. Secret combinations can be created and operated at every level of society, including so-called 'religious groups'. Whatever the appellation, priest crafts, gangs, cabals, collusions, plots, and etc.; they are all forms of secret societies and secret combinations, and are the brainchild of Satan himself. Once a person is involved with one of these groups, it is virtually impossible to withdraw; Satan will not allow his organizations to be threatened by someone having second thoughts. Once you sell your soul to the devil, there's no return policy.

Reading from an article given to me by a close friend, I learned of a secret combination called the 'Deep Web' which is essentially the hidden internet or 'dark side' of the internet. The Deep Web is used explicitly for illegal activity of every imaginable kind. The Deep Web, to put it simply, is Satan's social media channel. These are the kinds of things the article pointed out as accessible on the Deep Web: child pornographers, thieves, human sex traffickers, forgers, assassins, and peddlers of state secrets, and nuclear weapons. Quoting from the article, "The FBI, DEA, the ATF, and the NSA, are spending tens of millions of dollars trying to figure out how to crack it." In the meantime they are also 'using it' to trap the entrepreneurs of evil.

Prophets of old saw our day, and witnessed that the land of America would be a promised land and a bastion of freedom, as long as, 'the people are righteous and believe in the Lord God and his Son Jesus Christ'. I fear that we as a nation have turned away from God and risk destruction because of our unbelief.

I suspect that the branches of our government have been infiltrated and are becoming controlled by secret combinations. There are still good and honest people being elected to high offices; but they face an up-hill battle as they try to get to the truth; and curtail those who would sacrifice our freedoms in exchange for social relativism. Whether it's flagging support for our protection from 'enemies both foreign and domestic'; or the tacit blind-eye turned to the will of the people on same-gender marriage; or the curtailing of Second Amendment rights; we as a free, god-fearing people must NOT let this happen. Christians around the world are being persecuted in the name of Christ. Our freedoms are eroding and being confiscated every day by unrighteous men in high office. We are witnessing the same wickedness that prevailed in the cities of Sodom and Gomorrah. The prophets have foretold the destruction of all the wicked at the coming of Jesus Christ. Unlike the days of Noah, where water destroyed the wicked, this time it will be by fire.

From the ancient empires of Europe and the Middle East; to the ancient civilizations of the Americas; many great nations have been destroyed because of pride, power, and secret combinations; the same may be said of our day unless we repent, eschew evil and embrace the teachings of the Father of our spirits, and our Brother Jesus Christ. History will repeat itself, if we don't remember the lessons of the past.

For our preservation we must destroy the secret combinations, repent of our evil doings and come unto Christ. Recognize Satan and his tactics, cast everything he promotes aside; and turn to righteousness. Take a STAND for freedom; STAND in holy places; and be not moved. I testify of these things in the name of Jesus Christ our Lord and Savior; Amen.

(Scripture References: *King James Version of the Holy Bible, Book of Mormon, Doctrine and Covenants, and Pearl of Great Price*: Gen. 4:23; Ps 64:5; John 3:19; Eph. 6:12; 2 Thes. 2:7; Rev. 17:5; 2 Ne. 27:27; Alma 37:21; Hel. 16:21; 3 Ne. 9:5; D&C 123:13; Rev. 2:6; D&C 117:11; Moses 5:30; Moses 5:51; Moses 6:15; 2 Ne. 9:9; 2 Ne. 10:15; 2 Ne. 26:22; 3 Ne. 6:27-30; 3 Ne. 28:9; Alma 37:30; Hel. 2:8; Ether 11:15; Hel. 6:26; 3 Ne. 3:9; 4 Ne. 1:42; Morm. 8:27; Ether 8:18; Ether 10:33; and Ether 11:22)

Conclusion

If I have taught anything of importance in this reading, it would be this: We all enter this world as 'Truly Innocent'. Children remain truly innocent to the age of accountability (which in the modern Church of Jesus Christ is accepted to be eight years of age). As we begin to exercise our 'moral agency' to choose right from wrong, Satan begins his quest to control us. Through the Atonement of Christ, and his Priesthood Power - shared with righteous men; Satan's influence can be vanquished and our true innocence renewed.

In the days and weeks following our son's death, Cassie and I received personal inspiration through the Spirit of the Holy Ghost testifying that we needed to tell our story. We have come to the realization that four of Satan's most pernicious tools covered in this book, were experienced by our son Joseph. The first is depression. Joseph felt he had lost everything including the hope and willpower to go on with life. Second, the natural man within him had taken control through the use of alcohol. Third, Satan had gained control of his life; and he was possibly possessed by multiple evil spirits. The Holy Ghost had borne witness to me that he needed a priesthood blessing and the demon cast out; but he simply refused. I knew we were in trouble, and could possibly lose our son. And fourth, Satan had convinced Joseph that there was no hope that his life could get better; and the only way to rid him of the pain, was to commit suicide. Since Joseph's death, the spirit told Cassie and me (individually) that we could help others prevent such a tragedy by sharing our story. If this book could help even one person avoid the possibility of depression, control of the natural man, and the possession of Satan, that leads to suicide; we feel it would have been worth the effort and sacrifice. I boldly pronounce that the wish of my heart and the desire of my whole being would be that I could go to every family in the world and tell them these things and awaken them to the reality of Satan and his designs.

The Spirit directed me to the scriptures, LDS conference talks, words of hope, and doctrine related to these subjects. I apologize for procrastinating for over ten years to bring this book to print and digital media. I also ask your forgiveness for my shortcomings in the written word. I would love the opportunity to stand before large groups of people and bear testimony of these things; I would feel much better about that than simply writing a book. Hopefully having my written thoughts will help preserve these words for review and future reference; whereas the spoken word has a tendency to slip away and be forgotten.

This book is necessary, and written for our day. It isn't written out of self-pity for what we've been through; but to boldly declare to the world these truths. I ask that after you've read the entire book, that you kneel in prayer and ask your Heavenly Father if these words are true. I testify that the spirit will bear witness to you that they are true; that its contents can help you, members of your family, friends, neighbors, and coworkers.

Reading the scriptural references cited here, will bring an awareness of Satan and his plan; as well as the Saviors counter-measures. Cross-reference it, read it over and over to understand and bring clarity to these concepts; they are needed to strengthen the armor of faith, hope, and encouragement so we might carry on, and endure to the end. As in our family, perhaps suicide has impacted your relationships and you are trying to cope or understand. My hope and prayer is that this reading will help you to get through the mourning, the depression, and future trials that will surely come in this life of learning and character-molding experiences.

Each chapter of this book has been a step-by-step journey. I have tried to outline what is crucial to our obtaining the ultimate goal of Life Eternal; with our Heavenly Father and his son Jesus Christ. I promise that if you'll read, ponder, and pray about the contents of this book, you will honestly be able to overcome the natural man, and the adversary: Satan the father of all lies.

My goal is to prevent another suicide; and to enlighten God's children to realize their potential; to understand the reality of Satan, and to recognize his tools of destruction. To understand that when we look in the mirror there are two distinct individuals: our perfect immortal spirit body; and a mortal body, which is the natural man. Our goal in life is that our spirit bodies and minds learn to control the flesh or natural man.

Another important learning from this book has been the knowledge of the two enemies of God. The first enemy is the 'natural man' (or woman). If we choose to follow the natural man or the enticements of Satan, then he becomes our master. All children born to this earth accepted God's plan of happiness, gaining a physical body, and coming to this earth to be tried and tested in preparation to return to God's presence. It is God and his son we must choose to follow. When the perfect spirit within each of us has control over the natural man, we are well on our way to achieving our Earthly mission. We will never be perfect in this life; but through the Atonement of Christ, we know that when we fall short, the Savior's love will lift us up. God only asks us to keep trying to be better. Through repentance and the merciful plan of the Atonement of Christ, we can obtain perfection after the resurrection.

The second enemy of God and man is Satan. He is the 'opposition' that allows us to have a choice, and exercise our agency; which next to life itself, is the greatest gift from God. We must be able to choose good or evil in this earthly experience. If we choose evil, our agency is destroyed. Darkness enters in, and the light of Christ is diminished as Satan becomes our master.

There are only two ways to release or cast out evil spirits when they have possessed a person:

1. Physical death. When the body dies, evil spirits depart; as does the person's spirit. The person's spirit goes back first to the God that created them. Then depending upon their works here on earth being good or evil, they are sent to either paradise or spirit prison, where they can continue progressing if they desire. What happens to the evil spirits? They go to find another place in another body.

2. Cast out evil spirits through the power and authority of the Holy Melchizedek Priesthood and in the name of Jesus Christ*. Christ ordained his Apostles and members of the Seventy by the laying on of hands; bestowing the Priesthood upon their heads. In the time of Jesus Christ there were a few other men holding this same Priesthood. Today there are many thousands who hold this same Priesthood Power. It's a sacred gift from God to act in the name of Jesus Christ to bless the lives of God's children. I was ordained an Elder in the Priesthood at age 18, and then by the age of 24 ordained a High Priest. I testify this is the power of God given to man, and I've witnessed many mighty miracles throughout my life through the blessings of the Priesthood. Anyone needing help should seek out someone holding the Holy Priesthood of God.

*Note: When preparing to help someone possessed by evil spirits, it is essential that (to be the most effective in casting them out) the process be done in a discrete way.

Talking about the process to or around the person, allows the spirits to become aware of what is going to happen; and they will temporarily depart of their own accord, so as not to be subject to the process (they literally feel fear and dread in the name of Jesus Christ). The fact that they leave is good, but not as effective or possibly as permanent as when they can be rebuked directly. Realizing a Priesthood blessing will still make them whole and clean of evil spirits.

The Apostle Paul describes who this enemy is:

"For we *wrestle*[a] not *against*[b] *flesh and blood*[c], but against principalities, against powers, against the *rulers*[d] of the *darkness*[e] of this world, against spiritual *wickedness*[f] in high places." (Ephesians 6:12 – *emphasis* added)

a.　JS-H 1:15　Real enemy to righteousness & spiritual death - the Devil himself and his followers one-third of the hosts of heaven wrestling them every day each of us our entire life.
b.　TG: Opposition (again Satan)
c.　TG:　Mortals
d.　2 Cor4:4 God of this world (or worldly people) the Devil
e.　TG: Darkness, Spiritual; Secret Combinations (Devil)
f.　TG: Governments; Wickedness (governments lead by Satan)

According to Paul, we should not fear men, but should fear the unseen evil spirits, including their master Satan himself. When secret combinations take over governments, those nations will eventually fall into corruption; and wickedness will abound until they are destroyed.

Paul gives us the formula to escape the chains of Satan:

"Finally, my brethren, be *strong* in the Lord, and in the power of his might.

Put on the whole *armour* of God, that ye may be able to stand against the wiles of the devil.

Wherefore take unto you the whole armour of God, that ye may be able to withstand in the evil day, and having done all, to Stand therefore, having your loins *girt* about with *truth*, and having on the *breastplate* of *righteousness*;

And your feet shod with the preparation of the gospel of *peace*;

Above all, taking the shield of *faith*, wherewith ye shall be able to quench all the fiery *darts* of the wicked.

And take the helmet of *salvation*, and the sword of the Spirit, which is the word of God:

Praying always with all prayer and supplication in the Spirit, and watching thereunto with all *perseverance* and supplicationfor all saints;" (Ephesians 6:10-11, 13-18 – *emphasis* added)

In my daily prayers, I often pray for the Second Coming of Jesus Christ. Why? The answer is simple; when he comes again, Satan and all his followers will be cast off to spirit prison for a thousand years. Evil spirits will be removed from the earth including those people who are possessed by such demons. A spirit cannot be killed. 'Spiritual death' or 'the second death' takes place after the final judgment, when Satan and his spirit followers are cast into Outer Darkness; along with mortals like Cain, who have sinned against the Holy Ghost; they will at some point be resurrected, but will still become Sons of Perdition, and be cast into Outer Darkness. Because they chose God's plan in the preexistence and gained a mortal body, they will rule over Satan who will never have a body of flesh and bones.

"Blessed are the pure in heart: for they shall see God."
(Matthew 5:8)

"And blessed are all the pure in heart, for they shall see
God.   (3 Nephi 12:8)

"O then ye unbelieving, turn ye unto the Lord; cry mightily
Unto the Father in the name of Jesus Christ, that perhaps ye
may be found spotless, pure, fair, and white, having been
cleansed by the blood of the Lamb, at that great and last day.
(Mormon 9: 6)

"O all ye that are pure in heart, lift up your heads and receive the pleasing word of God, and feast upon his love; for ye may, if your minds are firm, forever." (Jacob 3:2)

"Now they, after being sanctified by the Holy Ghost, having their garments made white, being pure and spotless before God, could not look upon sin save it were with abhorrence; and there were many, exceeding great many, who were made pure and entered into the rest of the Lord their God." (Alma 13:12)

"But charity is the pure love of Christ, and it endureth forever; and who so is found possessed of it at the last day, It shall be well with him.

Wherefore, my beloved brethren, pray and to the Father the energy of heart, that ye may be filled with this love, which he hath bestowed upon all who are true followers of his Son, Jesus Christ; that ye may become the sons of God; that when he shall appear we shall be like him, for we shall see him as he is; that we may have this hope; that we may be purified even as he is pure. Amen." (Moroni 7: 47-48)

The words of the Master contained in the scriptures, are given to us to study, ponder and pray. What great hope it brings to the soul to know of the great blessings we have in store when we can become pure; both inwardly and outwardly. Let us never allow anything that isn't pure and wholesome to enter our bodies; nor speak unkind words to others. Let us only speak of our Savior Jesus Christ and our Heavenly Father, with reverence and respect; never taking the Lord's name in vain.

Let's eliminate the use of any substance that can harm our bodies, or which may have detrimental side effects. Let's stay in control of our bodies and our senses. Let us have faith to call upon our Heavenly Father in fasting and prayer for relief from our ailments and rely upon him first through priesthood blessings, before doctors and drugs. When these are needed, have discretion and wisdom in their use.

The Word of Wisdom found in the *Doctrine and Covenants* (section 89) is a good reference for staying healthy. God expects us to use wisdom when taking anything into our body; and to take care of it. Exercise, get proper amounts of rest, and show God you are thankful for the temple of our spirit.

Of all the human senses, the eyes seem to affect the desires of the natural man the most. It has been said that the 'eyes are the window of the soul'. The eyes can be used by Satan to entice the natural man; and blind our spiritual eyes with lustful thoughts, which can lead to actions such as fornication and adultery. Satan tempts or entices the natural man with little sins first, which then can open the door to more grievous sins.

Years ago I watched an interview on *60 Minutes* with Ted Bundy. He was one of America's worst serial killers before he was put to death. One of the questions he was asked, "What started you on this path of killing?" His answer has always stuck in my mind, "I started with pornography and looking at dirty magazines." He put out a plea to all the listeners not to indulge in such filth, to look at him and see what it led to in his life. Since that time, and the arrival of the internet, pornography has proliferated throughout every form of media. There is great societal and religious concern for what this is doing to men, women and children of all ages. Pornography is one of Satan's most effective tools in today's world.

The things that we see help form our character and actions. The most popular television programs and theater movies are those that promote violence and promiscuity. These things wear down and desensitize the human mind, such that Satan's evil acts seem to be a 'normal' part of life. Millions of people look up to and worship Hollywood actors and actresses and emulate the evil that is depicted on the screen.

The widespread popularity of graphic video games has become an expensive time-waster; and given two generations a penchant for violence and killing. This desensitization of death and dying has been linked to the increase of violence in our society. I believe this activity helped desensitize Joseph to the point that suicide would be just a common thing. Many years ago I read some staggering statistics. The report stated that by the time a boy reaches the age of 18, he has 'fictionally murdered' about 20,000 beasts, animals, or humans playing such 'games'. As parents we must pay attention to the forces that are at work destroying the family. When we patronize movies, subscribe to premium movie channels, purchase game decks, or services that stream media into our homes; we *may* be promoting Satan's work, and making those that follow him rich. Consider how those precious hard-earned funds could be put to better use.

> "Wherefore, we shall have a perfect knowledge of all our guilt, have and are uncleanness, and our nakedness; and the righteous shall have a perfect knowledge of their enjoyment, and their righteousness, being clothed with purity, yea, even with the robe of righteousness." (2 Nephi 9:14)

I love to go to the Temple and be clothed in pure white; where we don't know the other's position in life, where we are all equal before the Lord, having been found worthy and clothed modestly in His House. With that as a standard, we should evaluate our appearance and how it may affect those around us. Let's strive to set the example of modesty. When we look in the mirror each morning; do we see a disciple of Christ? A God-given human attribute is attraction to the opposite sex. When sons or daughters of God wear clothing that exposes private and sacred parts of the body, it can result in the daughter or sons of God thinking impure thoughts. These thoughts of lust can if unchecked result in sin, which allows Satan to bind that person with his chains. The Scriptures say that our physical body is a Temple and a covering for our spirits.

"Moreover, the Lord saith: Because the daughters of Zion are haughty, and walk with stretched-forth necks and

wanton eyes walking and mincing as they go, and making a tinkling with their feet-

Therefore the Lord will smite with a scab the crown of the head of the daughters of Zion, and the Lord will discover their secret parts.

In that day the Lord will take away the bravery of their tinkling ornaments, and cauls, and round tires like the moon;

The chains and the bracelets, and the mufflers;

The bonnets, and the ornaments of the legs, and the

headbands and the tablets, and the ear-rings;

The rings, and nose jewels;

The changeable suits of apparel, and the mantles, and the wimples, and crisping-pins;

The glasses, and the fine linen, and hoods, and the veils.

And it shall come to pass, instead of sweet smell there shall be stink; and instead of our girdle, a rent; and instead of well set hair, baldness; and instead of a stomacher, a girding of sackcloth; burning instead of beauty.

Thy men shall fall by the sword and thy mighty in the war.

And her gates shall lament and mourn; and she shall be desolate, and shall sit upon the ground." (2 Nephi 13:16-26)

In these scriptures we understand that the Lord is talking to women of all ages that are members of his Church: 'in our day'. It's very clear that he doesn't want us tampering with his creation; this mortal body that he has entrusted to us. This body should be pure and without excessive decorations. This is desecrating and downgrading God's most special creation. This includes any disfiguring (such as tattoos, piercing and scarifying) that takes away from the natural beauty of a son or daughter of God. We only have one body; let's make it a Holy Temple for our perfect spirits by taking care of our bodies and following healthy routines.

If only we could see with our spiritual eyes, what glorious visions would we behold? Tears of joy would fill our eyes and we would seek the kingdom of God and nothing else. We would certainly take more seriously the task of perfecting ourselves. It's a harsh reality that every sin and transgression of which we don't repent during our Earth life; will remain with us into the Spirit World, where it will be 100 times more difficult to repent without our mortal body. Our eternal progression and resurrection timing depends on this repentance. The powers of the Atonement must be utilized for our eternal destiny. God's love is so great that he gives us (every human being) a lifetime (and until the end of the thousand year Millennium) to prove our worthiness to return to His presence for all eternity.

Mercy overcomes the demands of justice through the power of the Atonement of Jesus Christ. If we don't choose freely through our agency to repent, then we will suffer as the Savior did:

> "For behold, I God, have suffered these things for all, that they might not suffer if they would repent;
>
> But if they would not repent they must suffer even as I;
>
> Which suffering caused myself, even God, the greatest of all, to tremble because of pain, and to bleed at every pore, and to suffer both body and spirit – and would that I might and drink the bitter cup, and shrink---
>
> Wherefore, I command you again to repent, lest I humble you with my almighty power; and that you confess your sins, lest you suffer these punishments of which I have spoken , of which in the smallest, yea, even in the least degree you have tasted at the time I withdrew my spirit." (D & C 19:16-20)

We all must confront these two enemies each day of our mortal life; the one seen, and the other unseen. Make a commitment now to stand in holy places! Control the natural man and win the battle over the unseen enemy, Satan. Make the shadow of his presence in your life slowly fade away, and become pure light; having a perfect brightness of hope. Then let that light shine forth because you are living a Christ-centered life.

The prophecies of old about the last days are literally being fulfilled. Mothers killing daughters, and fathers killing sons. The love of men is 'waxing cold'. The whole earth is in commotion, and men's 'hearts' are failing. Astoundingly, one of the national political parties voted recently to eliminate the name of God from their political platform. Luckily, they decided to keep God around; but sadly it was only by a narrow margin.

The guilty one is the invisible but real enemy that's being exposed in the pages of this book. If every father and mother throughout the world knew this doctrine, and taught it to their children, then violence, hate, war, suicide, murder, and all evil and darkness could be *controlled*. As we open our eyes to what's going on throughout the world, we see Satan gaining power every day. The only permanent solution is the second coming of Jesus Christ. As horrible as it may be, the Earth will be cleansed by fire, and the wicked servants of Satan will be burned; and his hosts bound for a thousand years.

The scriptures say that in the end, all of God's children will look upon Satan and say: "Is this the man that made the earth to tremble, that did shake kingdoms?" (*The Book of Mormon*, 2 Nephi 24:16). We all will be staring in unbelief at his lack of glory, his darkness, and his nothingness; incredulous that he was the one who deceived nations, and stole the souls of men.

As I end this book, allow me to relate two touching stories that illustrate innocence and Christ-like love. As you read each story, you'll be able to identify the behaviors and characteristics that denote human love that goes beyond self, and extends to others without guile.

You're familiar with two of my sons, Grant and Joseph. They were close in age and were very close as brothers. As boys they played together and hunted together. As young adults they worked together and helped each other through thick and thin. When Joseph lost his driving privileges, Grant stepped in and became his driver, taking him to work and everywhere he went. This placed Grant in the same situations as Joseph; drinking parties and exposure to drugs. Many times Grant left the parties but he was worried about his brother and stayed nearby. On a couple of occasions when fighting broke out, Grant was there to step in and save his brother from serious injury and even death. Grant was there for him and even stepped in to fight the other guy; then gathered Joseph up, and took care of him.

Grant witnessed the verbal and physical abuse that Tracy gave Joseph; and saw how Joseph would just take it without a single negative response. Eventually, Grant gave into the natural man and the enticing of Satan, and was picked up and charged with a DUI. Grant was to stand before the judge was March 6th; the day after Joseph's suicide. The judge postponed it for a couple of months because of Joseph's death.

In the last few months previous to his death, Joseph was chastised for being a bad influence on Grant, by several family members, and I'm embarrassed to say, including me. Joseph would just take it without retort, as if he accepted it as true; even though we all knew Grant was responsible for his own choices. Joseph took those words of blame personally. He advised Grant never to go to jail because he was raped in jail. He also told Grant he would rather kill himself than step foot in a jail again.

So here's the situation; Grant knows he'll be going to court and likely be going to jail for at least a few days. Joseph has just told Grant never to go to jail because of the likelihood of assault; and told him he [Joseph] would rather kill himself than go to jail ever again.

Now Joseph thinks he is to blame for Grants situation; and believes his family will blame him, if Grant commits suicide (he knew of Grant's suicide letter he had previously written). Adding to this dilemma, the family is fasting and praying for Grant not to go to jail and for the judge to have mercy on him. In my prayers I also asked my Heavenly Father to separate my two sons; that one would find work elsewhere because neither of them were handling well the consequences of their actions that now confronted them.

Joseph felt he could save his brother by taking his own life, thinking all blame would leave with him. I heard Joseph's voice that morning saying, "I love you Dad and Mom good night." I wish I could've been awakened by his words of love, and maybe I could have saved his life.

The final story is about identical twin boys. They were so identical, that is was difficult even for their parents to sometimes tell them apart. As the boys grew into their teenage years, life's decisions separated them into different paths. One joined a gang, and left home. He started using drugs, dropped out of school, and couldn't hold a job. When he ended up in jail, his parents came and paid the fines, lovingly embraced him, and asked him to come home; instead he returned to the gang. During a fight with a rival gang, he killed a person. He was a minor, but was tried as an adult; and convicted of First Degree Murder. The judge sentenced him to death by lethal injection. His life became a small cell in prison. He was on death row for years as the inevitable date of his execution ultimately approached. All alone, hope was just a dream.

The other brother loved the Lord and kept his life in order. He served an LDS mission, graduated from college, and became a doctor. He served faithfully in his church and community. His home was a Christ-centered place. He knew that he was ready to face God if death came his way. He had always loved his brother and constantly felt concern for his eternal welfare. It worried him that his brother's eternal progression had been halted by his errant ways; and especially anxious with his brothers impending death.

After considerable fasting and prayer, he decided to visit his brother just prior to his scheduled execution. Due to the circumstances, he was allowed a final visit with his brother, inside his cell. As they talked, the brother that was going to die expressed how he regretted the decisions he had made, and the bad life he had experienced. He had been thinking of the teachings of his youth, and realized he wasn't ready to meet his maker.

The brother, who had come to visit, explained that he had lived a righteous life and WAS prepared to meet God. He told his brother he had come to switch places. They exchanged clothes and the righteous brother died for his brother. What love; giving his own life so his brother could go free!

Each of these stories ended with one brother giving his life for another. Although the individual circumstances are significantly different, each brother felt that by sacrificing their own life, another could live; and start fresh on their pathway back to God. I am grateful that Jesus Christ knows the beginning from the end; and he knows each of us personally.

The road will be tough for my son Joseph. Suicide is not God's way; but I know he can become truly innocent again and still come forth in the first resurrection. He can be with his family for all eternity. I believe the same is possible for the boy who committed murder; if he repents and comes unto Christ. Forgiveness from God can only happen when full measure has been paid in His eyes; and in His own due time. Thanks to Joseph's choice for his brother, Grant has married in God's temple and now has two beautiful sons. Grant also did Joseph's temple work by proxy one year after his death. I believe Joseph continues to progress; and I know we will embrace again someday.

As we strive to make our homes a place of refuge from the storms of life, and the influences of Satan; they will become a Christ-centered and holy place where the Savior may come and dwell. Jesus Christ overcame both physical and spiritual death for us. For now, we must live by faith; because a veil of forgetfulness has been drawn over our pre-earth memory. But I believe that in that Great Council in Heaven, where we heard and accepted Christ's Plan; we had the privilege to witness our brother Jehovah carry out the work of the Creation, direct His labors among the ancients of Israel and come to earth as the Only Begotten of the Father; to conduct His Earthly Ministry and take upon himself our pain, infirmities and sins. I believe we witnessed His atoning sacrifice in Gethsemane and Golgotha's hill where He hung on the cross. I believe we saw the awful moment in this horrible scene, when the Savior was all alone and uttered these words: "Father Forgive Them, for They Know Not What They Do."

With this declaration he proclaimed to God our 'INNOCENCE'. He paid the price for sin; He loved us so much that he bled and died for us; A sinless ransom for all mankind. I call that 'True Innocence'.

(References: King James Version of the Holy Bible, Book of Mormon, and Doctrine and Covenants)

END

Made in the USA
San Bernardino, CA
13 April 2016